SONIA ALLISON'S
New Complete Microwave Cookery

SONIA ALLISON'S

New Complete Microwave Cookery

Kaye & Ward · Kingswood

To all my many friends in the microwave industry who have given me so much co-operation and assistance over the last eight years.

Copyright © 1984 by Sonia Allison

Designed by David Gibbons

Published by Kaye & Ward Ltd.
The Windmill Press, Kingswood, Tadworth, Surrey

Second impression 1985

Filmset by BAS Printers Limited
Printed in Great Britain by
William Clowes Ltd, Beccles and London

ISBN 0 7182 1560 5

Contents

Introduction

As far as I am concerned, there was life BM (Before Microwaves) and, over the past eight years or so, life AM (After Microwaves), a much more contented, relaxed and leisurely in between time with my microwave oven or cooker – either term will do! – working flat out for me, a sharp drop in our electricity bills as a consequence, many less demands made on my busy working schedule and the opportunity to be more creative than I ever imagined possible with a comparatively new form of cooking: swift, cool, hygienic, economical and, as it transpired, reliable and undemanding into the bargain.

I admit quite freely that microwave ovens cannot replace, in toto, conventional ovens and hobs but they go a long way towards it and my intention when writing this book was to put together a package of innovative recipes in addition to old favourites, proving what a wide range of dishes can be cooked successfully and fast in the microwave. The exceptions are Yorkshire Pudding (it collapses), pancakes, soufflés, meringues and éclairs which fail with irritating predictability for reasons best known to themselves. And deep frying is taboo as well because controlling the temperature of the fat or oil is problematic and overheating could result.

Many colleagues, friends and acquaintances still regard a microwave as something to use strictly for defrosting and reheating frozen foods. A pity. Others, more enthusiastic and in tune with my way of thinking, understand and appreciate a microwave's capabilities and potential, accepting its qualities with gratitude. They know that it can be used safely by the young, the old and the disabled; that given minimal time in the evening after a day's work, anyone, male or female, can put together an admirable two or three course meal in about three-quarters of an hour; that microwave ovens are as safe as houses, with as many protective, built-in safety devices as Fort Knox; that work top models are easily transportable from one part of the kitchen to another – or room to room – and plug into a 13 amp socket without further ado.

New users, and even a few old hands, may encounter feelings of frustration, bewilderment and insecurity as they try to absorb a welter of literature, master new techniques and run with the microwave before they can walk. But given time and a modicum of patience, there will be no looking back and the progression from heating baked beans on toast to making a glamorous Chocolate Roulade will be astonishingly rapid. All I ask is that everyone read the section headed Guide to Microwave Cooking *before* they get carried away on a wave of enthusiasm and rush into the kitchen to experiment. Forewarned is forearmed.

Guide to Microwave Cooking

Just pause. Bear in mind that microwave cooking is comparatively new so, to prevent confusion and disappointment, carefully read through the instruction/recipe book supplied with your own make of oven. This should give you an understanding of the different techniques involved, as should my guidelines below.

What are Microwaves?

Based on the principle of radar, microwaves are a form of energy which are electromagnetic, short-length, non-ionising, high frequency radio waves at the top end of the radio band. They are close to infra-red rays but not as powerful, and the frequency is 2450MHz or megahertz which literally translates into millions of cycles or vibrations per second. The word 'hertz' comes from Heinrich Hertz, the scientist who first discovered the nature of the waves.

Inside the cavity of a microwave oven, with its extraordinary number of compulsory cut-outs and safety devices, the microwaves are completely confined and will be unable to leak out and attack you. In any event, microwaves are a different kettle of fish altogether from X-rays, Gamma-rays and ultra-violet rays which are ionising and known to cause dangerous cellular alterations to the body with minimal or no temperature change. Microwaves have none of these effects and, more importantly, are non-cumulative. Exposure to the sun, sitting under heat lamps and giving oneself infra-red treatment for rheumatic aches and pains will cause, long term, infinitely more harm than using a microwave oven where the waves are literally locked in and cease as soon as the door is opened or the 'off' switch operated. Leaks, when and if they occur, will do so only if the oven is worn, damaged or mishandled and for safety reasons, it should be checked from time to time by a qualified engineer to make sure the door fits snugly, the seal around the door is secure, and the hinges are not rusty. If the door front fractures, stop using the oven at once and request a service call as soon as possible. What would happen if one were, briefly, exposed to microwaves? The answer is a burn which is never pleasant. Therefore look after the oven, keep it serviced, clean it regularly and you should have nothing at all to fear.

How Microwaves cook food

When the microwave is plugged into a socket, the door closed and the oven switched on, microwaves are emitted from a magnetron (or microwave energy generator), usually at the top of the oven and placed to one side. The magnetron is protected by a cover, generally plastic. The microwaves are transmitted into the inside of the oven cavity down a channel called a waveguide, bounce off the sides, and 'beam' on to the food from all directions. Instantaneously, the food absorbs the

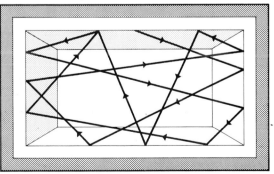

Microwaves deflecting in an oven

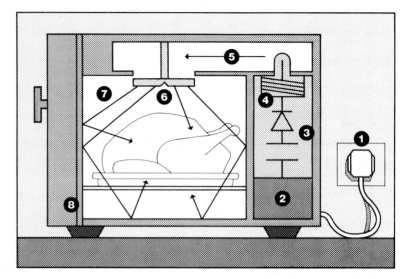

1. *Flexible cord*
2. *Power transformer*
3. *High voltage rectifier and capacitor*
4. *Magnetron*
5. *Waveguide*
6. *Wave stirrer (paddle)*
7. *Oven cavity*
8. *Oven door and frame with special seals*

microwaves which in turn cause the water molecules within the food itself to vibrate frantically at 2400 million cycles or vibrations per second. The result is excessively rapid friction which creates enough heat to cook food fast and furiously, effectively and cleanly. For a simple comparison of how friction makes heat, rub your hands together vigorously and feel how warm they become. Now multiply this umpteen times and you will understand how the microwaves work. For even cooking, most models are fitted with what is called either a wave stirrer, stirrer blade or paddle (invisible and again at the top) which helps to distribute the waves. Other models have a round and rotating turntable as well. Turntables do restrict the shape and size of the dishes to some extent, and therefore consider a model where the turntable can be switched off or removed.

Successful Cooking

Because microwaves are short-length, high-frequency radio waves, they are able to penetrate only 1 inch ($2\frac{1}{2}$cm) of the food in all directions. Thus shallow dishes are better than deep ones, except those used for some cakes and puddings which need headroom in order to rise satisfactorily. Round dishes give the most satisfactory results, followed by oval.

Sometimes food in oblong or square dishes cooks unevenly, especially at the corners. The food will also cook more satisfactorily if thick pieces are placed towards the outside edges of the dish and *never* piled up. Stirring during the cooking cycle helps to distribute heat and, where practical, this has been recommended in the recipes. If possible, whole potatoes and other similar-shaped foods (apples for example) should be arranged, on a plate or in a dish, in the shape of a hollow triangle, square or ring.

Resting and Standing Times

In order for heat to penetrate the food and work its way gently from the outside to the centre, it is recommended that the food be allowed to rest or stand after or between cooking. Individual recipes will specify. If some dishes were cooked without a rest (and this applies especially to large quantities, turkeys etc.), the outside would become overdone and the middle remain underdone. Depending on what is more convenient, food may be left to rest or stand inside or outside the microwave. *As a further precaution*, it is advisable to undercook a dish and return it briefly to the oven if necessary, rather than add extra time for 'good measure'. The microwaves act so swiftly that even a few seconds too many could sometimes spoil the food.

Seasonings

As salt tends to toughen meat, poultry and offal cooked in a microwave, it should be added half way through the cooking cycle or at the very end. Other seasonings, such as herbs and spices, may be added at the beginning.

Caution

Never operate the oven while empty because without food or drink to absorb the microwaves, they will bounce straight back to the magnetron and shorten its life span. Similarly, melting 1 or 2 teaspoons of fat, or heating a tiny amount of liquid, will have the same effect, so it is best to place a cup or tumbler of water into the oven at the same time. Just in case an empty oven gets switched on by accident, it is a wise safety measure to keep a container of water inside until the oven is needed for cooking.

To Clean

Suggestions for cleaning have been given in the Hints and Tips Section on page 230. As fresh food spills are so easy to remove from the cool interior of a microwave (nothing burns on in the conventional sense), a wipe over with a damp cloth immediately after use will ensure that it stays spotless and fresh.

Selection of suitable microwave containers

Cookware

Metal containers reflect microwaves away from the food and prevent it from cooking. Therefore *never* use metal containers or tins of any sort in the oven. It is also important to note that crockery with metal trims, and manufacturers' names or pattern designs printed in gold or silver underneath, could cause arcing which resemble tiny flashes of lightning. The arcing not only damages the magnetron but also ruins the metallic decorations. The exceptions here are small amounts of foil used to cover poultry wing tips and ends of legs to prevent scorching; also metal skewers for kebabs which are well covered by the surrounding food. However, *ensure* that the skewers do not come into contact with any part of the oven interior.

In order for the microwaves to reach the food and subsequently cook it, the dishes chosen should be made of materials through which the microwaves can pass most readily – like sun rays through a window pane. These are listed below and although most stay cool and even cold, some kinds absorb heat from the cooked food and feel hot to the touch. For comfort, the cookware should be removed from the oven with oven gloves.

BASKETS

These may be used for *brief* reheating of rolls etc. Prolonged spells in the microwave cause dryness.

CLING FILM (See-through plastic wrap)

Excellent for covering and lining dishes. To prevent the film from ballooning up in the oven and bursting, or being sucked back on to the food (the latter a disaster if this happens to a pudding which is supposed to rise), I have recommended puncturing the film twice with the tip of a knife to allow steam to escape. By puncturing, I mean a small slit and not a tiny pin-prick.

GLASS

Not your best crystal but Pyrex type glassware is ideal. Corningware, which is ceramic glass, is also excellent. Other, sturdy, glass may also be used.

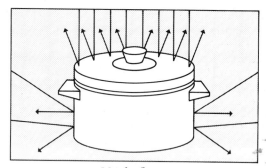

Metal reflects

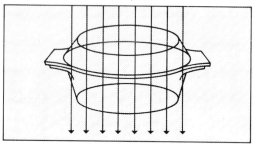

Ceramics transmit

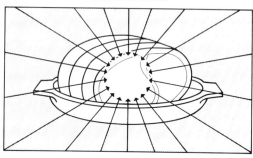

Food absorbs

PAPER

Kitchen paper or serviettes may be used to line the oven base if food is to be cooked directly on it (it is a great absorber), and also to cover food to prevent spluttering.

PLASTIC

Rigid plastic only please to prevent collapse, and *not* used yogurt or cottage cheese containers! Look for special microwave utensils made by Thorpac, Lakeland Plastics in Windermere or Anchor Hocking. Just 3 examples though there are more makes stocked by microwave centres, some kitchen boutiques and departmental stores. Note that plastic spatulas are useful in that they can be left, say, in a sauce while it is cooking and then used for stirring as and when required.

POTTERY AND PORCELAIN

Both may be used but not a best tea or dinner set. Avoid dark utensils as they become very hot.

ROASTING BAGS (also called Boiling Bags)

With a hundred and one uses, see-through plastic roasting bags are convenient to use and also clean. Ideal for cooking joints of meat or poultry, close the tops with elastic bands or string, *not* metal ties.

WAXED PAPER PRODUCTS

Rather like basketware, these should be used *very briefly* or the wax will begin to melt.

WOOD

Wood, like basketware, dries out in the microwave and should be used only for brief reheating.

Extras

BROWNING DISH

This is a white ceramic dish, the base of which is coated with a special tin oxide material. It becomes very hot indeed when preheated, making it possible to sear food prior to cooking in the microwave. This gives the food a brown finish associated with conventional grilling or frying. As the dish needs to be preheated, empty, for varying lengths of time (depending on the food being cooked), be guided by your own microwave oven instruction book. As a general rule, the preheating time should be

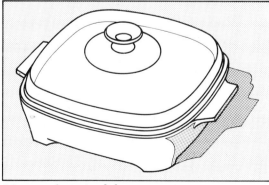

Microwave browning dish

around 6 minutes for steaks and chops and 2 to 3 minutes for eggs. It should *never* be preheated for longer than 8 minutes, nor used in a conventional oven. Every time a batch of food has been cooked, the browning dish will need cleaning and preheating again but for *half the length of time allowed initially.* Although it will take on a yellowy tinge when hot, the dish will return to its original colour when cool. Preheating this type of dish does not harm the oven.

TIP

The larger the dish, the longer the preheating time required. Thus 5 minutes in a small dish will equate to 7 minutes in a large one. Browning dishes are usually optional extras, to be purchased separately from the oven.

TEMPERATURE PROBE AND THERMOMETERS

This looks like a thick knitting needle attached to a plastic-coated lead and is generally available with the more sophisticated models of microwave ovens. One end slots into the side of the oven while the other end (the needle part) is inserted into the food to be cooked and registers the internal temperature.

The cooking cycle is therefore geared to temperature and not time and when, for example, a joint of well-done beef registers 160°F (71°C), the oven will switch off automatically. As every make of cooker varies, please refer to your own microwave book before using the probe and setting the temperature.

Thermometers for use in microwave ovens are now obtainable and they, too, must be used according to the manufacturers' instructions.

TIP FOR PROBE

The temperature given above is just one example. Pork requires a higher internal temperature; rare beef a lower one.

Choice of Microwave Ovens

When I first started working with microwave ovens, some had an on/off switch and a timer and that was it. More up-to-date models had a defrost button and, later on, I progressed to one with a third power setting, namely 'heat'. Looking around today, many of the newer microwave ovens have every gadget and gimmick one can think of: variable power settings, electronic touch controls, double decker interiors, turntables, pre-set programmes and memory banks, browning elements, microwave and conventional ovens combined to give you the best of both worlds in one unit, buzzers, warning bells, bleeps, flashing lights, digital figures, sleek, elegant lines in dark, sophisticated colours and automation.

People ask me, often, which model I would recommend and I always find this a difficult question to answer. Those who are non-technically minded will be best off with a fairly basic model which does its job efficiently and is, additionally, straightforward to operate. Others, who are into electronics, will find the new models a joy in that they bear some relation to computers and can easily be programmed and manipulated to suit all purposes. The only advice I can give on the selection front is to suggest that you call in at your nearest microwave centre, Electricity Board or departmental store, have a thorough look at as many ovens as you can, and ask for a demonstration. You will then be in a better position to buy what suits you, not what looks fabulous, is very expensive and turns out to be more complex to cope with than you bargained for.

Power Controls

Microwave ovens vary between 500 and 700 watt output with a corresponding input of 1000 and 1500 watts. Though the wattage output is what controls cooking times, the input of electricity is utilised by the transformer, the magnetron, stirrer blades and turntable, cooling fan, browning elements and assortment of lights inside the oven and on the control panel.

All recipes in this book have been prepared in a 600 watt output oven using only *two*

power settings: COOK/HIGH which is 100% power (600 watts), and DEFROST which is 50% (300 watts). If your oven has a different output, the guide below may prove useful

For a 500 watt output oven, *increase* cooking time by about one-fifth (20%). e.g. 10 minutes becomes 12 minutes.

For a 550 watt output oven, *increase* cooking time by about one-tenth (10%). e.g. 10 minutes becomes 11 minutes.

For a 650 watt output oven, *decrease* cooking time by one-tenth (10%). e.g. 10 minutes becomes 9 minutes.

For a 700 watt output oven, *decrease* cooking time by about one-fifth (20%). e.g. 10 minutes becomes 8 minutes.

Using these figures will give a fairly accurate conversion time but for greater accuracy, refer to your own microwave oven recipe book.

If you are uncertain of the output of your own oven, carry out this water test:

Pour $\frac{1}{4}$ pint (150ml) cold water into a jug. Heat at full power until it boils. This should take approximately $2\frac{1}{4}$ minutes. If it boils more quickly, this would indicate that the output is higher – 650 watts perhaps – and the recipe timings should be adjusted accordingly as given above. Similarly, if the water boils more slowly, then the output is probably lower, so again refer to the adaptation of timings given above.

Variable power settings can range from 1 to 10 and are to be found in some of the more up-to-date and technically advanced microwave ovens. The variable settings enable a selection of dishes to be cooked more slowly than others and some users find this advantageous, especially when making meat stews and casseroles which respond better to a more gentle approach and a lower power setting than full. Some models have a system whereby the power comes on and off automatically for short bursts for so many seconds at a time. Listen and you can hear it happening. Other models have an automatic reduction in output at the lower settings and this is silent.

Summary of the Settings

Setting 1 equates to 10% of power output and is also termed warm. It is used to keep cooked dishes warm or take the chill off cold ones. It is called either warm or low.

Setting 2 equates to 20% of power output and is recommended for warming or very gentle simmering. It is called either warm or low as well.

Setting 3 equates to 30% of power output and is used for slow defrosting and simmering. It is called either defrost, low, simmer or soften.

Setting 4 equates to 40% of power output and is often chosen for defrosting, braising and stewing. It is called either slow cook, medium, low defrost, stew, simmer or braise.

Setting 5 equates to 50% of power output and is the one used most frequently for defrosting. It can also be used for simmering and stewing. It is called either medium, defrost, simmer or stew.

Setting 6 equates to 60% of power output and is used chiefly for reheating cooked dishes, baking or simmering. It is called either reheat, bake or simmer.

Setting 7 equates to 70% of power output and is used primarily for roasting. It is called either medium high, bake or roast.

Setting 8 equates to 80% of power output and is also used for reheating and baking. It is called either reheat or bake.

Setting 9 equates to 90% of power output and is used for fast cooking of vegetables in fat (i.e. when making a stew). It is called either medium high, roast, fast reheat or sometimes sauté.

Setting 10 equates to 100% of power output and is used for the majority of recipes in this microwave book. It is called either full power, high, maximum or fast cook.

If you have a microwave with variable power settings such as listed above, follow the instructions for use in your own microwave guide book and *do not try* to convert my recipes which were cooked at full power or defrost setting.

It is a consoling thought to know that when cooking in the microwave, the electricity saved is between 50 and 70%. Also no pre-heating is necessary and there is minimal residual heat in the oven cavity. It has been estimated that using a microwave is four times as efficient as conventional cooking because *all* the energy is directed to the food with no 'over-spill'.

Colour

Microwaved foods can look pale when cooked and also insipid. Hence bastes for roast meat and poultry, brown gravy cubes for stews and casseroles, and icings for cakes. I have also incorporated a number of other tricks – like using Red Leicester cheese instead of Cheddar for toppings – as you will soon find out when you make up some of the recipes in the book. *None* lack colour!

Reheating

Slow reheating of meat and poultry, or keeping plates of food warm in a cool oven, can sometimes cause a build-up of bacteria, resulting in mild food poisoning.

With a microwave oven, the action is so fast that germs have no time to breed, and the food stays daisy fresh and moist without looking frayed round the edges.

Bonuses

Freshness of flavour and colour, plus retention of nutrients, characterise most foods cooked in a microwave oven. The foods also tend to shrink less, and cooking smells do not invade the kitchen or the rest of the house.

And on a Final Note

Standard recipes are *not* convertible to microwave ovens, so please use only those which have been specifically designed for the appliance – as those in my book. NEVER pre-heat a microwave oven as it is both unnecessary and damaging to the magnetron. Where the letter (F) appears by the recipe title, this indicates the dish is suitable for freezing.

Convenience Foods

Convenience Foods – Frozen

	DEFROST (50%)	COOK/HEAT (100%)	COMMENTS/GUIDELINES
BACON RASHERS 8oz (225g)	3 minutes Stand 6 minutes	3 minutes, turn over, cook 2 minutes.	Separate after defrosting. Transfer to large plate, arranging rashers in single layer. Cover with kitchen paper. Drain after cooking.
BEEFBURGERS 2 × 2oz (50g)	2 minutes Stand $\frac{1}{2}$ minute	$1\frac{1}{2}$ minutes	Put on to plate to defrost and cook. Cover with kitchen paper. Turn over once during cooking.
4 × 2oz (50g)	3 minutes Stand 1 minute	$2\frac{1}{2}$ to 3 minutes	As above.
2 × 4oz (125g)	2 minutes Stand 2 minutes	3 minutes	As above.
4 × 4oz (125g)	6 minutes Stand 3 minutes	$5\frac{1}{2}$ to 6 minutes	As above.
BEEF, roast in gravy 8oz (225g)	6 minutes Stand 4 minutes	4 minutes	Remove from foil container. Put into glass or pottery dish. Cover with film. Slit twice. Alternatively cover with matching lid.
12oz (350g)	8 minutes Stand 4 minutes	6 minutes	As above.
BREAD 1 slice	20 to 30 seconds Stand 1 minute		Stand on kitchen paper or plate. Time depends on size and thickness of slice.
2 slices	30 to 40 seconds Stand 1 minute		As above.
4 slices	1 to $1\frac{1}{2}$ minutes Stand $1\frac{1}{2}$ to 2 minutes		As above.
6 slices	2 minutes Stand 2 minutes		As above.
Small loaf	4 minutes Stand 5 to 6 minutes		Wrap loaf in kitchen paper or clean tea towel.
Large loaf	6 to 8 minutes Stand 8 to 10 minutes		As above.
BREAD ROLLS 2 rolls	$\frac{1}{2}$ to 1 minute		Put on to a plate. Cover with kitchen paper.
BURGER BUNS 2 buns	$\frac{1}{2}$ to 1 minute		Put on to a plate. Cover with kitchen paper.
4 buns	$1\frac{1}{2}$ to 2 minutes		As above.

	DEFROST (50%)	COOK/HEAT (100%)	COMMENTS/GUIDELINES
BUTTER			
4oz (125g)	15 seconds Stand 15 seconds 10 seconds Stand 15 seconds		Remove from foil. Put on to plate. Repeat the 10 seconds defrost and 15 seconds standing until thawed. Check often to be sure the butter does not become too soft.
8oz (225g)	30 seconds Stand 30 seconds 15 seconds Stand 30 seconds		As above.
CAKES AND PUDDINGS			
Cake 1 slice	$\frac{3}{4}$ minute to $1\frac{1}{4}$ minutes		Put on to paper or plate. Time to defrost will depend on size of slice.
Cream cake/Pastry Individual	$\frac{3}{4}$ minute Stand 3 minutes		Put on to paper or plate.
Cream sponge 10oz (275g)	1 to $1\frac{1}{2}$ minutes Stand 20 to 25 minutes		Put on to paper or plate. Stand until cream thaws through.
3 Layer cake 17oz (475g)	1 to $1\frac{1}{2}$ minutes Stand 2 to 3 minutes		Put on to plate.
Cheesecake 10oz (275g)	$1\frac{1}{2}$ to $2\frac{1}{2}$ minutes Stand 10 minutes		Remove from foil container. Place on paper or plate.
17 to 19oz (475 to 525g)	2 to 4 minutes Stand 10 to 15 minutes		As above.
Doughnut, cream 1 doughnut	30 seconds Stand 4 minutes		Put on to paper or plate. Check that cream is not melting too fast.
2 doughnuts	45 seconds Stand 5 minutes		As above.
4 doughnuts	$\frac{3}{4}$ to 1 minute Stand 8 minutes		As above.
Doughnut, jam 1 doughnut	$\frac{1}{2}$ to 1 minute Stand 3 minutes		Put on to paper or plate.
2 doughnuts	1 minute Stand 5 minutes		As above.
4 doughnuts	1 to $1\frac{1}{2}$ minutes Stand 8 minutes		As above.
CANNELLONI			
14oz (400g)	7 minutes Stand 4 minutes	5 to 6 minutes	Remove from foil container and place in a similar-sized dish. Cover with film and slit twice. Turn dish several times during cooking.

	DEFROST (50%)	COOK/HEAT (100%)	COMMENTS/GUIDELINES
CHICKEN, coated and fried (pre-cooked) 2 to 3 pieces 7 to 9oz (200 to 250g)	4 minutes Stand 4 minutes	2 to 3 minutes Stand 2 to 3 minutes	Separate and arrange on plate or dish with thickest pieces round edge. Cover with kitchen paper. Half way through cooking time, re-arrange the pieces and re-cover.
4 pieces 12oz (350g)	6 minutes Stand 4 minutes	3 to 4 minutes Stand 2 to 3 minutes	As above.
5 to 7 pieces 16oz (450g)	8 minutes Stand 6 minutes	6 to 8 minutes Stand 3 to 4 minutes	As above.
Chicken Cordon Bleu 12oz (350g)	4 minutes Stand 4 minutes	6 minutes	Remove wrapping and put on to plate. Cover with kitchen paper. Turn dish half way round after cooking 3 minutes.
Chicken Kiev 12oz (350g)	As above	As above	As above.
CHIPOLATAS 8oz (225g)	3 minutes Stand 2 minutes	3 minutes	Stand on kitchen paper on a plate. Cover with more paper.
16oz (450g)	5 minutes Stand 3 minutes	$4\frac{1}{2}$ minutes	As above.
COTTAGE/SHEPHERD'S PIE Individual	3 minutes Stand 2 minutes	3 minutes	If in foil, remove to plate or dish and cover with lid or kitchen paper.
16oz (450g)	8 minutes Stand 4 minutes	7 minutes	Remove from foil and place in similar-sized dish. Cover with film and slit twice. Alternatively, cover with matching lid. Turn dish several times during cooking.
CREAM $\frac{1}{2}$ pt (approximately 275 to 284ml)	$1\frac{1}{2}$ minutes Stand 5 minutes $\frac{1}{2}$ minute Stand 2 minutes Repeat until thawed		Place in bowl and break up with fork while thawing. If in carton, remove lid. Transfer to bowl as soon as cream can be removed easily.
ECLAIRS – CHOCOLATE 4	1 to $1\frac{1}{2}$ minutes Stand 15 to 20 minutes		Stand on kitchen paper on a plate. Check to make sure cream does not melt too quickly or it will begin to run.
FAGGOTS in sauce 4 by 13oz (375g)	3 minutes Stand 3 minutes	$4\frac{1}{2}$ to 5 minutes	Remove from foil container and put into dish. Cover with film and slit twice. Alternatively, cover with matching lid. When faggots have defrosted, uncover and arrange round edge of dish to cook. Re-cover as above.
6 by 18oz (500g)	5 minutes Stand 5 minutes	7 to 9 minutes	As above.

	DEFROST (50%)	COOK/HEAT (100%)	COMMENTS/GUIDELINES
FISH CAKES 4	3 minutes Stand 2 minutes	1½ to 2 minutes	Put on to plate. Cover with kitchen paper. Turn over at half time during defrosting.
FISH FINGERS 4	2 minutes Stand 1 minute	2 minutes	Put on to plate. Cover with kitchen paper. Turn over half way through cooking time.
8	4 minutes Stand 2 minutes	2 minutes	As above.
FISH IN SAUCE, cod, plaice etc (boil-in-bag) 1 by 6 oz (175g)	4 to 4½ minutes Stand 2 minutes	2½ to 3 minutes	Put on to plate. Make a slit with scissors in a corner of each bag. This is necessary as the bag might balloon up and burst. Do not cook more than one bag at a time because the sauce heats up faster than the fish and may seep out, on the longer time, before the fish is cooked. After cooking, the sauce will be hot, so carefully cut along slit end of bag and slide fish and sauce on to same plate.
2 by 6oz (175g)	6 to 6½ minutes Stand 2 minutes	4½ to 5 minutes	
FRUIT JUICE, to soften 6 to 6½ fluid oz (170 to 176ml)	3 minutes		Remove lid. Stand container upright on paper. If metal top and bottom, or if container has a metallic lining, soften block of juice by running under warm water then transfer to jug or bowl to defrost.
HADDOCK, buttered, smoked 7oz (200g)	4 minutes Stand 4 minutes	4 minutes	Put on to plate. Make a slit with scissors in a corner of the bag so that the bag will not balloon up and burst. After cooking the butter will be hot, so carefully cut along slit end of bag and slide fish and butter gently on to same plate.
ICE CREAM, to soften 1¾pt (1 litre)	30 to 45 seconds		Leave, covered, in original container. Check to see that ice cream is not melting.
KIPPERS, fillets with butter in bag 6 to 8oz (175 to 225g)	4 minutes Stand 2 minutes	2 to 3 minutes	Put on to plate. Make a slit with scissors in a corner of the bag so that the bag will not balloon up and burst. After cooking, the butter will be hot, so carefully cut along the slit end of the bag and slide fish and butter gently on to same plate.
10oz (275g)	6 minutes Stand 2 minutes	5 minutes	As above.

	DEFROST (50%)	COOK/HEAT (100%)	COMMENTS/GUIDELINES
LASAGNE 16oz (450g)	8 minutes Stand 4 minutes	6 minutes	Remove from foil container and place in a similar-sized dish. Cover with film and slit twice. Alternatively, cover with matching lid. Turn dish several times during cooking.
MACKEREL, smoked fillets (2) to serve cold, 8oz (225g)	2 to 2½ minutes Stand 2 to 3 minutes		Put on to plate and cover with kitchen paper.
to serve warm/hot, 8oz (225g)	2 to 2½ minutes Stand 2 to 3 minutes	2 to 3 minutes	As above.
MACKEREL, buttered smoked fillets (boil-in-bag) 6oz (175g)	4 minutes Stand 2 minutes	3 minutes	Put on to plate. Make a slit with scissors in a corner of the bag so that the bag will not balloon up and burst. After cooking, the butter will be hot, so carefully cut along the slit end of bag and slide fish and butter gently on to same plate.
MOUSSAKA 14oz (400g)	7 minutes Stand 4 minutes	5 to 6 minutes	Remove from foil container and place in a similar-sized dish. Cover with film and slit twice. Alternatively, cover with matching lid. Turn dish several times during cooking.
MOUSSE, individual	30 seconds Stand 15 minutes		Remove lid.
OVEN CHIPS		2½ minutes and re-arrange. 2½ minutes Stand 3 minutes	Arrange in single layer on 10 inch (25cm) plate. Cover with kitchen paper.
PANCAKES (4 filled)	5 minutes	1½ to 2 minutes	Put on to plate. Cover with kitchen paper.
PATÉ 1 portion	2 to 2½ minutes Stand 5 to 10 minutes		Transfer to plate and cover with kitchen paper.
PIZZA 5 inch (7oz or 200g)	2 minutes Stand 2 minutes	2 minutes	Snip wrapping after defrosting and before cooking/heating.
7 inch (9 to 10oz or 250 to 275g)	3 minutes Stand 2 minutes	2½ minutes	As above.
PIZZA, French bread 2 pieces	2 minutes Stand 2 minutes	2 minutes	As above.

	DEFROST (50%)	COOK/HEAT (100%)	COMMENTS/GUIDELINES
PIZZA BUNS 2 buns	1 minute Stand 1½ minutes	2 minutes	As above. NOTE: If any of the above are not wrapped top and bottom, stand on a plate and cover with kitchen paper while defrosting and cooking/heating.
PLATE MEAL, home-prepared and frozen	1 minute Stand 5 minutes	2 to 3 minutes	If covered with cling film, slit twice before defrosting and cooking. If not, cover with kitchen paper. Turn plate twice or three times while cooking.
PORK PIES, individual	2 minutes Stand 15 minutes		Place on paper on plate. Do not overheat or jelly will melt.
PREPARED MEALS (Shop-bought) e.g. Sweet and Sour Chicken 6 to 8oz (175 to 225g)	3 to 4 minutes Stand 3 minutes	3 to 4 minutes	Remove from container and put into suitable dish. Cover with film and slit twice. Alternatively, cover with matching lid. Turn twice during cooking/heating. Stir before serving.
SALMON, smoked in a pack 7oz (200g), sliced	45 seconds Stand 25 to 30 minutes		Turn over after 20 seconds defrosting.
SAUSAGE ROLLS, cooked 1	45 seconds Stand 2 minutes	15 seconds	Stand on kitchen paper on plate. Cover with more paper.
4	1½ to 2 minutes Stand 3 minutes	45 seconds	As above.
SAUSAGES, large (6 to the lb or 450g) 2 sausages	1½ minutes Stand 2 minutes	3½ minutes	Stand on kitchen paper on plate, cover with more paper.
4 sausages	2 minutes Stand 2 minutes	5 minutes	As above.
medium (8 to the lb or 450g) 2 sausages	1½ minutes Stand 1 minute	2½ minutes	As above.
4 sausages	2 minutes Stand 2 minutes	3½ minutes	As above.
SAUSAGES Cocktail or Chipolatas 8oz (225g)	3 minutes Stand 2 minutes	3 minutes	Stand on kitchen paper on plate, cover with more paper.
16oz (450g)	5 minutes Stand 3 minutes	4½ minutes	As above.
TRIFLES, individual (Shop-bought)	1 to 2 minutes Stand 5 minutes		Remove lid.

	DEFROST (50%)	COOK/HEAT (100%)	COMMENTS/GUIDELINES
WAFFLES, 2		1 to 2 minutes Stand 2 minutes	Place on kitchen paper, cover with more paper.
YOGURT, individual	2 to 3 minutes Stand 5 minutes		Remove lid. Stir before serving.

Convenience Foods – Canned

	COOK/HEAT (100%)	COMMENTS/GUIDELINES
CASSEROLE, soya-type chunks or meat 15½oz (439g)	4 minutes Stand 2 minutes	Place in bowl. Cover with plate. Stir after 2 minutes cooking.
CORN 12oz (350g)	4 to 4½ minutes	Place in bowl. Cover with film and slit twice. Alternatively cover with plate or lid.
CUSTARD to warm 15oz (425g) can	1½ to 2 minutes	Pour custard into bowl. Cover with plate. Stir once or twice. Do not allow to boil.
to heat until hot, 15oz (425g) can	3½ minutes	As above.
to heat until hot, (500ml container)	4 to 4½ minutes	As above.
PASTA, spaghetti hoops, etc. 15½oz (439g)	3 minutes Stand 2 minutes	Place in bowl. Cover with plate. Stir once or twice.
RICE PUDDING 15½oz (439g)	3 minutes	Place in bowl. Cover with plate. Stir once or twice.
SOUP, condensed about 10oz (295g)	6 to 6½ minutes	Empty soup from can into bowl. Add 1 can cold water. Mix in well. Cover with plate. Stir every minute while cooking. Do not allow to boil. Time will vary depending on consistency of soup.
SOUP, ready-to-serve 15oz (425g)	4 to 5 minutes	Place in bowl. Cover with plate. Stir every minute. Time will depend on personal taste in hot soup but DO NOT allow to boil vigorously.
SPONGE PUDDING 8 to 10oz (225 to 275g)	1½ to 2 minutes	Remove from tin and place in bowl. Cover with film and slit twice. Alternatively, cover with plate.
STEAK AND KIDNEY PUDDING 15½oz (439g)	4 to 5 minutes Stand 5 minutes	Remove from tin and place in bowl. Cover with film and slit twice. Alternatively, cover with plate.

	COOK/HEAT (100%)	COMMENTS/GUIDELINES
VEGETABLES Small (peas, beans etc.) 8 to 10oz (225 to 275g)	2 to 3½ minutes Stand 2 minutes	Pour 2 tablespoons of liquid from can into serving dish or bowl. Drain off rest of liquid and discard. Put vegetables into dish. Cover with film. Slit film twice. If vegetable is in sauce, e.g. baked beans, *do not drain*. If preferred, cover dish or bowl with plate. Stir vegetables at least once during cooking/ heating. Drain before serving.
14 to 15½oz (400 to 439g)	3 to 4 minutes Stand 3 minutes	As above.
Large (artichoke, asparagus etc) 15 to 15½oz (425 to 439g)	4 to 5 minutes Stand 3 minutes	As above but do not stir. Turn dish or bowl twice or 3 times during cooking/heating.

Convenience Foods (Miscellaneous)

	DEFROST (50%)	COOK/HEAT (100%)	COMMENTS/GUIDELINES
BUTTER, to soften from refrigerator 8oz (225g)	40 to 50 seconds		Remove from foil wrapping. Stand on plate.
to melt, from room temperature ½oz (15g)	40 to 50 seconds		Put into glass cup or jug. Cover with saucer or plate. Do not overheat or butter will splutter.
1oz (25g)	1 to 1½ minutes		As above.
2oz (50g)	1½ to 2 minutes		As above.
3oz (75g)	2 to 2½ minutes		As above.
4oz (125g)	2½ to 3 minutes		As above.
8oz (225g)	3 to 3½ minutes		As above.
If from refrigerator, allow a little extra time			
CHRISTMAS PUDDING, (at kitchen temperature) 1 portion to heat		45 seconds Stand 1 minute	Stand on plate. Cover with kitchen paper.
1lb (450g) to heat		3 to 4 minutes Stand 2 minutes	In bowl. Cover with kitchen paper or plate.
2lb (900g) to heat		5 minutes Stand 5 minutes 5 minutes Stand 5 minutes	In bowl. Cover with kitchen paper or plate.

	DEFROST (50%)	COOK/HEAT (100%)	COMMENTS/GUIDELINES
CHEESE, to bring back to serving temperature if taken directly from refrigerator			
Firm cheese 8oz (225g)	30 to 45 seconds		Put on to plate. Leave uncovered.
Soft cheese 8oz (225g)	15 to 45 seconds		As above.
CHOCOLATE, to melt from kitchen temperature			
1 bar 3½oz (100g)	3 to 3½ minutes		Put into bowl in pieces. Stir once and watch carefully as soon as it starts to melt. If over-heated, chocolate may become granular.
1 bar 7oz (200g)	4 to 5 minutes. Allow an extra ½ to 1 minute if taken straight from refrigerator.		As above.
GELATINE, to dissolve 1 packet (0·4oz or 11g)	1½ to 1¾ minutes		Add 2 tablespoons cold liquid to granules in jug or bowl. Cover with plate. Swirl round after 1 minute. Stir thoroughly after removing from microwave to ensure gelatine has dissolved.
JAM, to soften			
4oz (125g)		30 to 45 seconds	Put into bowl or leave in jar. Cover with kitchen paper or plate. Make sure metal jar lid is removed.
8oz (225g)		1 to 1¼ minutes	As above.
JELLY, to melt 1 packet (4¾oz or 135g)	2 to 2½ minutes		Break into cubes and put into jug. Cover with plate.
MEAT PIE, Individual		¾ to 1¼ minutes	Remove from foil tray. Stand on kitchen paper. Cover with more paper.
Family size 16oz (450g)		3 minutes Stand 4 minutes 3 minutes Stand 4 minutes	As above.
MINCE PIES, cooked			
1 pie		15 seconds Stand 1 to 2 minutes	Stand on paper. Leave uncovered.
4 pies		1 minute Stand 2 to 3 minutes	As above.
PLATE MEAL, 1 serving, from refrigerator		2 to 3 minutes Stand 30 to 40 seconds	Cover with film if not already done. Slit twice. Alternatively, cover with inverted plate or kitchen paper.

Snacks and Breakfasts

Granola
Makes about 1½lb (675g), allowing for evaporation

One of America's most popular breakfast cereal mixes and fast catching on over here, my version contains bran for added fibre and a sprinkling of plump raisins. I confess it is very sweet and needs toning down with milk.

4oz (125g) butter or margarine
4oz (125g) golden syrup
9oz (250g) porridge oats
1½oz (40g) coarse bran
4oz (125g) dark brown soft sugar
3oz (75g) walnuts, finely chopped
4oz (125g) Californian seedless raisins

1. Put butter or margarine into a 10 inch (25cm) round glass or pottery dish. Add syrup. Leave uncovered and melt 4 minutes at defrost setting.

2. Mix in all remaining ingredients except raisins. Leave uncovered and cook 9 to 9½ minutes at full power, stirring 4 or 5 times so that Granola browns evenly and becomes the colour of brown bread crust.

3. Remove from oven, add raisins and mix in well. Leave to stand until crispy and cold, stirring from time to time until crumbly. Store in an airtight container.

HONEY GRANOLA
Use honey instead of golden syrup.

HAZELNUT GRANOLA
Use chopped hazelnuts instead of walnuts.

Porridge

For 1 portion
Put 2 rounded tablespoons porridge into a bowl. Add ¼ pint (150ml) water or milk and a pinch of salt. Leave uncovered and cook 1¾ to 2 minutes at full power, stirring. Stand 1½ minutes. Serve with milk or cream and either sugar or salt.

For 2 portions in 2 bowls
Cook 3 to 3½ minutes at full power.

For 3 portions in 3 bowls
Cook 3½ to 4 minutes at full power.

For 4 portions in 4 bowls
Cook 4 to 4½ minutes at full power.

Bacon

Bacon cooks extremely well in the microwave and shrinks less than if grilled or fried conventionally. To prevent sticking, do not line, as some books suggest, the dish or plate with kitchen paper. However, the bacon should be loosely covered with paper while cooking to prevent spluttering and dirtying the oven. Drain at the end by wiping with more paper.

1 rasher
Cook $\frac{3}{4}$ to 1 minute at full power.

2 rashers
Cook $1\frac{1}{2}$ to $1\frac{3}{4}$ minutes at full power.

3 rashers
Cook 2 to $2\frac{1}{4}$ minutes at full power.

4 rashers
Cook $2\frac{1}{2}$ to $2\frac{3}{4}$ minutes at full power.

5 rashers
Cook 3 to $3\frac{1}{2}$ minutes at full power.

6 rashers
Cook 4 to $4\frac{1}{2}$ minutes at full power.

NOTE: Timing is a guide only and depending on the type of bacon and size of rashers, you may need to allow a little more time or even a few seconds less.

Welsh Rarebit   Serves 3

A favourite snack which adapts beautifully – and fast – to microwave cooking. The topping is enriched with egg yolk and has a warm, round flavour.

4oz (125g) Cheddar cheese, finely grated
1 level tsp powder mustard
1 level tsp cornflour
1 egg yolk
2 tsp milk
salt and pepper to taste
3 large slices freshly made brown or white toast
paprika

1. Mix cheese with mustard, cornflour, egg yolk and milk. Season to taste.

2. Spread over 3 slices of toast. Put on to individual plates.

3. Leave uncovered and cook 1 minute each at full power. Dust lightly with paprika and serve straight away.

BUCK RAREBIT   Serves 3

Make as above. Pop a poached or fried egg (pages 68–69) on top of each. Sprinkle very lightly with paprika.

BACON RAREBIT   Serves 3

Make as Welsh Rarebit then top with one or two bacon rashers, cooked as given in either the Convenience Food Chart (page 14) or above.

Baked Beans on Toast   For 1

Stand a large slice of fresh toast on a plate and spread with butter or margarine. Top with 4 rounded tablespoons canned baked beans in tomato sauce. Leave uncovered and heat $1\frac{1}{2}$ to 2 minutes at full power.

BAKED BEANS ON TOAST   for 2

Make as above but allow 3 to $3\frac{1}{2}$ minutes for 2 plates.

RAREBIT BEANS   For 1 or 2   (Picture p. 49)

Make as above, sprinkling each with 1oz (25g) grated cheese. Allow $\frac{1}{4}$ minute extra cooking time.

CANNED SPAGHETTI (or any of its variants) ON TOAST

Follow directions for Baked Beans on Toast, using any of the canned pastas in sauce.

Starters

Starters, more appropriately appetisers, should be just that and set the taste buds tingling for the culinary pleasures still to come. Thus, keep to smallish portions, garnish attractively, and thank your lucky stars that some of the dishes can be made in the microwave while you are relaxing over a pre-meal drink.

Although the selection is relatively short, there are also soups to choose from should you so desire, while some of the fish, vegetarian, egg and vegetable dishes are also appropriate to serve as hors d'oeuvres.

Please bear in mind that the number of servings is a guide only. You may wish to offer less if the meal is robust, more if the meal is light.

Stuffed Tomatoes   Serves 6

A light starter and just right for spring and summer evenings.

6 medium tomatoes
1oz (25g) butter or margarine
4oz (125g) onion, peeled and chopped
2oz (50g) fresh white breadcrumbs
1 level tsp prepared mustard
1 level tsp salt
1 level tsp dried basil or mixed herbs
2oz (50g) cooked chopped meat, poultry, tongue, prawns or grated Cheddar

1. Cut tops off tomatoes, reserve for lids and scoop centres into bowl. Discard hard cores. Stand tomato cups upside down to drain on kitchen paper.

2. Put butter or margarine into a dish and melt 1 to 1½ minutes at defrost setting. Add onion and cook 2 minutes at full power, leaving uncovered.

3. Stir in crumbs, tomato pulp, mustard, salt, basil or herbs and the meat, fish or cheese.

4. Pile into tomato cups and top with lids. Arrange in a ring round the edge of a dinner plate.

5. Cover with kitchen paper and heat 6 to 7 minutes at full power. Serve straight away while hot.

Vol-au-Vents   Serves 6

Always welcome, these are made from ready-made puff pastry vol-au-vents cases or those bought frozen and conventionally baked.

Make up ½ pint (275ml) coating white sauce or Béchamel sauce as given in the Sauce Section on page 40. Add 8oz (225g) cooked and coarsely-chopped poultry, ham or meat. Alternatively, use the same amount of cooked and flaked fish, crab-meat or prawns. Spoon into 6 by 3 inch (7·5cm) vol-au-vent cases and top with lids. Arrange in a ring in a 10 inch (25cm) round shallow dish or round the edge of a dinner plate. Cover with kitchen paper and reheat until very hot, allowing 5 to 5½ minutes at full power and turning dish or plate 3 times unless oven has a turntable. Garnish with parsley and serve.

Artichokes in Red Wine with Gribiche Dressing   Serves 4

A powerful blend of flavours, slightly exotic and with plenty of French flair. Make the sauce first and set it aside in the cool while preparing the artichokes.

GRIBICHE DRESSING

4 Grade 3 eggs

1 rounded tsp French mustard

1 level tsp salt

½pt (275ml) salad oil

3 tblsp light-coloured malt vinegar

1 rounded tblsp parsley

1 rounded tblsp *fresh* chopped herbs to include chives, tarragon, savory and thyme (leaves only)

2 rounded tblsp mixture of drained chopped capers and gherkins

pepper to taste

ARTICHOKES IN RED WINE

4 large globe artichokes

salted water

¼pt (150ml) dry red wine

1 garlic clove, peeled

1 rounded tsp salt

1. For sauce, break 3 eggs carefully into a medium-sized greased dish. Pierce each yolk in 2 places with tip of pointed knife to stop them bursting and spluttering while cooking.

2. Cover with a plate then 'hardboil' by microwaving for 8 minutes at defrost setting. Stand 3 minutes. Carefully remove yolks with a spoon and put into blender goblet or food processor. Reserve whites.

3. Add whole egg, mustard and salt to yolks. Blend until very smooth. With machine still running, add oil in a thin, continuous stream. The mixture will gradually thicken to mayonnaise consistency.

4. Blend in vinegar then spoon out into a bowl. Cut egg whites into strips then add to sauce with remaining ingredients. Cover and leave in the cool.

5. To cook artichokes, cut away stalks, leaving bases flat. With a sharp and non-serrated knife, cut tops off upper leaves as though you were slicing a loaf of bread. You will find the easiest way to do this is to place each artichoke on its side.

6. Soak for 20 minutes in cold, salted water. Lift out and shake to remove surplus liquid.

7. Pour wine into a large dish, about 10 inches square by 2 inches in depth (25 by 5cm). Crush in garlic then stir in salt. Add artichokes, placing them upright with leaves facing.

8. Cover with cling film, then puncture twice with the tip of a knife. Alternatively, cover with a matching lid.

9. Cook 25 minutes at full power, turning dish 4 times unless oven has a turntable. Leave to stand 10 minutes. Uncover and put on to serving plates. Accompany with Gribiche Dressing.

TIP: To eat, pull off leaves one at a time and dip fleshy part nearest the stalk end in dressing. Pass through the teeth. Continue until you come to a cone of inedible leaves. Lift these off and underneath you will find the 'choke', a mass of very fine spikes which look like silken threads or fine bristles. Lift off by pulling with the fingers then eat the heart, the luxury portion, with a knife and fork plus extra dressing.

To prepare artichokes for guests or for stuffing, cook as above then gently ease leaves apart until you come to the centre. Remove core of inedible leaves and the spiky choke, then either fill with dressing or stuff and reheat. Water, white wine or cider can be used instead of red wine, and garlic omitted completely if preferred.

PERNOD ARTICHOKES Serves 4

For an elusive taste, microwave artichokes in 2 tablespoons Pernod, 6 tablespoons water and 1 rounded teaspoon salt. Cover and cook as previously directed. Leave until cold then serve with French dressing.

Veal Stuffed Peppers Serves 4, allowing 1 per person (F)

With peppers to be found all the year round from countries near and far, Stuffed Peppers may be made from the vivid red variety or the more subdued green. Either way they are colourful and tasty and can be served hot or cold, basted with juices from the dish for added succulence.

4 medium red or green peppers, each 4oz or 125g

1oz (25g) butter or margarine, at kitchen temperature

5oz (150g) onions, peeled and chopped

8oz (225g) minced veal

2oz (50g) easy-cook, long grain rice

1 level tsp salt

5 tblsp tomato juice, chicken stock or water

½ level tsp dried thyme

COOKING LIQUID

4 tblsp tomato juice or chicken stock

1. Wash and dry peppers. Cut off tops and set aside for lids. Remove inside seeds and fibres. Cut a sliver off the base of each so that it stands upright without falling.

2. Put butter or margarine into a dish and heat, uncovered, for ¾ to 1 minute at full power. Stir in onions. Continue to cook, still uncovered, for 3 minutes. Mash in veal and cook another 3 minutes.

3. Remove from oven and add all remaining ingredients. Spoon equal amounts into peppers. Top with lids.

4. Stand upright in a 3pt (1·75 litre) deep dish. Add cooking liquid. Cover with cling film, then puncture twice with the tip of a knife. Alternatively, cover with a matching lid.

5. Cook 15 minutes at full power, turning twice unless oven has a turntable. Leave to stand 10 minutes. Serve hot or cold, coated with juices from dish.

BEEF STUFFED PEPPERS Serves 4, allowing 1 per person (F)

Make as Veal Stuffed Peppers, using minced beef instead of veal.

PORK SAUSAGE STUFFED PEPPERS Serves 4, allowing 1 per person (F)

Make as Veal Stuffed Peppers, using pork sausage meat instead of veal.

Chicken Liver Pâté in a Ring   Serves up to 20

Ideally suited to entertaining, this is a splendidly mild pâté made from chicken livers with creamy and spicy additions to give it its own distinguished character and texture. It does need rather more attention than many microwaved dishes but the end justifies the means.

1lb (450g) chicken livers, washed and dried

4oz (125g) onions, peeled and cut into fairly large pieces

1 garlic clove, peeled and cut into 4 pieces

2oz (50g) plain flour

2oz (50g) butter, melted about 1½ to 2 minutes at defrost setting

¼pt (150ml) single cream

1 Grade 2 egg, beaten

⅛ tsp ground allspice

1 level tsp salt

1. Line a 7 inch (17·5cm), straight-sided soufflé dish with cling film. Also cover the outside of a tumbler (3 inches or 7·5cm tall by 2 inches or 5cm in diameter) with cling film and stand in the centre of the soufflé dish, open end facing; in other words, *do not* invert the glass. You now have what virtually amounts to a self-made ring mould.

2. Finely mince raw livers with onions and garlic. The appearance is messy but bear with it! Tip into a bowl and stir in flour, butter, cream, egg, allspice and salt. Beat gently until all ingredients are well amalgamated. The mixture is very liquidy but this is as it should be.

3. Pour carefully into 'mould', taking care not to disturb the tumbler. Cover with cling film, taking it right across the dish and over the tumbler. Puncture twice with the tip of a knife.

4. Cook 10 minutes at defrost setting, turning dish 4 times unless oven has a turntable. Stand inside or outside the oven for 10 minutes. Cook a further 3 minutes at defrost setting. Uncover and remove tumbler. Pack cavity with crumpled kitchen paper towels to absorb surplus moisture.

5. Re-cover with film, puncture as before and leave to stand 15 minutes. Return to oven and microwave 5 minutes at defrost setting, turning twice. Uncover and pack centre cavity with more crumpled kitchen paper towels. Cover loosely and leave to stand until cold. Remove paper.

6. Cover pâté more securely (either with cling film or foil), and refrigerate overnight. Invert on to a dinner plate and gently peel away film. If any moisture appears, mop up with kitchen paper.

7. Garnish as desired (see below) and serve with toast or crackers.

GARNISHES

1. Top ring with slices of hardboiled egg and fill centre cavity with shredded lettuce. Dust egg with paprika.

2. Shower with very finely grated carrot and fill centre with watercress.

3. Top with alternate slices of tomato and cucumber. Fill centre with mustard and cress.

Liver Paste   Serves about 10 to 12 (F)

Luxury personified. A glorious paste which is, I think, as top class as anything the gastronomes of France could produce. It cooks in 10 minutes but does depend on a food processor or blender for its ultra-smooth texture.

6oz (175g) salted butter

1 garlic clove, peeled and sliced

1lb (450g) chicken livers, washed and dried

$\frac{1}{8}$ level tsp nutmeg

seasoning to taste

about 2 to 3oz (50 to 75g) extra butter for the top

1. Put butter into a 3pt (1·75 litre) dish and heat 2 minutes, uncovered, at full power.

2. Add garlic and chicken livers. Cover with cling film, then puncture twice with the tip of a knife.

3. Cook 8 minutes at full power, turning dish 4 times unless oven has a turntable.

4. Remove from microwave then add nutmeg and seasoning to taste. Spoon butter and cooked liver together into a food processor or blender goblet. Do this in 2 batches and run machine each time until mixture is very smooth.

5. Spread evenly into a smallish, soufflé-type dish. For an airtight seal (the best there is) melt extra butter and pour over the top. Leave, without moving, until butter sets then 'store', covered, in the refrigerator.

6. To serve, spoon out on to plates and serve with hot toast.

Aubergine Dip   Serves 4 to 6

Characterfully Middle Eastern, this is a simply made dip to mop up with pieces of Greek-style bread – either Pitta or the crustier sesame seed. It responds best to being mixed in a blender or food processor and I have the State of Louisiana to thank for teaching me how to cook aubergines; boiling and not frying which renders them delicate, non-greasy and better able to harmonise with other foods and absorb their flavours.

1lb (450g) aubergines, peeled and cut into 2 inch (5cm) pieces

4 tblsp boiling water

$\frac{1}{2}$ to 1 level tsp salt

1 tblsp fresh lemon juice, strained

3 tsp corn or sunflower oil (for a typically South European taste, use olive oil instead)

1 small garlic clove, peeled and sliced

1. Tip aubergines into a dish and add the water. Cover with cling film, then puncture twice with the tip of a knife. Alternatively, cover with a matching lid.

2. Cook for 6 minutes at full power, turning dish twice unless oven has a turntable. Remove from oven, stand 2 minutes and drain.

3. Transfer aubergines to a blender goblet or food processor. Add salt, lemon juice, oil and garlic. Run machine until mixture forms a smooth purée.

4. Spoon into a small serving bowl, cover securely and refrigerate until completely cold before eating.

Mushrooms a la Grècque   Serves 2

Supposedly Hellenic, this is a popular restaurant starter, quite simple to emulate at home and refreshingly piquant.

2 bouquet garni bags
1 garlic clove, peeled and crushed
1 large bay leaf, broken into 4 pieces
2 tblsp water
1 tblsp lemon juice
1 tblsp malt vinegar
1 tblsp corn oil
$\frac{1}{2}$ level tsp salt
8oz (225g) button mushrooms, washed and gently wiped dry
1 rounded tblsp chopped parsley

1. Put all ingredients, except mushrooms and parsley, into a medium glass or pottery bowl.

2. Cover with a plate and cook $2\frac{1}{2}$ minutes at full power.

3. Gently toss in mushrooms. Cover as above. Cook 3 minutes at full power, turning dish twice unless oven has a turntable.

4. Remove from oven and leave until cold. Lift mushrooms into a dish. Coat with juices, strained through a fine mesh sieve.

5. Chill several hours before serving. Transfer mushrooms and juices to 2 dishes and sprinkle with parsley.

Potted Prawns   Serves 6 (F)

In the old days, it used to be tiny pink shrimps that were potted but, coastal regions apart, where are they to be found morning fresh other than in cans from far away places? On the assumption that shrimps are not readily available, I have substituted prawns with equal success.

8oz (225g) unsalted butter
10oz (275g) peeled prawns, thawed if frozen
3 tsp lemon juice
$\frac{1}{8}$ level tsp nutmeg
$\frac{1}{2}$ level tsp paprika
GARNISH
6 unpeeled prawns or 6 watercress sprigs

1. Melt 6oz (175g) butter in a dish for 3 minutes at defrost setting. Leave uncovered.

2. Coarsely chop prawns and add to butter with the lemon juice, nutmeg and paprika. Leave in the cool until mixture just begins to firm up.

3. Spread neatly and smoothly into 6 baby pots or dishes. Chill until firm in the refrigerator.

4. Melt rest of butter and spoon over each. Chill again until butter has set in an even layer.

5. To serve, run a knife dipped in hot water round inside of each pot, and invert on to a plate. Garnish with prawns or watercress and eat with hot toast.

Smoked Salmon Quiche   Serves 8

Why not luxuriate in a stylish Quiche, filled with Pacific smoked salmon, notable for its own character and interesting flavour? Not in the same league as the much costlier Scotch, it is nevertheless well suited for Quiche and also makes a fine pâté to go with fingers of hot toast.

shortcrust pastry made with 6oz (175g) plain flour and 3oz (75g) fat etc

1 egg yolk

FILLING

6oz (175g) Pacific smoked salmon, finely chopped

3 Grade 3 eggs

½pt (275ml) single cream

½ level tsp salt

½ level tsp finely grated lemon peel

1. Roll out pastry fairly thinly and use to line a lightly-greased, 8 inch (20cm) round glass or pottery fluted flan dish.

2. Prick well all over with a fork, especially where sides of pastry meet base. Leave uncovered and cook 6 minutes at full power, turning dish 4 times unless oven has a turntable.

3. Remove from oven, brush all over with egg yolk to seal holes and cook a further minute at full power.

4. Remove from oven and cover base with the chopped salmon.

5. Beat all remaining ingredients well together. Pour into flan over salmon. Cook 10 to 12 minutes at full power or until bubbles just begin to break in the middle.

6. Turn 4 times unless oven has a turntable then remove from oven, cut into wedges and serve hot, warm or cold.

ASPARAGUS QUICHE   (Picture p. 50)   Serves 8

Make exactly as the Smoked Salmon Quiche but use 1 can (12oz or 350g) green asparagus spears which, when drained, will yield about 6oz or 175g. Reserve 6 spears for decoration, coarsely chop remainder and use to cover base of pastry.

QUICHE LORRAINE   Serves 8

Make as Smoked Salmon Quiche, but cover base of pastry with 6oz (175g) microwaved bacon, finely chopped and used cold. Sprinkle filling with a little nutmeg before cooking.

CHEESE AND BACON QUICHE   Serves 8

Make as Smoked Salmon Quiche, but cover base of pastry with 4oz (125g) microwaved bacon, finely chopped and used cold. Sprinkle filling with 2oz (50g) grated Red Leicester or Cheshire cheese before cooking.

SPINACH QUICHE   Serves 8

Make as Smoked Salmon Quiche, but cover base of pastry with 6oz (175g) cooked spinach, *very well drained*. Sprinkle filling with a little nutmeg before cooking.

Soups

The warmth and comfort of homemade soup is undeniable, so is its flavour, and this short selection offers some vintage favourites in addition to what I call 'modern' soups, concocted from cans and other fast-cooking ingredients.

Curry Rice Soup   Picture p. 51   Serves 6 (F)

More like a broth than a soup, this is a blissfully heart-warming brew to come home to on chilly days and takes only 20 minutes to cook.

2oz (50g) butter or margarine
4oz (125g) onions, peeled and chopped or grated
6oz (175g) well-scrubbed celery, cut into thin strips
1 level tblsp curry powder
2 tblsp medium sherry
1¾pt (1 litre) chicken stock (use cubes and water in the absence of the real thing)
4oz (125g) easy-cook, long grain rice
1 level tsp salt
1 tblsp soy sauce
6oz (175g) cooked cold chicken, cut into strips
thick yogurt or soured cream for serving

1. Put butter or margarine in a 4pt (2·25 litre) dish and melt, uncovered, 1½ to 2 minutes at defrost setting.

2. Add onions and celery. Leave uncovered and cook 5 minutes at full power, stirring once.

3. Mix in curry powder, sherry, stock, rice, salt and soy sauce. Cover with a plate and cook 10 minutes at full power, stirring twice.

4. Add chicken and continue to cook a further 5 minutes at full power. Stir round, ladle into soup plates or bowls and top each with 1 tablespoon of yogurt or soured cream

Cream of Carrot Soup   Serves 6 (F)

Perhaps one of my favourite soups with its rich texture, subtle flavour and delicate orange colour. It is also incredibly convenient and inexpensive, based on little more demanding than cornflour, a can of carrots, milk, water and seasoning.

2 level tblsp cornflour
1 large can (about 1¼lb or 550g) carrots
¾pt (425ml) milk (skimmed if liked)
1 level tsp onion salt
1 level tsp salt
¼ to ½pt (150 to 275ml) extra boiling water

1. Put cornflour into a 4pt (2·25 litre) glass or pottery dish. Mix smoothly with liquid from can of carrots.

2. Blend carrots to a purée in a food processor, blender goblet or by rubbing through a fine mesh sieve. Add to dish with milk and both the salts.

3. Leave uncovered and cook 12 minutes at full power, stirring 4 times. By this time, the soup should have come to the boil and thickened.

4. Remove from oven and thin down to taste with the boiling water. Adjust seasoning to taste and serve straight away.

CREAM OF VEGETABLE SOUPS   Serves 6 (F)

Pea, broad bean, celery soup and so forth may be made in exactly the same way as the Carrot Soup, using appropriate cans of vegetables.

Avocado Soup   Serves 6

Totally uncomplicated, comfortably warming and pleasingly light; a change from chilled avocado soups and perfect for entertaining. Add 2 teaspoons of cooked grated beetroot to each and get a fascinating colour combination but for conservative eating, sprinkle with chopped parsley, a few croûtons or a dusting of paprika.

1½pt (just under 1 litre) hot chicken stock
2 medium sized and ripe avocados
1 tblsp lemon juice
1 level tsp onion powder
½ to 1 level tsp salt

1. Pour chicken stock into a bowl and cover with a plate. Heat for 4½ minutes at full power.

2. Meanwhile halve avocados, remove flesh and mash *very finely* with lemon juice and onion powder. Alternatively, work to a purée in a blender or food processor.

3. Whisk into soup with salt. Cover as above. Reheat for 3 minutes at full power, turning bowl twice unless oven has a turntable.

4. Ladle into warm bowls or plates and serve straight away.

TIP: Do not reheat leftovers as flavour and colour will spoil.

Rustic Tomato Soup   Serves 6 to 8 (F)

A wealth of flavour and rugged texture characterise this vivid red soup based on summer-ripe tomatoes. Serve it with crusty brown bread or rolls spread with either butter or peanut butter.

2lb (900g) blanched tomatoes, skinned and quartered
2oz (50g) butter or margarine
4oz (125g) celery, scrubbed and finely chopped
4oz (125g) onions, peeled and finely chopped
4 rounded tsp dark brown soft sugar
1½ level tsp salt
½pt (275ml) hot water
2 level tblsp cornflour
8 tblsp cold water

1. Blend tomatoes to a purée in a blender or food processor. Leave aside temporarily.

2. Put butter or margarine into a 3pt (1·75 litre) glass or pottery dish and heat 1 minute at full power.

3. Mix in celery and onions. Cover dish with plate or lid and cook 3 minutes at full power.

4. Add sugar, salt, hot water and the tomato purée (made under point one). Cover as above or use cling film, puncturing twice with the tip of a knife. Cook 8 minutes at full power, turning dish 4 times unless oven has a turntable.

5. Uncover. Blend in cornflour, mixed smoothly with water.

6. Leave uncovered and cook a further 8 minutes at full power, stirring 4 times. Ladle into bowls and serve while still very hot.

Lettuce Soup   Picture p. 52   Serves 6

Delicately balanced in colour and flavour, creamy Lettuce Soup is unusual and well-recommended for summer eating. Serve plain, or top each portion with a tablespoon of soured cream and a hint of chopped parsley. The soup may also be served chilled, garnished with lemon slices and mint leaves.

2oz (50g) butter or margarine
6oz (175g) onions, peeled and grated
8oz (225g) green lettuces (round variety), washed well then rinsed and shredded
1pt (575ml) cold milk
2 level tblsp cornflour
½pt (275ml) boiling water or chicken stock
1 to 2 level tsp salt

1. Put butter or margarine into a 3pt (1·75 litre) deepish casserole dish. Melt 1½ to 2 minutes at defrost setting.

2. Mix in onions and lettuces. Cover with plate or matching lid and cook 3 minutes at full power.

3. Transfer to blender goblet with one third of the milk. Run machine until ingredients are mixed to a purée.

4. Return to dish. Mix in cornflour, remaining milk, boiling water or stock and the salt.

5. Cover as before then cook soup for 15 minutes at full power, whisking gently at the end of every 3 minutes.

BELGIAN-STYLE LETTUCE SOUP   Serves 6

Use single cream instead of milk and add 1 teaspoon butter to each portion.

SPINACH SOUP   Serves 6

Make as Lettuce Soup, substituting 8oz (225g) spinach leaves for the lettuce.

Chilled Cream of Cheshire Soup   Picture p. 53   Serves 6 to 8

Rich and quite different from the usual run-of-the-mill soups, this one is based on the two famous Cheshire cheeses – blue and white. Amply endowed with the best things of life and therefore filling, it should be treated only as a prelude to a light meal.

1oz (25g) butter or margarine
6oz (175g) onions, peeled and chopped
3oz (75g) celery stalks, scrubbed and chopped
1oz (25g) plain flour
1½pt (850ml) warm chicken stock
3 tblsp dry white wine
seasoning to taste
4oz (125g) blue Cheshire cheese, crumbled
4oz (125g) white Cheshire cheese, crumbled
¼pt (150ml) double cream
finely chopped parsley for garnishing.

1. Put butter or margarine into a 4pt (2·25 litre) glass or pottery dish. Melt, uncovered, 1 to 1½ minutes at defrost setting.

2. Add onions and celery. Mix in well. Cover with a plate and cook 8 minutes at full power.

3. Remove from oven. Stir in flour then gradually blend in the stock and wine. Cover as above and return to oven. Cook 10 to 12 minutes at full power, whisking every 2 to 3 minutes to keep mixture smooth.

4. Remove from oven and season to taste. Add cheeses and stir until melted. Leave soup until cold. Blend to a smooth purée in blender goblet. Pour into large bowl and whisk in two-thirds of the cream.

5. Cover and chill several hours or overnight. Before serving, stir round gently to mix then pour into bowls. Swirl in rest of cream and sprinkle each with parsley.

TIP: If soup is too thick after cream has been added, thin down with a little cold milk.

Tomato Soup with Avocado Mayonnaise   Picture p. 54   Serves 8

A bright and breezy soup, on the sophisticated side and well-suited to an intimate dinner party.

2 medium, ripe avocados
1 tblsp lemon juice
1 garlic clove, peeled and sliced (optional)
4 tblsp mayonnaise
½ to 1 level tsp salt
2 cans condensed cream of tomato soup
1pt (575ml) warm water
12oz (350g) blanched and skinned tomatoes, cut into strips
seasoning to taste

1. Make the Avocado Mayonnaise first and leave aside temporarily while preparing the soup. Scoop avocado flesh into food processor bowl or blender goblet.

2. Add lemon juice, garlic, mayonnaise and salt. Run machine until smooth. Spoon out into a dish.

3. Tip both cans of soup into a 4pt (2·25 litre) dish. Mix in water and tomatoes.

4. Cover with a plate and cook 8 to 10 minutes at full power or until soup is hot but not boiling. Stir 4 times.

5. Adjust seasoning to taste then ladle into warm soup bowls or plates. Add a tablespoon of the avocado mixture to each and serve straight away.

Minestrone   EXCELLENT   Serves 8 to 10 (F)

An old treasure we have adopted with love and heartfelt thanks from Italy! It cooks quickly in the microwave, retaining its full flavour and glowing colours.

12oz (350g) topped and tailed courgettes, unpeeled and thinly sliced
8oz (225g) carrots, peeled and thinly sliced
8oz (225g) onions, peeled and coarsely chopped
4oz (125g) green cabbage, washed and shredded
4oz (125g) white cabbage, washed and shredded
2oz (50g) celery, scrubbed and very thinly sliced
6oz (175g) potatoes, peeled and diced
4oz (125g) fresh or frozen sliced green beans
4oz (125g) fresh or frozen peas
1 can (14oz or 200g) tomatoes
2 rounded tblsp tomato purée
2oz (50g) small pasta or long grain rice
$1\frac{3}{4}$pt (1 litre) boiling water
3 to 4 level tsp salt

1. Put all the fresh and frozen vegetables into a 6 pt (about 3·5 litre) bowl. Mix in canned tomatoes, purée and either pasta or rice.

2. Cover with a large plate. Cook 15 minutes at full power, stirring 3 times. Pour in two-thirds of the boiling water. Cover as above.

3. Cook 20 to 25 minutes at full power, stirring 4 times. Remove from cooker and stir in rest of water with salt. If soup is too thick for personal taste, add an extra $\frac{1}{4}$ pint (150ml) boiling water.

4. Ladle into dishes and pass grated Parmesan cheese separately.

Packet Soups (Dried Ingredients)   Serves 4 to 5

Tip packet of soup into a deepish glass or pottery dish. Gradually add cold water as directed on the packet, stirring continuously. Cover with a plate and leave to stand 15 minutes so that vegetables have time to soften slightly. Cook 6 to 8 minutes at full power when soup should come to the boil and thicken. Stir 2 or 3 times. Remove from cooker. Leave to stand 5 minutes then stir round and serve.

Canned Condensed Soups   Serves 2 to 3

Spoon soup into a bowl or dish and add 1 soup can of warm water. Cover. Cook 6 to 7 minutes at full power when soup should be hot but not boiling. Whisk thoroughly, but gently, 3 or 4 times. Ladle into 2 or 3 soup bowls and serve.

Sauces and Dressings

I admit where basic white sauces are concerned, there is no saving in time when made in the microwave, measured, that is, against conventional cooking. But on the plus side there is less likelihood of the sauce 'lumping', hardly a chance of it boiling over, and no tacky pan to clean up afterwards. Also all the sauces seem to be more flavoursome, extra glossy and superbly smooth.

Hollandaise and Béarnaise sauces, the pièce de resistance of aspiring and great chefs, work miraculously in seconds with no tantrums, Bread sauce turns out deliciously creamy and pale as ivory, Egg Custard sauce is a labour of speed and Cranberry sauce, poultry's best friend, tastes as though the berries had just been gathered.

Even Apple sauce is more aromatic than usual, and the Bolognese and Neapolitan sauces have a distinctive, fresh and pungent taste, so reminiscent of Mediterranean cooking.

When I first embarked on microwave cooking all those years ago, I had certain reservations about making sauces in the oven but time and success have changed my mind completely. If any of *you* still have reservations, just try out a selection and judge the results for yourselves.

White Sauce · Serves 4 (F)

The coating variety and multi-purpose, this is everybody's favourite sauce with its glossy appearance and velvety smooth texture. A selection of popular variations follow.

½pt (275ml) milk, taken from the refrigerator

1oz (25g) butter or margarine

1oz (25g) plain flour

seasoning to taste

1. Pour milk into a glass or pottery jug. Leave uncovered and heat 1½ minutes at full power until fairly hot. Remove from oven.

2. Put butter or margarine into a bowl. Leave uncovered and melt 1 to 1½ minutes at defrost setting.

3. Stir in flour to form a roux and cook ½ minute at full power. Remove from oven and gradually blend in the warm milk.

4. Return to oven and cook, uncovered, until sauce comes to the boil and thickens. Allow about 3 to 4 minutes at full power and beat at the end of every minute to ensure sauce stays smooth.

5. Season to taste, stir well and use as desired.

CAPER SAUCE · Serves 4 (F)

Make as White Sauce, adding 1 rounded tablespoon drained and chopped capers half way through cooking time. Serve with herrings, mackerel, skate and either roast lamb or mutton.

CHEESE SAUCE   Serves 4 to 5 (F)

Make as White Sauce, adding 2 to 3oz (50 to 75g) grated cheese
(variety to taste) and 1 level teaspoon prepared mustard half
way through cooking time. Serve with bacon, pork, fish, poultry
and vegetables.

HARDBOILED EGG SAUCE   Serves 4 to 5

Make as White Sauce, adding 2 Grade 3 hardboiled and chopped
eggs at the end with the seasoning. Do not reheat as eggs may
become rubbery. Serve with fish and poultry.

MUSHROOM SAUCE   Serves 4 to 5

Make as White Sauce, adding 2oz (50g) chopped mushrooms
half way through cooking time. The mushrooms should first
be cooked in a little butter or margarine for about 1 to $1\frac{1}{2}$
minutes at full power. A light shake of nutmeg, added with the
seasoning, gives a 'lift' to the flavour. Serve with fish, poultry
and light meat dishes.

MUSTARD SAUCE   Serves 4 (F)

Make as White Sauce, adding 2 level teaspoons prepared English
mustard and 2 teaspoons of lemon juice at the end with the
seasoning. Serve with pork, bacon, offal and fish.

ONION SAUCE   Serves 4 to 5 (F)

Put 4oz (125g) peeled and quartered onions into a smallish glass
or pottery dish. Add 2 tablespoons water and $\frac{1}{2}$ level teaspoon
salt. Cover with cling film, then puncture twice with the tip of
a knife. Cook 4 to 5 minutes or until very soft. Drain and chop.
Make up the White Sauce and stir in the chopped onions half
way through cooking time. Serve with lamb and boiled bacon.

PARSLEY SAUCE   Serves 4 (F)

Make as White Sauce, adding 2 heaped tablespoons chopped
parsley about 1 minute before sauce is ready. Serve with fish,
vegetables, poultry and boiled bacon.

WATERCRESS SAUCE   Serves 4

Make as White Sauce, adding 2 heaped tablespoons chopped
watercress leaves at the same time as the seasoning. Serve with
fish or poultry.

BÉCHAMEL SAUCE   Serves 4 (F)

*This is the more aristocratic version of White Sauce, and is simply
the result of adding flavourings to the milk.*

Pour $\frac{1}{2}$ pint (275ml) milk into a glass or pottery jug. Add 1
bouquet garni bag, 1 bay leaf, 1 small peeled and quartered
onion, 2 parsley sprigs and a pinch of nutmeg. Cover with a
saucer and bring just up to the boil, allowing 5 to 6 minutes

at defrost setting. Cool to lukewarm outside the cooker. Strain and use as directed for White Sauce and its variations.

POURING SAUCE — Serves 4 to 6 (F)

Make White Sauce or Béchamel Sauce but reduce the flour to ½oz (15g) only. The sauce is useful if food is dry and moisture is needed – rather like gravy but made with milk. If sweet, it makes a pleasing substitute for custard over steamed puddings.

TIP: Any of the White Sauce variations may be made into a pouring consistency by reducing the flour as given above.

Cornflour Sauce — Serves 4 to 6 (F)

The most simple of all sauces which takes well to sweet or savoury additions. It is easy to digest and perfectly suitable for children and the elderly.

2 level tblsp cornflour

½pt (275ml) cold milk (skimmed if preferred)

salt *or* sugar to taste

1. Tip cornflour into a 1pt (575ml) dish and blend smoothly with some of the cold milk.

2. Carefully blend in remainder. Leave uncovered and cook 4 to 5 minutes at full power until thickened, beating at the end of every minute. The sauce *must* come to the boil and may need an extra ½ to 1 minute, depending on the temperature of the milk.

3. Remove from microwave and season to taste with salt. Alternatively, add 1oz (25g) caster sugar and stir until dissolved. Use as desired.

CORNFLOUR JAM OR HONEY SAUCE — Serves 4 to 6 (F)

Instead of sugar, sweeten sauce to taste with about 1 heaped tablespoon of jam or 1 rounded tablespoon clear honey.

Bread Sauce — Serves 6 to 8 (F)

A vintage tradition – Bread Sauce with poultry and the Christmas turkey in particular. It works like a charm in the microwave.

½pt (275ml) milk, heated with the same additions as given for the Béchamel sauce then strained

2½oz (65g) fresh white breadcrumbs (crusts excluded)

½oz (15g) butter or margarine

pinch of nutmeg

salt and pepper to taste

1. Pour warm milk into a clean bowl. Add crumbs. Leave uncovered and cook until thickened, allowing about 4 to 6 minutes at defrost setting and stirring at the end of every minute.

2. Mix in butter or margarine, nutmeg and salt and pepper to taste. Leave uncovered. Reheat about 1 minute at defrost setting. Serve as suggested.

BROWN BREAD SAUCE — Serves 6 to 8 (F)

A good choice for game, make exactly as the Bread Sauce above, using brown breadcrumbs instead of white, and no crusts.

Bolognese Sauce
Serves 6 generously (F)

A long time favourite, this is a fulfilling and glowing sauce for 'Spag Bol' or any other pasta dish. It cooks in about 20 minutes and is best made one day for the next.

1lb (450g) raw minced beef
1 garlic clove, peeled and crushed
4oz (125g) onions, peeled and grated
4oz (125g) green pepper, deseeded and finely chopped
1 level tsp Italian seasoning or mixed herbs
1 can (14oz or 200g) tomatoes, mashed down in their own liquid
2 rounded tblsp tomato purée
1 brown gravy cube
5 tblsp dry red wine or water
3 level tsp brown sugar
1 level tsp salt

1. Put beef and garlic into a 3pt (1·75 litre) glass or pottery dish. Thoroughly mix in onions and pepper. Leave uncovered and cook 5 minutes at full power.

2. Stir in Italian seasoning or mixed herbs, the mashed tomatoes and liquid, tomato purée, crumbled gravy cube, wine or water and the sugar.

3. Cover with cling film, then puncture twice with the tip of a knife. Cook 15 minutes at full power, turning dish twice unless oven has a turntable. Uncover, season with salt, stir round and serve or use as required.

TIP: If for serving the next day, uncover and stir round as soon as sauce is ready. Re-cover as above. Refrigerate when cold. Reheat at defrost setting until hot enough for personal taste.

Neapolitan Sauce
Serves 6 to 8 (F)

Delicious, whether spooned over pasta or cooked steaks. A slimmers' version follows.

1½lb (675g) blanched tomatoes, skinned and cut into eighths
1 garlic clove, peeled and sliced
2 level tblsp tubed or canned tomato purée
3 level tsp caster or soft brown sugar
½ level tsp salt
1 level tsp dried basil
1 heaped tblsp chopped parsley
1 level tblsp cornflour
1 tblsp cold water

1. Put tomatoes, garlic and purée into food processor or blender goblet and run machine until smooth.

2. Pour into a 3pt (1·75 litre) glass or pottery dish. Mix in sugar, salt, basil and parsley.

3. Blend cornflour smoothly with water. Add to tomato mixture and stir in well.

4. Cover with a plate and cook 6 minutes at full power, stirring 4 times. Leave to stand 4 minutes before serving.

SLIMMERS' NEAPOLITAN SAUCE   Serves 6 to 8 (F)

Make as above but omit cornflour and water mixture.

Basting Sauces

Bastes are brushed over meat joints and poultry to increase browning and make them look more appetising. They also add to the flavour and can be used as a basis for traditional gravy or sauce.

1oz (25g) butter or margarine, at kitchen temperature
2 rounded tsp tomato ketchup or purée
1 level tsp paprika
1 tsp Worcestershire sauce

BUTTER BASTE

1. Melt butter or margarine, uncovered, for 1 to $1\frac{1}{2}$ minutes, at defrost setting.

2. Stir in rest of ingredients. Use as required.

1oz (25g) butter or margarine, at kitchen temperature
2 rounded tsp tomato ketchup or purée
1 level tsp paprika
1 tsp Worcestershire sauce
1 slightly rounded tsp mild curry powder
1 level tsp powder mustard
$\frac{1}{4}$ level tsp garlic granules

SPICY CURRY BASTE

1. Melt butter or margarine, uncovered, for 1 to $1\frac{1}{2}$ minutes at defrost setting.

2. Stir in rest of ingredients. Use as required.

1 rounded tblsp tubed or canned tomato purée
1 level tsp prepared English mustard
1 tsp malt vinegar
1 tsp Worcestershire sauce

TOMATO BASTE

This is completely non-fat and therefore useful for dieters and those who are on a limited fat intake for health reasons. It is also the baste to choose for lamb, duck and poultry already impregnated with fat and/or oil (self-basting).

1. Mix all ingredients well together.

Hollandaise Sauce   Picture p. 55 | Serves 6 to 8

Magic, or so it seems, to be able to create a perfect Hollandaise sauce, one of the trickiest of all sauces, in a matter of seconds with no complicated mixing techniques. It is the classic sauce to serve with microwaved salmon and salmon trout, with broccoli and cauliflower, with oven-hot globe artichokes and asparagus, in avocado pear halves (a very rich combination) or spooned over freshly cooked fennel.

4oz (125g) slightly salted butter
1 tblsp fresh lemon juice
2 Grade 3 egg yolks
salt and pepper to taste
pinch of caster sugar

1. Put butter into a smallish jug or dish and leave uncovered. Melt until hot and bubbly for 1 to $1\frac{1}{2}$ minutes at full power.

2. Add lemon juice and egg yolks. Whisk well. Return to oven and cook 30 seconds at full power.

3. Remove from oven and stir briskly. The sauce is ready if it is thick as cold custard and clings to whisk, fork or spoon – whichever implement you have used. If not, cook a further 15 seconds.

4. Season with salt and pepper to taste, then add sugar to counteract sharpness coming from the lemon. Serve warm.

NOTE: If Hollandaise refused to thicken and looks curdled, it means it has been overcooked. One remedy is to beat in 2 tablespoons double cream; another to blend the sauce smoothly in blender goblet and reheat about 5 seconds at full power in the microwave. If none of the treatments work, you will have to regard the sauce as a write-off and start again!

BÉARNAISE SAUCE (SHORT-CUT)   Serves 6 to 8

A harmonious sauce, perfect with grilled steaks and thick slices of underdone roast beef. Make exactly as Hollandaise, substituting mild vinegar for lemon juice. Add $\frac{1}{2}$ level teaspoon dried tarragon with seasonings and sugar.

MALTAISE SAUCE   Serves 6 to 8

Another beauty for freshwater fish, veal and poultry, you make this exactly as Hollandaise then add 2 level teaspoons finely grated orange peel with seasonings and sugar.

Short-Cut Curry Sauce — Serves 6 to 8 (F)

A lazy cook's sauce but what does it matter when the end result is so rewarding! Serve it spooned over hardboiled eggs, portions of microwaved chicken, thick slices of roast lamb or even sausages! And for using up leftovers, it is the best yet. Just add diced meat or poultry to the sauce, cover with a plate and microwave a few minutes until hot – the time will depend on the original temperature of the sauce and the quantity of cooked food added. Just stir fairly often to ensure even heating.

1 can condensed cream of celery soup

¼pt (150ml) boiling water

2 level tblsp tomato purée

1 level tblsp curry powder

1 garlic clove, peeled and crushed

1 level tsp turmeric

2 level tblsp mango chutney

1 level tblsp peanut butter

1 rounded tblsp desiccated coconut

1. Put soup into a 2pt (1·25 litre) glass or pottery dish and beat in half the water. Stir in all remaining ingredients except coconut.

2. Cover with a plate and heat 4 minutes at full power, stirring twice. Stand 2 minutes then gently whisk in rest of boiling water. Finally mix in the coconut.

Balalaika Sauce — Serves 6 to 8

Flavours of Eastern Europe merge together splendidly in this original sauce, especially designed for any fish you can think of, from sole to plaice, salmon to prawns, even fish fingers to fish cakes.

1oz (25g) butter or margarine

2 level tblsp cornflour

4 tblsp dry white wine

¼pt (150ml) water

1 carton (5oz or 142ml) soured cream

2 level tblsp lumpfish 'caviar', red or black and available from supermarket chains and delicatessens

1½ level tsp salt

1 rounded tblsp scissor-snipped chives or fresh dill

8oz (225g) blanched tomatoes, skinned and finely chopped

1. Put butter or margarine into a 2pt (1·25 litre) glass or pottery dish. Cover with a plate and heat for 2 minutes at full power.

2. Mix cornflour smoothly with wine then stir in water. Blend soured cream into mixture. Leave uncovered and cook at full power for 4 to 5 minutes or until sauce bubbles gently and thickens. Beat hard at the end of every minute.

3. Stir in the lumpfish 'caviar', salt, chives or dill and the tomatoes. Cook, uncovered, a further 1½ to 2 minutes at full power, stirring twice.

Gravy
Serves 6 (F)

This can be made very easily in the microwave, using fat-skimmed pan juices left over from roasting poultry or meat. If there is insufficient juice, it may be topped up with water, wine or cider.

THIN GRAVY FOR POULTRY   Serves 6 (F)

Tip 1 level tablespoon cornflour into a 1¾pt (1 litre) glass or pottery bowl or basin. Mix smoothly with 1½ tablespoons cold water. Crumble in 1 brown gravy cube or blend in 1½ level teaspoons brown gravy powder. Stir in ½ pint (275ml) pan juices with, if necessary, extra water, wine or cider to make up the amount. Leave uncovered and cook 4 to 5 minutes at full power, beating at the end of every minute. Gravy is ready when it has thickened slightly and therefore may need an extra ½ to 1 minute; much will depend on the temperature of the pan juices to begin with. Season to suit personal taste and serve.

THICK GRAVY FOR MEAT   Serves 6

Make exactly as above, using 2 level tablespoons cornflour, smoothly mixed with 3 tablespoons cold water.

Cranberry Sauce
Serves 6 to 8 (F)

Bright, glistening, sweet-sour. A most stylish accompaniment to serve at any festive occasion with turkey, goose, gammon and pork, and a delight to make in the microwave. Though the sauce tends to be runny when hot, it thickens up on cooling to a jelly-like consistency.

8oz (225g) cranberries, thawed if frozen

¼pt (150ml) water

6oz (175g) caster sugar

1 level tsp finely grated lemon peel

1. Put all ingredients into a 2pt (1·25 litre) dish. Cover with a plate.

2. Cook 8½ minutes at full power, stirring sauce twice and crushing fruit against sides of bowl as you do so.

3. Remove from oven, keep covered and serve when cold. Store leftovers in an airtight container in the refrigerator.

CRANBERRY WINE SAUCE   Serves 6 to 8 (F)

Make as Cranberry Sauce, but use red wine instead of water.

CRANBERRY ORANGE SAUCE   Serves 6 to 8 (F)

Make as Cranberry Sauce, adding the finely grated peel of 1 medium washed and dried orange with all remaining ingredients.

Apple Sauce

Serves 8 to 9 (F)

The traditional sauce for pork, it also goes well with duck, goose and, surprisingly, roast lamb.

Cook 1lb (450g) peeled, cored and sliced apples to a pulp as directed in Cooking Fresh Fruit Chart on page 162. Beat to a purée then stir in 1 level tablespoon caster sugar and a little salt to taste. Reheat, uncovered, $\frac{1}{2}$ to $\frac{3}{4}$ minute at full power to melt sugar. Stir round. Serve cold.

Egg Custard Sauce

Makes about 1pt or 575ml

Full of childhood reminders, this is a true, old-fashioned and authentic custard sauce which, with the aid of a microwave, can be made in under 10 minutes with minimal beating and no curdling. It keeps well, can be served hot or cold and is a dream in trifles, spooned over stewed fruits and steamed puddings, or used as a topping for strawberries and raspberries instead of the more customary cream. Custard Sauce, based on eggs and milk, dates back to the reign of Queen Elizabeth the First and reached its heyday in Victorian and Edwardian times when it was approved by Nanny for nursery teas, along with the wobbly jelly and bright pink blancmange!

1pt (575ml) milk (long life gives an enriched flavour), or use half milk and half single cream
3 level tsp cornflour (prevents curdling as it acts as stabiliser)
1 tblsp cold water
4 Grade 2 eggs
2 rounded tblsp caster sugar
1 tsp vanilla essence

1. Heat milk, uncovered in jug, for 2 minutes at full power.

2. Meanwhile, tip cornflour into a 2pt (1 litre) bowl, add water and stir until smooth. Break in eggs individually then add sugar.

3. Whisk until smooth then gradually blend in the hot milk. Leave uncovered. Cook 5 to $5\frac{1}{2}$ minutes at full power, whisking at the end of every minute. When ready, custard should cling to the wooden fork or spatula used for whisking or, in the case of a wooden spoon, coat the back of it in an even layer. Mix in vanilla.

4. Tip into a clean bowl and either serve straight away or leave until cold. Cover leftovers and store in the refrigerator.

ALTERNATE FLAVOURS

Use rum, sherry, almond or rose essence instead of vanilla.

LEMON OR ORANGE CUSTARD

Make as above, then stir in 2 level teaspoons finely grated lemon or orange peel instead of vanilla.

Hot Chocolate Sauce   Serves 6

The ultimate luxury for ice cream and banana splits. If allowed to cool, it may also be spooned over a dish of Profiteroles.

1oz (25g) butter
2oz (50g) dark brown soft sugar
2 level tblsp cocoa powder
1 rounded tblsp golden syrup
2 tblsp cold milk
1 tsp vanilla essence

1. Put butter into a basin and melt uncovered for 1 to 1½ minutes at defrost setting.

2. Add brown sugar then sift in cocoa powder. Stir in rest of ingredients thoroughly.

3. Leave uncovered and heat for 5 minutes at defrost setting, stirring twice. Serve hot or cold over ice-cream and ice cream sundaes.

HOT MOCHA SAUCE   Serves 6

Make exactly as above, adding 1 heaped teaspoon instant coffee powder or granules with syrup, milk and essence.

Rarebit Beans. See page 25.

Above: *Asparagus Quiche. See page 32.*

Opposite: *Curry Rice Soup. See page 33.*

Left: *Lettuce
Soup.
See page 35.*

Opposite:
*Chilled Cream of
Cheshire Soup.
See page 36.*

Tomato Soup with Avocado Mayonnaise. See page 36.

Hollandaise Sauce. See page 44.

Poached Salmon Steaks. See page 76.

Health Foods and Vegetarian Dishes

As interest in health foods and vegetarian dishes grows, I offer a short selection of both which fare extremely well in a microwave oven. They are primarily for main courses and accompaniments and I am sure will be well accepted by all cooks, of any persuasion, who enjoy appetising food without meat or fish.

Cauliflower Cheese   Serves 4 (F)

Cook cauliflower as directed in Vegetable Chart on page 128. Drain. Put into dish. Coat with freshly made Cheese sauce and sprinkle with paprika.

Leave uncovered and reheat 5 to 6 minutes at defrost setting.

Nut Burgers   Makes 10 (F)

Nothing especially original about these – vegetarians have been enjoying nut cutlets for years – but the blend of mixed nuts gives the Burgers an outstanding flavour and crunchy texture. Serve them hot with one of the sauces from the Sauce Section and two or three different vegetables. Or try them cold with salad. Or slice them in half and use as a sandwich filling with lettuce, pickle and mayonnaise. Or just eat them as they are for a snack.

4oz (125g) shelled but unskinned whole almonds, washed and dried
4oz (125g) walnut pieces
4oz (125g) cashew pieces, lightly toasted (page 224)
4oz (125g) fresh brown breadcrumbs (soft)
3oz (75g) onion, peeled and grated
$\frac{1}{2}$ level tsp salt
1 level tsp prepared mustard
1oz (25g) butter or margarine, melted 1 to $1\frac{1}{2}$ minutes in microwave
2 tblsp milk

1. Grind nuts finely in blender or food processor. Mix with rest of ingredients.

2. Shape into 10 even-sized ovals. Arrange round edge of large greased plate. Leave uncovered and cook 4 minutes at full power, turning over once. Serve as suggested.

NUT 'CAKE'   Serves 6 to 8 (F)

Make as above, using 6oz (175g) brazils, 2oz (50g) toasted but unsalted peanuts and 4oz (125g) unskinned but shelled almonds, first washed and dried. Shape into a round of 7 to 8 inches (17·5 to 20cm) on a greased plate. Leave uncovered. Cook 3 minutes at full power, stand 5 minutes, turn plate round and cook a further $2\frac{1}{2}$ minutes at full power. Cut into wedges and serve hot or cold.

Paprika Mushrooms   Serves 6

Reminiscent of the glories of the Austro-Hungarian Empire when the food was rich, lavish and very much to Queen Marie Theresa's taste, these paprika mushrooms are enveloped in lightly seasoned soured cream and attractively coloured with tomato purée. They make a regal meal with baby boiled potatoes or small pasta.

2lb (900g) button mushrooms
2oz (50g) butter or margarine
1 garlic clove, peeled and crushed
1 large carton (10oz or 284ml) soured cream
1 level tblsp paprika
1 rounded tblsp tubed or canned tomato purée
$1\frac{1}{2}$ level tsp salt

1. Trim mushrooms then wash and dry.

2. Put butter or margarine into a 4pt (2·25 litre) glass or pottery dish and melt $1\frac{1}{2}$ to 2 minutes at defrost setting. Leave uncovered.

3. Add mushrooms and garlic. Cover with a plate and cook 10 minutes at full power, stirring 3 times.

4. Mix in remaining ingredients, tossing over and over gently with a spoon. Cover as above. Cook 5 minutes at full power, stirring once.

5. Remove from oven and uncover. Stir once more then serve with suggested accompaniments.

Curried Mushrooms   Serves 6

Splendidly tempting, what better meal than these softly curried mushrooms? They make a sustaining lunch or supper dish, and are predictably at their finest accompanied by rice or bulgar with side dishes of chutney, sliced hardboiled eggs showered with chopped walnuts, yogurt mixed with 1 or 2 teaspoons chopped mint, and a salad of chopped tomatoes and cucumber.

2lb (900g) button mushrooms
2oz (50g) butter or margarine
1 level tblsp curry powder
1 level tsp salt
$\frac{1}{4}$pt (150ml) buttermilk
1 level tsp caster sugar
$\frac{1}{4}$ level tsp garlic powder
1 level tblsp cornflour
2 tblsp cold water

1. Trim mushrooms then wash and dry. Leave aside temporarily.

2. Put butter or margarine into a 4pt (2·25 litre) glass or pottery dish and melt $1\frac{1}{2}$ to 2 minutes at defrost setting. Leave uncovered.

3. Add curry powder, salt, buttermilk, caster sugar and garlic powder. Cover with a plate and cook 2 minutes at full power.

4. Toss in mushrooms. Add cornflour, smoothly mixed with water. Cover as above and cook 7 minutes at full power, stirring twice.

5. Uncover, stir again and serve as suggested.

Leek and Chestnut Casserole — Serves 4 (F)

A tempting arrangement, remarkably easy and a hearty meal with microwaved jacket potatoes and tomatoes.

2 large leeks

1oz (25g) butter or margarine

8oz (225g) dried chestnuts, cooked as described on page 227

½ to 1 level tsp salt

1. Trim leeks, leaving on 2 inches (5cm) of green 'skirt'. Slit and wash very thoroughly to remove earth and grit, then cut into ½ inch (1·25cm) slices.

2. Put butter or margarine into a 7 inch (17·5cm) round glass or pottery casserole and melt 1 to 1½ minutes at defrost setting.

3. Mix in leeks, cover with a plate and cook for 6 minutes at full power, stirring twice.

4. Break up chestnuts and combine with leeks. Sprinkle with salt. Cover as above and cook a further 3 minutes at full power. Stir and serve.

Kibbled Wheat Salad — Serves 4

Full of that slightly firm and 'al dente' texture so beloved by the Italians, kibbled wheat makes a sturdy salad indeed, and a very tasty one at that enhanced with onions, parsley, oil and fresh lemon juice. Nutritious enough for anyone into the 'naturals', the salad partners amicably with eggs and cheese.

8oz (225g) kibbled wheat

1½pt (850ml) hot water

1½ level tsp salt

1 tblsp salad oil

juice of a small lemon

3oz (75g) onion, peeled and finely grated

2 heaped tblsp finely chopped parsley

1. Rinse kibbled wheat and put into a 4pt (2·25 litre) glass or pottery dish. Add hot water and salt.

2. Cover with cling film. Slit three times with a knife. Cook 10 minutes at full power, turning dish 4 times unless oven has a turntable. Uncover.

3. Return to oven and cook at full power a further 15 minutes, stirring 3 times.

4. Remove from oven, cover with a plate and leave until completely cold. Drain if necessary but wheat should have absorbed all the moisture.

5. Fork in rest of ingredients, transfer to a dish or bowl and serve as suggested above when cold.

KIBBLED WHEAT CEREAL — Serves 6

Spoon freshly cooked kibbled wheat into bowls. Add milk and brown sugar or honey to each.

Bulgar ## Serves 4 to 6

Bulgar, also known as burghal or cracked wheat, is widely eaten in the Middle East and North Africa as a change from rice or potatoes, and is available over here from health food shops and oriental grocers. With its own nutty flavour and coarse texture, it is delicious whether served hot with main courses or cold in salads. As it is so popular with vegetarians, I thought it only fair to include microwave cooking instructions for a much underrated cereal in the West.

8oz (225g) bulgar

1pt (575ml) boiling water

1 to 1½ level tsp salt

1. Put bulgar into an 8 inch (20cm) round and fairly deep glass or pottery dish. Leave uncovered and toast, with no water, for 3 minutes at full power, stirring at the end of every minute.

2. Mix in boiling water. Cook, uncovered, for 5 minutes at full power, stirring 3 times. Season to taste with salt then fluff up with a fork. Draining should be unnecessary as the bulgar will absorb the water in the cooking time recommended.

ONION BULGAR — Serves 4 to 6 (F)

Put 1oz (25g) butter or margarine, or 1 tablespoon salad oil, into an 8 inch (20cm) round and fairly deep glass or pottery dish. Heat 1 to 1½ minutes at defrost setting. Add 4oz (125g) peeled and finely grated onion. Cook, uncovered, for 3 minutes at full power. Remove from oven. In separate dish, toast 8oz (225g) bulgar as directed in previous recipe. Stir in onions with 1pt (575ml) boiling water. Leave uncovered. Cook for 5 minutes at full power, stirring 3 times. Season with salt and fluff up with a fork. Serve with vegetable dishes or eggs.

SULTAN'S SALAD — Serves 4

Cook bulgar as directed in first recipe then leave until lukewarm. Stir in 1 peeled and crushed garlic clove, 2oz (50g) grated carrots, 1 level tablespoon chopped fresh mint, 4 rounded tablespoons chopped parsley, the strained juice of 1 medium lemon and 3 to 4 tablespoons corn or sunflower oil. Adjust seasoning to taste with extra salt and a light sprinkling of pepper. Spoon into a dish and stud with black and green olives. Serve with Pitta bread.

Blue Cheese and Walnut Flan   Serves 4

Quiche-related, this makes a superb lunch dish with a crunchy chicory and orange salad, tossed in a zesty French dressing and sprinkled here and there with watercress leaves.

PASTRY

6oz (175g) plain flour

pinch of salt

3oz (75g) butter or margarine, at kitchen temperature

1oz (25g) walnuts, finely chopped

about 7 tsp cold water to mix

1 egg yolk from Grade 3 egg

FILLING

1 packet (7oz or 200g) full fat cream cheese, at kitchen temperature

2 level tblsp snipped fresh chives or the light green part of very well-washed leek, finely chopped

4oz (125g) soft blue cheese such as Lymeswold or Gorgonzola, at kitchen temperature

1 level tsp paprika

2 Grade 3 eggs, at kitchen temperature and well-beaten

4 tblsp cold milk.

1. For pastry, sift flour and salt into a bowl. Rub in fat finely, toss in walnuts then mix to a stiff paste with cold water.

2. Turn out on to floured surface, knead lightly until smooth then roll out fairly thinly into a circle. Use to line a lightly greased, 8 inch (20cm) glass or pottery pie plate. Pinch top edge into flutes between finger and thumb then prick all over with a fork. Cook 6 minutes, uncovered, at full power, turning 4 times unless oven has a turntable. If pastry has bulged in places, press down very gently with fingers protected by oven gloves.

3. Remove from oven and brush all over with egg yolk. Cook a further minute at full power to seal holes. Leave to stand while preparing filling.

4. Beat cream cheese until light and very soft. Add chives. Mash in blue cheese then add rest of ingredients. Beat well until completely smooth. Pour into pastry case. Cook, uncovered, 14 minutes at defrost setting, turning 4 times unless oven has a turntable. Serve warm or cold, cut into wedges.

62

Vegetarian Stuffed Aubergines   Serves 2

With a mellow egg filling and golden brown pine nuts, these stuffed aubergines may be served hot or cold and team especially well with jacket potatoes and salad. I like them for lunch but they also make a pleasing light supper dish accompanied by an assortment of cooked vegetables and perhaps some homemade soup for starters.

2 medium aubergines (about 1¼lb or 575g)

2 tsp lemon juice

3oz (75g) fresh brown breadcrumbs

1oz (25g) toasted pine nuts (see page 225)

1½ level tsp salt

1 level tsp garlic or onion powder

3 hardboiled eggs (see page 67), chopped

4 tblsp milk

1 level tsp mixed herbs

4 tsp salad oil

1. Slit skin of aubergines all the way round with a sharp knife, as though you were going to cut each aubergine in half lengthwise.

2. Put on to a plate, cover with a piece of kitchen paper and cook 6 minutes at full power when aubergines should be tender.

3. Remove from oven and cut each in half along split lines. Spoon pulp into blender or food processor. Add lemon juice. Run machine until mixture is smooth and purée-like.

4. Scrape into a bowl. Mix in crumbs, nuts, salt, garlic or onion powder, chopped eggs, milk and herbs.

5. Return to aubergine halves then stand on a plate, narrow ends towards centre. Trickle oil over tops, cover with kitchen paper and reheat 4 minutes at full power.

Tomato Upside Down Cheese Pudding   Serves 4

Nutrition-packed and colourful, this is an easy savoury dish to make and is ready for the table in about 10 minutes. Serve with a green vegetable.

8oz (225g) self-raising flour

1 level tsp powder mustard

½ level tsp salt

4oz (125g) butter or margarine

4oz (125g) Cheddar cheese, finely grated

2 Grade 3 eggs, beaten

¼pt (150ml) cold milk

1lb (450g) tomatoes, blanched and skinned

½ level tsp salt

1 rounded tblsp chopped parsley

1. Well-grease a 3pt (1·75 litre) deep round dish.

2. Sift flour, mustard and salt into a bowl. Rub in butter or margarine finely. Toss in cheese.

3. Using a fork, mix to a soft consistency with eggs and milk. Spoon into dish and spread evenly with a knife.

4. Cook, uncovered, for 6 minutes at full power, turning dish 4 times unless oven has a turntable.

5. Meanwhile skin tomatoes and chop. Mix with salt. Put into a shallow bowl and cover with a plate.

6. Remove pudding from oven and invert into a dish. Return to oven and cook a further 2 minutes at full power.

7. Remove from oven, cover with kitchen paper and leave aside temporarily. Heat tomatoes for 3 minutes at full power. Spoon over pudding, sprinkle with parsley and serve while still hot.

Lentil Dhal   Serves 6 generously (F)

Distinctly oriental with origins in India, this Lentil Dhal is an elegantly-flavoured and nutritious dish which makes a fine meal with freshly cooked long grain rice and side dishes of yogurt, chutney and sliced onions.

8oz (225g) orange lentils
2oz (50g) butter or margarine, or 3 tblsp salad oil
12oz (350g) onions, peeled and chopped
1 garlic clove, peeled and crushed
1 rounded tsp turmeric
1 rounded tsp paprika
$\frac{1}{2}$ level tsp ground ginger
1 rounded tblsp garam masala
$\frac{1}{8}$ level tsp cayenne pepper
4 cardamon pods, broken open to release seeds
1 rounded tblsp tubed or canned tomato purée
$1\frac{1}{4}$pt (725ml) boiling water
$1\frac{1}{2}$ level tsp salt
fresh coriander leaves, chopped

1. Rinse lentils under cold, running water. Leave on one side temporarily.

2. Put butter, margarine or oil into a 3pt (1·75 litre) dish and heat, uncovered, for 1 minute at full power. Mix in onions and garlic. Cover with a plate. Cook 3 minutes at full power.

3. Stir in rest of ingredients. Cover with cling film, puncturing twice with the tip of a knife. Cook 15 minutes at full power, turning dish 3 or 4 times unless oven has a turntable.

4. Fluff up with a fork before serving and, if too thick for personal taste, add a little extra boiling water until the right consistency is achieved. Garnish by sprinkling with chopped coriander.

Way Down Yonder Aubergine Casserole   Serves 4

Another hand-picked special, discovered during my travels to Louisiana. It is blissful for vegetarians, pertly-flavoured, and with just the right amount of crunch to add interest to the fairly soft texture of the aubergines. It may be 'hotted-up' by the addition of a few drops of Tabasco after the salt.

1oz (25g) butter or margarine

2oz (50g) celery, scrubbed and finely chopped

6oz (175g) onions, peeled and finely chopped

2oz (50g) red or green pepper, de-seeded and finely chopped

1lb (450g) cooked and puréed aubergines (for method, see recipe for Aubergine Dip on page 30)

6oz (175g) blanched tomatoes, skinned and chopped

3oz (75g) fresh white breadcrumbs

½ to 1 level tsp salt

2oz (50g) Double Gloucester cheese, grated

1. Heat butter or margarine, in 2pt (1·25 litre) dish, for 1 minute at full power. Leave uncovered.

2. Stir in celery, onions and pepper. Cover with plate or matching lid and cook 3 minutes at full power. Mix in aubergine purée, tomatoes, crumbs and salt.

3. Cover with plate or lid as above and cook another 3 minutes at full power, turning dish twice unless oven has a turntable.

4. Uncover, sprinkle with cheese and cook 2 minutes at full power, turning once. Stand 2 to 3 minutes and serve.

Avocado Farci   Serves 2

Perfect for vegetarians, this avocado dish is both unusual and delicious and may also be served as a meal starter for 4 people – vegetarian or not. In either case, the best accompaniment is crisp toast.

2 medium to large avocados, fully ripe but not squashy
juice of ½ medium lemon
2oz (50g) brown breadcrumbs
1½oz (40g) onion, peeled and finely grated
4oz (125g) blanched tomatoes, skinned and chopped
2oz (50g) Lancashire cheese, crumbled or grated
paprika
8 toasted hazelnuts

1. Halve avocados and carefully spoon flesh into a bowl. Add lemon juice and mash very finely with a fork.

2. Stir in crumbs, onion and tomatoes. Return to avocado shells and sprinkle with cheese and paprika. Top each with 2 hazelnuts.

3. Arrange on a plate with pointed ends towards centre. Cook, uncovered, for 5 to 5½ minutes at full power, turning plate twice unless oven has a turntable. Serve straight away.

Macaroni Pepperoni
Serves 2 as a main course or 4 as a side dish

An uncomplicated macaroni accompaniment, flavoured with peppers and coloured with tomato juice. If you heap grated cheese on to each serving and sprinkle with chopped parsley, you have a main meal of some substance.

½pt (275ml) tomato juice
4oz (125g) elbow macaroni
1 level tsp salt
2 tblsp hot wine or water
2oz (50g) frozen diced green and red peppers (used from frozen)
1 ½oz (40g) butter or margarine
FOR MAIN COURSE
3oz (75g) Cheddar cheese, finely grated
1 heaped tblsp chopped parsley

1. Pour tomato juice into a 2pt (1·25 litre) glass or pottery dish. Cover with a plate. Heat until boiling, allowing 3 to 4 minutes at full power.

2. Take out of oven and stir in macaroni, salt, wine or water, the frozen vegetables and butter or margarine. Mix well. Cover with cling film, then puncture twice with the tip of a knife. Alternatively, cover with matching lid.

3. Cook 10 minutes at full power, turning dish 4 times unless oven has a turntable. Leave to stand 5 minutes before serving.

Eggs

'I can't even boil an egg' is a cry from the heart I hear very often and although dab and experienced hands may find this hard to understand, egg cookery can be problematic and I, too, have eaten my way through tough and rubbery omelets, watery scrambled eggs, leathery fried ones, runny or overcooked boiled eggs and unfortunate poached ones with floppy whites and overcooked yolks. Why a microwave oven has such a superb effect on eggs is beyond my limited scientific scope but whichever way one cooks eggs the results are always perfect – or near perfect – and the speed of operation a joy. There is just one important factor to bear in mind: the yolks of eggs destined for poaching, frying and baking should be punctured twice, gently, with the tip of a knife or skewer to break the fine skin or membrane enveloping each. This will subsequently stop the yolks from bursting, spluttering and making a mess all over the oven.

Eggs   Warming

For those of you who decide to make a cake at the last minute, whether in the microwave or conventionally, and the recipe requires eggs at room temperature while yours are still in the refrigerator, I have overcome the problem completely by warming the eggs in a dish in the microwave.

For 1 Egg
Break into a small dish or cup. Puncture yolk twice with a metal skewer or tip of a knife to prevent bursting. Cover with plate or saucer. Warm $\frac{1}{2}$ minute at defrost setting.

For 2 Eggs
Break into a small dish or cup. Puncture yolks twice with a metal skewer or tip of a knife to prevent bursting. Cover with a plate or saucer. Warm $\frac{1}{2}$ to $\frac{3}{4}$ minute at defrost setting.

For 3 Eggs
Follow directions for 2 eggs but warm 1 to $1\frac{1}{4}$ minutes at defrost setting.

Eggs   Boiling

As far as I know, no-one has yet devised a simple technique for boiling eggs in the microwave. The nearest is to wrap the whole egg in foil, put it into a cup, cover with water and boil for so many minutes. Altogether a complicated procedure. My own technique works well and is based on 'egg in the cup'; a way of serving boiled eggs in many parts of Germany, usually for breakfast. Pursuing the same idea, I have worked out the following timings for boiled eggs with excellent results.

Soft Boiled Egg
Use 1 egg only. Break into a greased cup. Puncture yolk twice with a thin metal skewer or tip of a knife to prevent bursting.

Cover with a saucer. Cook 1 minute at defrost setting. Swirl gently round. Re-cover. Continue to cook a further $\frac{1}{2}$ minute at defrost. Stand $\frac{1}{2}$ minute. Either eat from the cup or invert on to a slice of toast.

Medium Soft Boiled Egg

Follow directions for Soft Boiled Egg but allow 2 minutes at defrost setting. Stand $\frac{1}{2}$ minute.

Hardboiled Egg

Follow directions for Soft Boiled Egg, but allow $2\frac{1}{2}$ minutes at defrost setting, depending on size. Stand $\frac{3}{4}$ minute. Tip out of the cup and use as required. Because the egg holds its shape so well, it can be used as a basis for egg mayonnaise. For garnishing purposes, the white can be separated from the yolk and either chopped or cut into thin strips. The yolk may be rubbed through a mesh sieve and sprinkled over other foods for a bright touch of yellow.

Hardboiled Eggs   cooking 2 at once

Follow directions for Soft Boiled Egg, but put into a greased dish and allow 4 minutes at defrost setting. Stand 1 minute.

Hardboiled Eggs   cooking 3 at once

Follow directions for Soft Boiled Egg, but put into a greased dish and allow $5\frac{1}{2}$ minutes at defrost setting. Stand 1 minute.

TIPS

1. Eggs taken from the refrigerator, or those larger than Grade 3, may need a few seconds longer than times given above.

2. For soft and medium boiled, it is best to cook eggs individually. Hardboiled eggs are less critical and you can microwave more than one at a time.

3. Wash the cup immediately after use as any leftover white has a tendency to congeal when cold.

4. It is important to keep eggs covered while cooking to prevent them from drying out.

5. The advantages of cooking eggs in this way is cleanliness, a saving in fuel costs, ease of eating and no little pieces of shell to cope with after the meal.

Poached Eggs

Appreciated by slimmers and others who are partial to poached eggs on toast, or on cooked spinach with a coating of cheese sauce for Eggs Florentine, the egg or eggs should be cooked individually in small dishes or cups. Up to 3 dishes may be placed simultaneously in the microwave but it is not advisable to cook 2 or 3 eggs together in 1 dish.

For 1 Egg
Pour 6 tablespoons hot water into a small glass or pottery dish. Add $\frac{1}{2}$ teaspoon of mild vinegar to prevent the white from spreading. Carefully break in 1 Grade 3 egg. Puncture yolk twice with the tip of a knife. Cover dish with a plate. Cook from 45 to 75 seconds at full power, depending on how firm you like the white to be. Leave to stand 1 minute. Remove from dish with perforated draining spoon.

For 2 Eggs in 2 Dishes
Cook $1\frac{1}{2}$ to 2 minutes at full power. Stand $1\frac{1}{4}$ minutes. If whites are too runny, cook an extra 15 to 20 seconds.

For 3 Eggs in 3 Dishes
Cook 2 to $2\frac{1}{2}$ minutes at full power. Stand 2 minutes. If whites are too runny, cook an extra 20 to 30 seconds.

Scrambled Eggs

Popular for all meals of the day, eggs scrambled in the microwave are light and soft in texture, almost non-fail and best made in a glass cup, bowl, dish or measuring jug so that one may monitor the action through the oven door. I offer 2 versions: one basic with a little milk, and the other enriched and softened with 1 tablespoon of milk per egg, which is slightly above the average amount usually recommended.

BASIC SCRAMBLED EGGS

For 1 Egg
Break 1 Grade 3 egg into a lightly buttered glass container. Add 2 teaspoons milk and seasoning to taste. Beat well. Cover with a saucer or plate. Cook 30 seconds at full power. Stir briskly. Re-cover and continue to cook a further 10 to 15 seconds when egg should be lightly set and start rising in the container. Remove from oven, again stir briskly and serve straight away. Do not overcook or egg will become leathery and liquid will seep out.

For 2 Eggs
Add 4 teaspoons milk to eggs. Season. Cook 45 seconds. Stir briskly. Cook a further 20 to 30 seconds. Stir briskly and serve.

For 3 Eggs
Add 6 teaspoons milk to eggs. Season. Cook 1 minute. Stir briskly. Cook a further 35 to 50 seconds. Stir briskly and serve.

For 4 Eggs

Add 8 teaspoons milk to eggs. Season. Cook 1½ minutes. Stir briskly. Cook a further 1 to 1¼ minutes, stirring briskly half way through and at the end. Serve straight away.

EXTRA CREAMY SCRAMBLED EGGS

For 1 Egg

Make as previously directed but add 1 tablespoon cold milk and seasoning to taste. Cook 3 minutes at defrost setting, stirring briskly twice.

For 2 Eggs

Make as previously directed but add 2 tablespoons cold milk and seasoning to taste. Cook 4¾ to 5 minutes at defrost setting, stirring briskly 3 times.

For 3 Eggs

Make as previously directed but add 3 tablespoons cold milk and seasoning to taste. Cook 6½ minutes at defrost setting, stirring briskly 4 times.

For 4 Eggs

Make as previously directed but add 4 tablespoons cold milk and seasoning to taste. Cook 8½ minutes at defrost setting, stirring briskly 5 times.

Fried Eggs

These turn out soft and tender, as only the best fried eggs should, brightly 'sunny side up', as the Americans say, and with a surround of white which never becomes frizzled and indigestible.

For 1 Egg

Brush a small dish lightly with melted butter or margarine (salad oil if preferred). Gently break in 1 Grade 3 egg. Puncture yolk twice with the tip of a knife. Sprinkle lightly with salt and pepper to taste and, if liked, some finely chopped fresh herbs. Cover with a plate. Cook 30 seconds at full power. Stand 1 minute. Cook an extra 15 to 20 seconds when white should be set. If not, allow an extra 5 to 7 seconds.

For 2 Eggs

Break 2 eggs into greased dish. Puncture yolks twice with the tip of a knife. Season. Cover. Cook 1 minute at full power. Stand 1 minute. Cook an extra 20 to 40 seconds when whites should be set. If not, allow an extra 6 to 8 seconds.

NOTE: Frying more than 2 eggs at a time is not recommended as the yolks would cook more quickly than the whites and become hard. This is due to the longer cooking time needed to set the whites.

Classic Omelet   Serves 1 to 2

A fine-textured and light omelet which is delicious both plain and filled. For a substantial meal, allow 1 omelet per person but for a lightish snack or breakfast, half an omelet should be adequate.

melted butter or margarine

3 Grade 2 or 3 eggs

¼ level tsp salt

2 tblsp cold water

pepper to taste

parsley to garnish

1. Brush a fairly shallow, 8 inch (20cm) round glass or pottery dish with melted butter or margarine.

2. Beat eggs *very thoroughly* with all remaining ingredients – breaking them up lightly, as for traditional omelets, is not enough.

3. Pour into dish and put into microwave. Cover with plate. Cook 1½ minutes at full power. Turn dish half round unless oven has a turntable.

4. Uncover then stir egg mixture gently with a wooden spoon or fork, bringing the partially set edges to the centre. Return to microwave and cover as before. Cook another 1½ minutes at full power.

5. Uncover and cook ½ to 1 minute or until top is just set. Fold into 3 like an envelope and carefully slide out on to a warm plate. Garnish with parsley (or watercress if preferred) and serve straight away.

HAM OMELET

Sprinkle half the cooked omelet with 1oz (25g) coarsely chopped ham.

AVOCADO OMELET

Cover half the cooked omelet with 1 round tablespoon mashed avocado, seasoned well to taste with salt and pepper and mixed with 1 teaspoon lemon juice to prevent browning.

PARSLEY OMELET

Shower omelet mixture with 1 heaped tablespoon chopped parsley after it has cooked for the first 1½ minutes.

CHIVE OMELET

Make exactly as Parsley Omelet.

MIXED HERB OMELET

France's Omelette aux Fines Herbs, this is a herb omelet flavoured with a mixture of 2 or 3 fresh herbs such as parsley, chives and basil. They should be very finely chopped and 1 heaped tablespoon, added as directed for the Parsley Omelet above, is enough for the quantity of eggs used.

Brunch Omelet Serves 1 to 2

This is an American-style omelet, very often served for Sunday brunch when people combine a relaxed late breakfast and early lunch.

Make exactly as the Classic Omelet but use 3 tablespoons cold milk instead of water. After uncovering, cook for 1 to $1\frac{1}{2}$ minutes. Fold in 3 and carefully slide out on to a plate. Garnish as suggested above.

Filled Omelets Serves 1 to 2

Either the Classic Omelet or Brunch Omelet may be filled, but then it should be folded in half and not into three.

TOMATO OMELET

Cover one half of the cooked omelet with 1 blanched tomato (2oz or 50g), skinned and chopped.

MUSHROOM OMELET

In small dish, melt $\frac{1}{2}$oz (15g) butter or margarine, uncovered, for $\frac{3}{4}$ minute at defrost setting. Add 2oz (50g) trimmed and coarsely chopped mushrooms. Stir well to mix and return to microwave. Cover and cook until soft, allowing $\frac{1}{2}$ to $\frac{3}{4}$ minute at full power. Use to cover one half of omelet.

CHEESE OMELET

Sprinkle half the cooked omelet with 1oz (25g) grated hard cheese (type according to individual preference) or with crumbled blue cheese.

Omelet Arnold Bennett Serves 2 to 3

This is a rich and luxurious omelet, said to have been masterminded by a chef at London's Savoy Hotel in honour of the famous writer. My adaptation follows.

Flake up 4oz (125g) freshly cooked smoked haddock fillet or smoked cod fillet and transfer to a small dish. Mix in 1 carton (5oz or 142ml) soured cream. Cover with a saucer or plate and cook for $1\frac{1}{2}$ minutes at full power. Remove from microwave and leave to stand while making the Brunch Omelet. Give it its full 3 minutes at full power (see directions above) then uncover and cook a further $\frac{1}{2}$ minute at full power. Spread all over with smoked fish and cream mixture and sprinkle with 1 to $1\frac{1}{2}$oz (25 to 40g) grated Red Leicester cheese. Leave uncovered and cook for a further $1\frac{1}{2}$ to 2 minutes at full power when omelet should be hot and cheese melted. Cut into 2 or 3 portions and serve with a crisp salad.

Tortilla   Serves 2

The famous Spanish Omelet is a flat and pancake-like egg dish containing onions and potatoes. Like the Omelet Arnold Bennett, and the Chinese one which follows, it is never folded but cut into portions and served flat. Accompany with rolls and butter. Also a crisp salad.

½oz (15g) butter or margarine
4oz (125g) onion, peeled and finely chopped
6oz (175g) cold cooked potatoes, cubed
3 Grade 2 eggs
¾ to 1 level tsp salt
2 tblsp cold water

1. Melt butter or margarine, uncovered, in an 8 inch (20cm) shallow round dish. Allow ¾ minute at defrost setting.

2. Mix in onion. Cover dish with plate then cook 2 minutes at full power. Uncover and stir in potatoes. Cover again with a plate and cook a further minute at full power. Remove from oven.

3. Beat eggs very thoroughly with salt and cold water. Pour evenly over onions and potatoes in dish. Cook, uncovered, for 4½ minutes at full power, turning dish twice unless oven has a turntable.

4. Stand 1 minute, cut into 2 portions and transfer to warm plates. Serve straight away.

Omelet Fu Yung   Serves 2

A personal adaptation of a Chinese egg dish. It teams well with rice or noodles and microwaved tomato halves.

½oz (15g) butter or margarine
3oz (75g) onion, peeled and finely chopped
2 rounded tblsp cooked peas
2 rounded tblsp canned bean sprouts, well-drained
2oz (50g) trimmed mushrooms, thinly sliced
3 Grade 2 eggs
¾ level tsp salt
2 tblsp cold water
1 tsp soy sauce
4 spring onions to garnish

1. Melt butter or margarine, uncovered, in an 8 inch (20cm) shallow round dish. Allow ¾ minute at defrost setting.

2. Mix in onion. Cover dish with plate then cook 2 minutes at full power. Uncover and stir in peas, bean sprouts and mushrooms.

3. Cover as above and cook 1½ minutes. Remove from oven. Beat eggs very thoroughly with salt, water and soy sauce.

4. Pour evenly over ingredients in dish. Cook 5 minutes, uncovered, at full power, turning twice unless oven has a turntable.

5. Stand 1 minute, cut into 2 portions and transfer to warm plates. Garnish with spring onions. Serve straight away.

Omelet in Pizza Style — Serves 2

Marvellous for slimmers and when one fancies something a bit Pizzaish but has neither time nor inclination to make a dough.

- ½oz (15g) butter or margarine
- 3 Grade 2 eggs
- 3 tblsp milk
- ½ level tsp salt
- 12oz (350g) blanched and skinned tomatoes, sliced
- 4oz (125g) Mozzarella cheese, sliced
- 8 canned anchovies in oil
- 8 black olives

1. Melt butter or margarine, uncovered, in an 8 inch (20cm) shallow round dish. Allow ¾ minute at defrost setting.

2. Beat eggs very thoroughly with milk and salt. Pour into dish. Cover with plate. Cook 1½ minutes at full power. Turn dish half round unless oven has a turntable.

3. Uncover then stir mixture gently with a wooden spoon or fork, bringing the partially set edges to the centre. Return to microwave and cover as before. Cook another 1½ minutes at full power.

4. Uncover and cook a further ½ minute. Spread with tomatoes and cheese then garnish with anchovies and olives. Leave uncovered and cook 4 minutes at full power, turning dish twice unless oven has a turntable. Cut into 2 portions and serve while piping hot.

Soufflé Omelet — Serves 2

Dreamy and soft, filled with jam and showered with icing sugar – a perfect sweet to end a light meal.

- 2oz (50g) jam, flavour to taste
- icing sugar
- melted butter
- 3 Grade 1 or 2 eggs
- 3 drops lemon juice
- 1 rounded tblsp caster sugar

1. Spoon jam into a small dish or cup. Cover with a saucer and heat for 1½ minutes at defrost setting. Remove from oven (it retains heat well) and leave to stand while preparing omelet. Cover a large piece of greaseproof paper with a thickish layer of sifted icing sugar.

2. Brush a 10 inch (25cm) round and fairly shallow dish all over with melted butter.

3. Separate eggs, putting yolks into one bowl and whites into another. Add lemon juice to whites and beat until stiff.

4. Add sugar to egg yolks and whip to a thick cream. Gently whisk into egg whites. When thoroughly combined, spoon into prepared dish.

5. Cook, uncovered, for 3½ minutes at full power, turning once unless oven has a turntable.

6. Invert on to the sugared paper, make a cut down the centre and spread one half with the warmed jam.

7. Fold in half and cut into 2 portions. Eat straight away.

Baked Eggs   Serves 1

Also called Oeufs en Cocotte, this way of preparing eggs is highly esteemed in France and certainly makes a classy starter for dinner parties. It also works well for lunch, delicious with toast or crackers and highly acceptable with a crunchy green salad. It is advisable to cook 1 egg at a time in an individual dish.

NEAPOLITAN BAKED EGG   Serves 1

Brush a small ramekin dish or baby soufflé dish with melted butter or margarine. Add 1 generous tablespoon of Neapolitan sauce (page 42). Gently break 1 Grade 3 egg on top. Puncture yolk twice with the tip of a knife. Season to taste. Cover with a saucer. Cook 3 minutes at defrost setting. Stand 1 minute and serve.

BAKED EGG WITH CREAM   Serves 1

Brush a small ramekin dish or baby soufflé dish with melted butter or margarine. Gently break in 1 Grade 3 egg. Puncture yolk twice with the tip of a knife. Season to taste. Coat with 1 tablespoon double cream and sprinkle with 1 level teaspoon finely chopped parsley. Cover with a saucer. Cook 3 minutes at defrost setting. Stand 1 minute and serve.

Fish

Fish and a microwave oven are great teammates, work harmoniously together and bring out the best qualities in each other. The microwave acts fast but sympathetically; the fish responds by turning out moist, tender and full of flavour. The colour is delicate, the texture superb. There is nothing to better this close relationship and anyone who has cooked fish in the microwave will agree what a success story it is.

Cooking Fish Generally speaking, cutlets, steaks and fillets should be cooked for approximately 5 to 6 minutes per pound (450g) if at kitchen temperature, 6 to 7 minutes if taken straight from the refrigerator, and 10 to 12 minutes if cooked from frozen. Obviously the times will vary depending on the type and thickness of fish and therefore it should be watched carefully and removed from the microwave when creamy-looking and slightly flaky. Overcooking will toughen the edges and must be avoided to prevent dryness.

BASIC METHOD

Arrange cod, haddock, coley, plaice, halibut, turbot and so on in a shallow dish. Brush with melted butter or margarine then sprinkle lightly with paprika, plain or seasoning salt and white pepper to taste. Cover with cling film, then puncture twice with the tip of a knife. Cook for times given above, turning dish twice unless oven has a turntable. Uncover, transfer to plates and serve straight away.

AMOUNTS

Allow 6 to 8oz (175 to 225g) per person and cook in no more than 1lb (450g) batches at a time unless following a specific recipe such as the Trout 'Rollmops' for example.

Whole Poached Salmon or Salmon Trout
Allow 8oz or 225g raw weight per serving

Now that farmed salmon and salmon trout are available all the year round and compare favourably in price with meat, the tendency is to buy a large fish and cook it whole – given one has a suitable saucepan or baking dish if it is to be oven-poached – and serve it for parties, hot or cold, with an appropriate sauce or dressing.

Although cutlets and steaks are easier to manage than a whole fish – and indeed cook fast and cleanly in the microwave – a large capacity oven without a turntable can cope with 1 big and uncut fish quite successfully, and does so speedily and conveniently with the minimum of fuss or mess. However, because of the technique involved, the fish does not look as handsome as one cooked conventionally and therefore should be skinned, portioned out and put on to plates (or one large dish) before serving.

To cook, have fish gutted but leave on the head. Wash thoroughly inside and out under cold, running water. Pat dry with paper towels then transfer to a giant roasting bag measuring about 22 by 19 inches (55 by 47·5cm). Close by winding

76

an elastic band round the top of the bag. Place diagonally across the glass tray on floor of oven. Cook at full power, allowing 4 minutes per lb (450g). Switch off half way through and leave the salmon to stand in the oven for 10 minutes. Complete cooking. Stand a further 10 minutes. Leave fish, in its bag, on the glass tray then lift out of the oven and place on the draining board. Open bag and allow liquid to trickle away into the sink. Alternatively, and if required for a particular sauce, collect in a measuring jug.

Cut off head then remove skin from the side facing you. Divide flesh into portions with 2 spatulas and put on to a serving dish or individual plates. When the first side has been dealt with, carefully and gently pull out bone and remove portions of fish as just described, this time leaving the skin where it is; you will find the flesh comes away quite easily. Garnish fish with watercress or parsley and lemon wedges.

TIP: Choose a fish of around 5lb or 2kg, weight after *gutting and cleaning. Alternatively, use half a very large fish.*

Poached Salmon Steaks   Picture p. 56   Serves 4

Classic in its simplicity, salmon cooked in the microwave retains its exquisite flavour and delicate pale pink colour, remaining succulent, well-shaped and tender. Serve it in a sauce of your choice taken from the Sauce Section on page 39, then garnish each with a slice of lemon and either a frond of dill or spray of parsley.

4 salmon steaks weighing 1½lb or 675g, thawed if frozen

¼pt (150ml) water

½ level tsp salt

1. Arrange steaks round the edge of an 8 inch (20cm) round and shallow glass or pottery dish.

2. Pour water into centre then sprinkle fish with salt. Cover with cling film, then puncture twice with the tip of a knife. Alternatively, cover with matching lid.

3. Cook for 8 minutes at full power, turning dish 4 times unless oven has a turntable.

4. Remove from microwave and leave to stand 5 minutes. Lift out of dish with slatted fish slice and transfer to warm plates. Garnish as described above.

SALMON MAYONNAISE   Serves 4
Cook fish as described above. Leave until cold then remove skin. Stand on lettuce-lined plates and garnish with other salad ingredients. Pass mayonnaise separately.

WINE-POACHED SALMON STEAKS   Serves 4
Cook fish as described under Poached Salmon Steaks, substituting dry white wine for water.

TARRAGON POACHED SALMON STEAKS   **Serves 4**

Cook fish as described under Poached Salmon Steaks but use 6 tablespoons water and 2 tablespoons tarragon vinegar. Sprinkle with ½ level teaspoon *each* of salt and dried tarragon.

Sole on the Plate   Allow 1 per person

For those indulgent times when one can afford to buy Dover soles, nothing treats them quite as kindly or as gently as a microwave cooker.

Choose as many soles as are required, each 12oz or 350g in weight, and cook each one individually. Wash and wipe dry. Put into a shallow, oblong glass or pottery dish. Add 1 tablespoon hot water. Cover with cling film, then puncture twice with the tip of a knife. Cook 4 minutes at full power, turning dish once unless oven has a turntable. Leave to stand 2 minutes. Continue to cook 5½ to 6 minutes, turning dish twice if no turntable. Using 2 fish slices or spatulas, carefully lift sole on to a large warm dinner plate. Coat with melted butter. Garnish with lemon wedges and parsley.

TIP: Instead of melted butter, coat with one of the sauces from the Sauce Section (page 39).

SOLE VERONIQUE   Allow 1 per person

Coat sole/soles with Béchamel sauce (page 40) and garnish with peeled, halved and de-seeded green grapes.

FILLETS VERONIQUE

Allow 6 to 8oz (175 to 225g) fish fillets per person and cook as directed under Cooking Fish, Basic Method. Coat with Béchamel sauce (page 40) to which has been added 3oz (75g) peeled, halved and de-seeded green grapes. Garnish with clusters of extra fresh grapes, either washed and dried or peeled.

Monk Fish with Egg and Lemon Sauce Serves 6

By virtue of demand and price, monk fish has risen from the ranks of the mundane to a very classy and highly acclaimed fish, justifiably esteemed for its creamy-white flesh and scampi-like texture. I am confident this recipe does it full justice.

1½lb (675g) monk fish
1oz (25g) butter, at kitchen temperature
3 level tblsp plain flour
½pt (275ml) milk, warmed for 2 minutes at full power
2 Grade 2 egg yolks
juice of 1 large lemon (about 6oz or 175g)
½ to 1 level tsp salt
2 rounded tblsp chopped chives, green part of leek or parsley

1. Cut monk fish away from bone then divide flesh into scampi-sized pieces with a sharp and non-serrated knife. Wash and dry.

2. Put butter into a 8 by 2 inch (20 by 5cm) round glass or pottery dish. Leave uncovered and melt 1 to 1½ minutes at defrost setting.

3. Coat pieces of monk fish with flour then add to dish of butter. Toss round until well-coated. Mix in milk.

4. Cover with cling film, then puncture twice with the tip of a knife.

5. Cook 7 minutes at full power, turning dish 4 times unless oven has a turntable.

6. Meanwhile, beat yolks and lemon juice well together. Season with salt. Add to fish at the end of its cooking time. Stir in well.

7. Cook a further 2 minutes at full power then leave to stand 5 minutes. Stir round, sprinkle with greenery and serve with plain boiled rice or new potatoes. French beans go well with the fish.

'Poached' Sea Bream Serves 4 generously

Expert anglers may be able to catch sea bream with relative ease and perhaps take it for granted, but to me, living inland, it's certainly a rare luxury. Available occasionally from our local fish market, the flesh of sea bream is slightly beige before and after cooking, but it is also creamy and light in texture with a mild and delicate flavour. It takes very well to microwaving and is especially good with Hollandaise sauce speckled with grated orange peel (called Maltaise and on page 44), and with vegetable accompaniments of broccoli and creamed potatoes.

1 by 3¼lb (1·5kg) sea bream, cleaned and scaled then cut in half by fishmonger across the middle (head and tail left on)
1 medium washed lemon, dried and sliced
3oz (75g) onion, peeled and sliced
2 bouquet garni bags
1 level tsp salt

1. Wash both pieces of fish under cold, running water then place side by side in large oval or oblong dish, head and tail at opposite ends.

2. Top with lemon and onion slices then add bouquet garni bags. Sprinkle with salt.

3. Cover dish completely with cling film, then puncture twice with the tip of a knife. Alternatively, cover with matching lid.

4. Remove turntable (if oven has one), or place turntable upside down, if model permits, to prevent it from rotating. This will stop the dish banging against the sides of the oven and causing damage.

5. Cook fish 14 minutes at full power, turning dish twice. Leave to stand 5 minutes inside or outside the oven, whichever is the most convenient.

6. Uncover. Peel away fish skin, gently remove fillets from bones and transfer to warm plates. Serve as suggested above.

Plaice with Celery Cream Sauce — Serves 4

Light and pleasing, this is an easy dish to put together with the novelty element being a sprinkling of toasted coconut over the top – unusual with fish but surprisingly tasty. Serve the plaice with brown rice or brown pasta, and a fresh green salad tingling with French dressing.

8 plaice fillets (about 2lb or 900g), washed and dried
1 can condensed cream of celery soup
$\frac{1}{4}$pt (150ml) boiling water
$\frac{1}{4}$ level tsp marjoram
2 level tblsp toasted coconut (page 225)

1. Wash and dry fish then roll up each fillet from head end to tail, flesh sides outside.

2. Arrange in 10 inch (25cm) round shallow dish, first brushed with butter or margarine.

3. Whisk soup and water well together. Stir in marjoram then spoon over fish.

4. Sprinkle with coconut. Cover with cling film, then puncture twice with the tip of a knife.

5. Cook 12 minutes at full power, turning dish 4 times unless oven has a turntable. Leave to stand 5 minutes inside or outside the oven, whichever is the most convenient.

6. Continue to cook a further 6 minutes at full power as above. Spoon out on to warm plates to serve.

PLAICE WITH MUSHROOM CREAM SAUCE

Make exactly as above, using cream of mushroom soup instead of celery.

Trout 'Rollmops'
Serves 4 as a main course or 8 as a starter

An ingenious way with trout, very appetising, typically British in concept and, served chilled with salad and brown bread and butter, a summer joy. All one needs is an obliging fishmonger or trout farmer who will scale and fillet the fish.

4 large trout, each 1lb or 450g, filleted

2 medium bay leaves, each broken into 4 pieces

6oz (175g) onions, peeled and cut into thin slices

1 level tblsp mixed pickling spice

¼pt (150ml) boiling water

2 rounded tsp granulated sugar

2 level tsp salt

6 tblsp wine or cider vinegar

1. Roll up each trout fillet from head end to tail, skin side inside. Arrange round edge of 10 inch (25cm) round glass or pottery dish which is 2 to 3 inches (5 to 7·5cm) deep.

2. Stud here and there with bay leaves and onion slices separated into rings. Sprinkle with pickling spice.

3. Mix boiling water with sugar, salt and vinegar. Stir well then spoon over fish.

4. Cover with cling film, then puncture twice with the tip of a knife. Cook 18 minutes at full power, turning 3 times unless oven has a turntable.

5. Cool, refrigerate until cold then uncover and serve.

SOUSED HERRINGS   **Serves 4 as a main course or 8 as a starter**

Make as above, substituting filleted herrings for trout. For half quantity, halve all ingredients and cook for 10 to 12 minutes at full power.

Trout with Almonds   Serves 4

One of our classic trout specialities, greatly enhanced by microwave cooking and totally unproblematic. Serve with any of the potato dishes given in the Vegetable Section on page 123 and accompany with a mixed salad or spinach.

2oz (50g) butter

1 tblsp fresh lemon juice

4 trout, each weighing 6 to 8oz (175 to 225g), cleaned and well-washed

2oz (50g) flaked and toasted almonds (page 224)

salt and pepper to taste

GARNISH

4 lemon wedges

parsley sprigs

1. Put butter into a small dish and melt for 1½ to 2 minutes at defrost setting. Stir in lemon juice.

2. Arrange trout, head to tail, in a buttered dish measuring about 10 by 8 inches (25 by 20cm). Remove turntable if necessary, referring to 'Poached' Sea Bream, points 4 and 5 of method (pages 78 and 79).

3. Coat with melted butter and lemon juice then sprinkle with almonds and seasoning.

4. Cover with cling film, then puncture twice with the tip of a knife.

5. Cook 9 to 12 minutes, turning dish twice. Leave to stand 5 minutes then transfer to 4 warm plates.

6. Coat with juices from dish and garnish with lemon wedges and parsley.

Hashed Fish　　　　　　　　　Serves 4

A nostalgic taste of the past, based on a Victorian recipe.

2oz (50g) butter or margarine

2 medium leeks, trimmed, slit then well-washed and sliced

1½lb (675g) fresh haddock or cod fillet, cooked and flaked (see directions under Cooking Fish, Basic Method on page 75)

12oz (350g) cold cooked potatoes, diced

¼pt (150ml) single cream

1 level tsp salt

4 poached or fried eggs

1. Put butter or margarine into an 8 inch (20cm) round glass or pottery dish and melt 1½ to 2 minutes at defrost setting. Leave uncovered.

2. Add leeks and mix in well. Cover with a plate and cook 5 minutes at full power.

3. Stir in fish, potatoes, cream and salt. Cover as above and reheat until very hot, allowing 5 to 7 minutes at full power. Stir once or twice.

4. Leave to stand then poach or fry eggs. Put hash on to 4 plates and top each with an egg.

Provençale Prawns　　　　　Serves 4 to 6

One of the most popular prawn dishes of all, the whole thing takes about 15 minutes to cook and is impressive served with freshly boiled rice fluffed with butter and a generous quantity of chopped parsley, watercress leaves or fresh basil – at least enough to give the rice a bold green colour.

1oz (25g) butter or margarine (or 1 tblsp olive oil, if preferred)

2oz (50g) onion, peeled and grated

1 garlic clove, peeled and crushed

1 can (14oz or 400g) tomatoes, drained

1 level tsp Italian seasoning or dried basil

1 level tsp dark brown soft sugar

1lb (450g) frozen peeled prawns, used from frozen

seasoning to taste

chopped parsley

1. Put butter, margarine or oil into a 3pt (1·75 litre) glass or pottery serving dish and heat 1½ minutes at defrost setting. Leave uncovered.

2. Stir in onion and garlic. Leave uncovered and cook 3 minutes at full power. Stir round.

3. Add tomatoes, Italian seasoning or basil and sugar. Cover with a plate and cook 5 minutes at full power, stirring twice.

4. Add prawns and cover as above. Cook 4 minutes then carefully separate. Re-cover and cook a further 3 to 4 minutes. Adjust seasoning to taste and sprinkle with parsley.

82

Mermaid Pie

Serves 4

Like Shepherd's Pie, but made with fish. A worthwhile midweek special.

Make up ½pt (275ml) Cheese, Onion or Mushroom sauce (see Sauce Section on page 40). Stir in 1lb (450g) cooked and flaked cod or haddock fillet, all skin and bones removed. Put into a 3pt (1·75 litre) serving dish and top with 1½lb (675g) creamed potatoes. Sprinkle lightly with nutmeg or paprika and 1½oz (40g) grated Red Leicester cheese. Leave uncovered and reheat for 6 to 7 minutes at full power, turning dish 3 times unless oven has a turntable. Serve with vegetables to taste.

Flan Arnold Bennett

Serves 6

Why not turn a successful and popular omelet into a flan, so well-suited to a light lunch, supper or even a buffet? This one has a charmed life and is best accompanied by a crackling salad of firm lettuce, celery, cucumber, grated carrot and some coarsely chopped toasted hazelnuts tossed together with a piquant French dressing.

shortcrust pastry, made with 6oz (175g) flour and 3oz (75g) fat etc

1 egg yolk

4oz (125g) cooked and flaked smoked haddock or cod fillet

3 Grade 2 eggs

1 carton (5oz or 142ml) soured cream

¼ to ½ level tsp salt

1 rounded tblsp mayonnaise

3oz (75g) Cheshire or Red Leicester cheese, grated

1. Roll out pastry and use to line an 8 inch (20cm) fluted flan dish. Prick well all over, especially where sides join the base.

2. Cook for 6 minutes at full power, turning twice unless oven has a turntable. If pastry has bulged in places, press down very gently with fingers protected by oven gloves.

3. Brush all over with egg yolk then cook a further 1 minute at full power to seal holes. Remove from oven and cover base with the fish.

4. Beat eggs well together with cream, salt and mayonnaise. Pour evenly over fish. Sprinkle with cheese and cook, uncovered, for 8 minutes at full power, turning dish 4 times unless oven has a turntable. Serve warm or cold.

Crab Mornay   Serves 4

Another fish classic to suit connoisseurs, it is speedy to make in the microwave and excellent served on freshly made toast or atop rice.

Make up Béchamel sauce as directed on page 40 them mix in 3oz (75g) grated Gruyère cheese or Cheddar if preferred. Season to taste with continental mustard. Stir in 8oz (225g) light and dark crab meat, either fresh or defrosted if using frozen. Cover with a plate. Reheat until hot, allowing 2 to 4 minutes at full power. Arrange on 4 slices of hot buttered toast and sprinkle each with paprika. Alternatively, arrange some hot cooked rice in a border around a large plate. Pile hot crab mixture into the centre and sprinkle with paprika. Garnish with watercress.

Kedgeree   Serves 4

A souvenir from the days of the Raj, along with the light snacks called Tiffin and Mulligatawny soup, Kedgeree used to be a breakfast dish but is now eaten for lunch or supper with cooked vegetables to taste. It is a mish-mash of smoked fish, rice, eggs and seasonings.

12oz (350g) smoked haddock fillet

4 tblsp cold water

2oz (50g) butter or margarine

8oz (225g) easy-cook, long grain rice

1pt (575ml) boiling water

3 Grade 3 hardboiled eggs, shelled and 2 chopped

¼pt (150ml) single cream

seasoning to taste

chopped parsley for garnishing

1. Put fish into a shallow glass or pottery dish and add the cold water. Cover with cling film, then puncture twice with the tip of a knife.

2. Cook 5 minutes at full power, turning dish once. Drain fish and flake up flesh with 2 forks, discarding skin and bones.

3. Put butter or margarine in a 3pt (1·75 litre) glass or pottery dish and melt, uncovered, $1\frac{1}{2}$ to 2 minutes at defrost setting. Stir in rice and boiling water.

4. Cover with film as above and cook 15 minutes at full power, turning dish 3 times unless oven has a turntable. Uncover then stir in flaked fish, 2 chopped eggs and the cream. Season to taste.

5. Fluff up with a fork, cover with a plate and reheat 5 minutes at full power. Remove from cooker then garnish with the third egg, first cut into slices or wedges. Add a heavy dusting of the parsley.

CURRY KEDGEREE   Serves 4

Make as above, adding 1 level tablespoon (or less) mild curry powder with the rice. Serve, as desired, with chutney.

Meat and Poultry

Most meat (and poultry too) responds well to microwave cooking but, where possible, prime cuts should be chosen as they tenderise more readily than the less expensive and muscular parts of the animal traditionally recommended for braises, stews and hot-pots. This may sound extravagant but 1lb (450g) rump steak, with additions, will make a generous and richly-flavoured meal for 4 to 6 people, lengthy cooking time is not called for, and the saving in fuel is substantial, especially when balanced against 2 to 2½ hours of conventional simmering on a gas or electric hob – the usual time recommended for stewing fairly tough cuts of meat.

More Plus Points

Meat stewed or braised in the microwave can be cooked in its own serving dish which saves on washing up, the whole process is clean and fast, no sticking or burning occurs, and strong smells rarely filter through the house. But I have to stress that there are still a few provisos. All meat should be cut into smaller than usual pieces, such as ½ inch or 1·25cm cubes instead of larger ones suggested for braising or stewing; it is advisable to 'dry' cook meat or poultry, and sometimes vegetables, for a given length of time *before* liquid is added as this technique helps to soften the meat; seasonings, and salt in particular, have a toughening effect and are therefore best added half way through cooking or, alternatively, at the very end. It is also useful to know that mince behaves perfectly in the microwave because it is virtually shredded into tiny pieces which tenderise easily. And another tip to note is that kosher meat, eaten by the Orthodox Jewish community, is salted by the butcher and reacts unfavourably to microwave cooking, the only exceptions being mince, poultry and offal such as liver.

Understanding the Charts

Although some potential buyers and even cautious users may doubt the ability of a microwave to do a satisfactory job on a roast, it *does* work remarkably well, the meat turns appetisingly brown and also remains moist, succulent and often more tender than a joint cooked conventionally. Obviously, as with all meat, it *must* be completely defrosted before cooking (please refer to the Defrosting Charts on page 87) and if you are at all uncertain about the cooking and standing times given in the Cooking Charts on page 97, let me explain in more detail. Large joints, as the chart says, require 7 minutes cooking time on full power for every 1lb (450g) and 5 minutes standing time. Thus you should cook a 6lb (about 3kg) joint for 21 minutes, leave it to stand for 15 minutes (inside or outside the microwave, depending on which is the most convenient), cook it for a further 21 minutes then leave it to stand another 15 minutes, completing the cooking and standing cycle as given in the charts. To hold in heat and moisture, the joint should be drained and then wrapped in foil for the last part of the standing time or left in its roasting bag. (More information on roasting bags follows.) Standing time is necessary to allow heat from the outside to transfer through to the centre, particularly when dealing with large joints. If no standing times were allowed or carried out only at the end, the outside of the meat would become dry and hard, leaving the centre area raw, cold or both. Joints of up to 2lb (1kg) can be cooked for 14 minutes, with no standing time between, and then left to stand as above for 10 minutes at the end.

Times

The times given in the charts for cooking and standing are fairly general. Thus pork and veal should have 2 minutes per 1lb (450g) added to the cooking time given, as should meat taken straight from the refrigerator. Medium to rare beef may be cooked 1 to $1\frac{1}{2}$ minutes *less* per 1lb (450g), but standing time remains the same. If your microwave oven has a temperature probe, denoting the degree of doneness of the joint, use it according to the instructions given in *your own* microwave oven guide book.

Shape of Joint

The more regular the shape the better and more evenly it will cook. As this is not always a viable proposition, wrap the narrow end of the joint (the bony part of a leg of lamb for example) with foil during the first half of cooking time to prevent frizzle and overcooking. The foil will have no detrimental effect on the workings of the oven, in that there will be much more meat in proportion to foil. If choice is possible, settle for the fillet end of pork or lamb, and a boned and rolled piece of beef or veal.

Roasting Bags

These are perfect for microwaved lamb, beef and veal and seem to encourage browning. Simply season and/or baste the joint, slide into a roasting bag and close the top by tying with an elastic band or a piece of string. Cook and stand as directed in the charts on page 97.

Tips on Roasting

1. If not using a roasting bag, stand the joint in dish, cover with film and puncture twice with the tip of a knife. If the cooking time recommended is 15 minutes or over at full power, the joint will brown of its own accord and will not require brushing with baste prior to cooking.
2. For very fat joints, stand a plastic trivet or 2 inverted saucers into a dish and place meat on top. Cover as directed under point 1.
3. When joints have fat on one side only, place into a bag or dish with the fat side down. Turn over half way through cooking.
4. For crisp crackling on pork, rub salad oil and salt well into the scored rind. 'Open' roast by standing in a dish and covering closely with paper to prevent spluttering and soiling the oven interior with splashes of grease. Do not turn at half time but keep crackling-side uppermost all the time.

Poultry Tips

1. The same defrosting and cooking rules apply to poultry as well as to meat but for a golden brown effect, a chicken or turkey should be brushed with baste (see page 43) prior to cooking. If the bird is of the self-basting variety, a light brush of soy sauce or sprinkling of paprika is all that is necessary.
2. It is advisable to stuff the crop end *only* and leave the body cavity empty. Wing tips and ends of legs should be foil-wrapped to prevent overcooking. If liked, prepared stuffings may be heated up separately in a greased dish. Times will vary from 3 to 6 minutes at full power, depending on whether the mixture is hot, warm, cold or taken from the refrigerator. And obviously quantity also determines the length of cooking time necessary.
3. Birds over 12lb ($5\frac{1}{2}$ to 6kg) should be roasted conventionally unless the capacity of the microwave is very large.

Defrosting Hints

1. To prevent slight cooking on the outside, large joints or birds are best left to defrost naturally, either overnight in a refrigerator or for several hours in the kitchen. This applies

particularly to quantities over 12lb or 5½ to 6kg.

2. As soon as chops, steaks and poultry joints have defrosted enough to be movable, arrange in a single layer on a plate or in a dish. *Never* heap up and, for maximum efficiency, arrange in a ring round the edge of the plate or dish.

3. When defrosting fairly large joints and birds in the microwave, refer to the Defrosting Chart on page 87 and add up the number of minutes standing time required. If it works out at about 40 minutes, rest for 20 minutes at half time then rest a further 20 minutes at the end of the defrosting period. If the joint or bird is still partially frozen, leave to thaw at kitchen temperature or in a sink of *cold* water.

4. Cover any piece of meat or poultry with cling film or kitchen paper as this speeds up defrosting and helps to keep in the moisture. If preferred, put meat or bird into a roasting bag for defrosting.

Browning Dish

For a grilled or fried effect, use a browning dish for steaks, chops etc., following the directions in your own microwave oven guide book or any that may come with the dish itself. For meat and poultry in general, the dish should be heated for 5 to 6 minutes at full power if small, and 7 to 8 minutes if large. The base should be brushed with melted fat or oil and then the food added.

1. For steaks weighing up to 8oz (225g), allow 3 to 5 minutes at full power, turning over once. For rare meat, keep to the shorter time; for well done meat, the longer time.

2. For 2 pork chops, each weighing 7 to 8oz (200 to 225g), allow a total of 15 minutes cooking time at full power, turning over after 3 minutes then once again after 10 minutes.

3. For 1lb (450g) chicken joints, allow a total of 9 to 10 minutes, placing them skin sides down. Turn over after 3 minutes then once again after 7 minutes.

Important Tip

It is essential to clean the dish thoroughly after every batch of cooking has been completed. It should then be re-greased and reheated at full power for half the original time given above.

Defrosting Meat and Poultry

	DEFROST (50%)	COMMENTS
JOINTS FOR ROASTING, on bone, per lb (450g)	9 minutes per lb (450g), allowing same length of standing time at end. Thus 1lb (450g) joint should stand 9 minutes after defrosting, a 2lb (900g) joint, 18 minutes, a 3lb (1·5kg) joint, 24 minutes and so on.	Stand joint on upturned plate or trivet in shallow dish. Turn over half way through defrosting. Wrap in foil before standing.
JOINTS FOR ROASTING, off bone, per lb (450g)	10 minutes Stand 10 minutes. Procedure as above.	As above.
CHOPS 4oz (125g)	3 minutes Stand 3 minutes	On plate, loosely covered with kitchen paper.
6oz (175g)	4 minutes Stand 4 minutes	As above.
8oz (225g)	5 minutes Stand 5 minutes	As above.
MINCED BEEF, per lb (450g)	10 minutes Stand 10 minutes	Remove mince from wrapper and stand on plate. Cover with second inverted plate or pudding basin. As the outside edges thaw, scrape away the soft mince and transfer to another plate. This prevents the outside meat from starting to cook before the inside has thawed.
STEWING CUBES, per lb (450g)	8 minutes Stand 8 minutes	Stand in shallow dish. Cover with plate. Turn cubes over half way through defrosting.
STEAKS 4oz (125g)	4 minutes Stand 4 minutes	On plate, loosely covered with kitchen paper.
6oz (175g)	5 minutes Stand 5 minutes	As above.
8oz (225g)	6 minutes Stand 6 minutes	As above.
LIVER 8oz (225g)	2½ minutes Stand 8 minutes	In a covered dish. Separate before standing.
16oz (450g)	4 minutes Stand 12 minutes	As above.

	DEFROST (50%)	COMMENTS
CHICKEN, whole per lb (450g)	8 minutes Stand 8 minutes following pattern for roasting joints on bone	Stand in shallow dish or leave in polythene bag, having first removed metal tab and snipped off end of bag. Turn over half way through defrosting and remove giblets as soon as possible.
CHICKEN PORTIONS 8oz (225g)	6 minutes Stand 6 minutes	Stand in shallow dish. Cover loosely with kitchen paper. Turn over half way through defrosting.
12oz (350g)	8 minutes Stand 8 minutes	As above.
DUCK, whole per lb (450g)	7 minutes Stand 7 minutes following pattern for roasting joints on bone	Stand in shallow dish. Turn over half way through defrosting.
DUCK PORTIONS 8oz (225g)	5 minutes Stand 5 minutes	Stand in shallow dish. Turn over half way through defrosting.
12oz (350g)	7 minutes Stand 7 minutes	As above.
GOOSE (about 10 lb or 4·5kg) per lb (450g)	4 minutes	Stand in large shallow dish. Cover loosely with kitchen paper. Turn over once during defrosting. Wrap goose in aluminium foil and stand overnight at room temperature until completely defrosted. Remove giblets.
TURKEY	See full instructions on page 118	

Basted Leg of Lamb, roasted in a microwave. See page 97.

90

Left: *Beef and
Mushroom
Kebabs.
See page 102.*

Opposite:
*Honeyed Pork,
studded with
cloves.
See page 99.*

Front: *Chicken with Chinese Gold Sauce. See page 114. Also shown in the oven is chicken spread with mayonnaise and sprinkled with tarragon before roasting.*

Centre: *Buffet Meat Slice. Metal dishes for serving only. See page 103.*

Chicken from the Forest. See page 115.

Opposite:
*Pineapple
Chicken Loaf.
See page 116.*

Spanish Chicken. See page 117.

Cooking Meat and Poultry

	COOK/HEAT (100%)	COMMENTS
JOINTS AND ROASTING, on bone, per lb (450g)	7 minutes per lb (450g) allowing 5 minutes per lb (450g) standing time. This should take place half way through cooking time for large joints with further standing time at end. Small joints may be left to stand when cooking time is completed.	Put into shallow dish. Cover with film and slit twice. Turn dish several times during cooking. When standing at the end, wrap joint in foil. Alternatively, cook and leave to stand in roasting bag.
JOINTS FOR ROASTING, off bone per lb (450g)	8 minutes per lb (450g) Stand 5 minutes per lb (450g). For technique, see above.	As above.
CHOPS 4oz (125g)	3 minutes Stand 3 minutes	Wash and dry chops and trim off surplus fat. Put on to plate or into shallow dish. Cover with film and slit twice. Turn plate or dish half way through cooking. Drain off melted fat before serving. Alternatively, cook in browning dish, following instructions given in *your own microwave oven guide book.*
6oz (175g)	4 minutes Stand 4 minutes	As above.
8oz (225g)	5 minutes Stand 5 minutes	As above.
STEAKS 4oz (125g)	As chops	Wash and dry steaks. Put on to plate and cover with kitchen paper. Turn over half way through cooking. Alternatively, cook in browning dish, following instructions given in *your own microwave oven guide book.*
6oz (175g)	As chops	As above. Allow up to $\frac{1}{2}$ minute longer for well done steaks; $\frac{1}{2}$ minute less for rare.
8oz (225g)	As chops	As above.
LIVER 8oz (225g)	3 minutes	Wash and dry liver. Put into greased shallow dish and cover with plate or matching lid. Stir and turn liver over half way through cooking. Season at end.
16oz (450g)	6 minutes	As above.

	COOK/HEAT (100%)	COMMENTS
CHICKEN, whole per lb (450g)	8 minutes Stand 5 minutes. For detailed technique, see joint on bone for roasting	Wash and drain chicken. Ensure that no giblets are left inside. Stand chicken in shallow dish. Brush with baste. Cover with film and slit twice. After standing time, remove film. Lift chicken out of dish, retaining hot juices for gravy, soup etc., though it is advisable to skim off fat before use. If preferred, cook in roasting bag.
CHICKEN PORTIONS 8oz (225g)	4 minutes Stand 5 minutes	Wash and dry chicken. Stand on plate, cover with film and slit twice. Turn plate half way through cooking.
12oz (350g)	6 minutes Stand 5 minutes	Wash and dry chicken. Stand on plate. If several portions, place thin parts towards centre of plate. Cover with film and slit twice. Turn plate half way through cooking.
DUCK, whole per lb (450g)	8 minutes Stand 5 minutes. For detailed technique, see joint on bone for roasting	Wash and drain duck. Stand on rack in shallow dish, breast side down. Cover with film and slit twice. Half way through cooking, remove film and carefully turn duck over. Re-cover with film and slit twice. After cooking remove film. Lift duck out of dish and wrap in foil for duration of standing time. Do not use roasting bag or duck will be greasy.
DUCK PORTIONS 8oz (225g)	4 minutes Stand 5 minutes	Wash and dry duck portions. Put into shallow dish. Cover with film and slit twice. Turn dish half way through cooking. After standing, drain off surplus juices.
12oz (350g)	6 minutes Stand 5 minutes	As above. If several portions, place thin parts towards centre of dish.
GOOSE (about 10lb (4·5kg)) per lb (450g)	7 minutes Stand 5 minutes. For detailed technique, see joints on bone for roasting	Wash and drain goose. Ensure that no giblets are left inside. Put into large roasting bag. Close up end with elastic band. Stand bag on large plate or in shallow dish unless oven has a removable base. Turn over once during cooking, taking care that no juices run out of bag. Carefully lift goose out of microwave (still on its plate, dish or glass oven base) and stand on draining board. Open up bag and allow juices to trickle out into a bowl placed in the sink. Transfer goose to carving board and wrap with foil. Leave to stand for however many minutes are left at the end. Do not use roasting bag or goose will be greasy.
TURKEY	See full instructions on page 119	

Honeyed Pork Picture p. 91 Serves 8

Before roasting leg of pork, brush scored rind with a baste made from 4 rounded tablespoons clear honey, 1 rounded teaspoon prepared English mustard, 1 level teaspoon salt and 2 teaspoons Worcestershire sauce. Before serving, stud with cloves as shown in the picture on page 91.

Chili Pork Chops VERY GOOD Serves 4 (F)

A simple imitation of Tex-Mex cooking with meaty pork chops submerged beneath canned tomatoes and red kidney beans. Serve it, piping hot and steaming, with jacket potatoes and sprouts – it will do wonders to enliven a blustery winter day.

4 spare rib of pork chops, each 8oz or 225g and fat trimmed

2 level tsp chili seasoning (purplish-brown from Schwarz)

1 level tsp onion salt

1 can (14oz or 400g) red kidney beans, drained

1 can (14oz or 400g) tomatoes

1. Arrange chops in a square, 8 inch (20cm) glass or pottery dish. Sprinkle with chili seasoning.

2. Cover with cling film, then puncture twice with the tip of a knife. Alternatively, cover with a matching lid.

3. Cook for 8 minutes at full power, turning dish 4 times unless oven has a turntable.

4. Uncover. Sprinkle with salt then top with beans and contents of can of tomatoes. Re-cover as before.

5. Cook 15 minutes at full power. Stand 5 minutes then serve as suggested above.

Pork 'n' Pineapple Serves 4 (F)

Always popular and very much a restaurant favourite, the dish can be microwaved to perfection in 20 minutes. I serve it with Mild Curry Rice (page 154) and a salad based on watercress, crisp lettuce and diced dessert apples, all tossed in a sharpish dressing. It contrasts beautifully with the mild flavour of the pork and the sweetness of the pineapple.

4 spare rib of pork chops, each 8oz or 225g and fat trimmed

1 can (15½oz or 439g) pineapple rings in syrup

1 level tsp paprika

4 tsp soy sauce

½ level tsp garlic granules

1. Wash and dry chops then arrange in a fairly shallow, 10 inch (25cm) round glass or pottery dish.

2. Drain pineapple. Reserve 2 tablespoons of the syrup for the baste and keep remainder for drinks or sauces.

3. Arrange pineapple rings over chops. Beat reserved pineapple syrup with all remaining ingredients. Spoon over chops.

4. Cover with cling film, then puncture twice with the tip of a knife. Alternatively, cover with a matching lid.

5. Cook 20 minutes at full power, turning dish 4 times unless oven has a turntable. Leave to stand 5 minutes before serving.

'Barbecued' Rib Bones   Serves 4

A real saving in time and kitchen smells when rib bones are cooked in the microwave, and the results are first rate. Serve the ribs with noodles (prepared ahead of time in the microwave and kept warm) and a fresh salad made from bean sprouts and thinly sliced raw mushrooms tossed in French dressing.

BASTE

2oz (50g) butter or margarine, at kitchen temperature

1 level tblsp tomato ketchup

2 tsp soy sauce

1 level tsp paprika

$\frac{1}{4}$ tsp garlic granules

$\frac{1}{2}$ tsp chili sauce (hot)

RIBS

2lb (1kg) fleshy pork rib bones which are also called sheet ribs or spare rib bones (and served in oriental restaurants)

1. To make baste, melt butter or margarine, uncovered, for about 1½ to 2 minutes at defrost setting. Stir in all remaining ingredients. Leave on one side temporarily.

2. Divide pork bones into single ribs then wash well and dry with kitchen paper. Arrange in a large dish with narrow part of bones pointing inwards.

3. Cover with cling film, then puncture twice with the tip of a knife.

4. Cook for 10 minutes at full power, turning dish 4 times unless oven has a turntable. Remove cling film, pour off fat then brush bones with baste, using about half the quantity.

5. Leave uncovered and cook 3 minutes at full power. Turn ribs over and brush with remaining baste. Cook, uncovered, a further 2 minutes. Arrange on 4 hot plates and serve coated with juices from dish.

Cooking a Large Piece of Gammon
Allow about 4oz (125g) per person (F)

Boil a large piece of gammon, weight up to 6lb or just under 3kg, conventionally in 2 or 3 changes of water to reduce saltiness. Cool. Wrap narrow end (unless middle cut) in a piece of foil. Put into a large roasting bag and close top with an elastic band. The allowance per pound (450g) cooking time is 8 minutes, so if the gammon weighs 6lb, cook 24 minutes at full power, stand for 30 minutes and then turn over. Continue to cook for another 24 minutes. Leave to stand 30 more minutes. Carefully take out of bag and remove foil if used. Strip off skin, cut fat into diamonds and rub all over with brown sugar. Stud each diamond with half a glacé cherry (green, red, yellow or a mixture), speared on to cocktail sticks. Also stud with cloves here and there. Serve cold.

Aubergine Moussaka   Serves 8 (F)

One of the top Greek favourites, Moussaka takes very well to being given the microwave treatment and is both moist and flavoursome.

AUBERGINES

1½lb (675g) aubergines, washed and dried

5 tblsp boiling water

2 tsp lemon juice

FILLING

2oz (50g) butter or margarine

8oz (225g) onions, peeled and grated

12oz (350g) cold cooked lamb or beef, minced

4oz (125g) fresh white breadcrumbs

1lb (450g) blanched tomatoes, skinned and chopped

1 to 1½ level tsp salt

SAUCE

¾pt (425ml) milk

1½oz (40g) butter or margarine

1½oz (40g) plain flour

3oz (75g) Cheddar cheese, grated

salt and pepper to taste

1. Cut stems off aubergines and discard. Slice fairly thinly and put into a large dish. Add water mixed with lemon juice.

2. Cover with cling film, then puncture twice with the tip of a knife. Cook 12 minutes at full power then leave to stand outside the oven for 15 minutes.

3. Prepare filling. Put butter or margarine into a dish and cook about 1¾ minutes at defrost setting. Mix in onions and cover with a plate. Cook 2 minutes at full power. Mix in rest of ingredients.

4. Drain aubergines thoroughly. Fill a 4pt (2·25 litre) greased dish with alternate layers of aubergine slices and meat mixture.

5. For sauce, heat milk in a jug for 3½ to 4 minutes or until hot but not boiling. Keep covered.

6. Melt butter or margarine, at defrost setting, for about 1¾ minutes in a fairly large basin. Stir in flour then gradually whisk in milk.

7. Return to microwave and cook 2½ to 3 minutes or until boiling, whisking gently at the end of every minute. Stir in cheese, season to taste and pour over Moussaka.

8. Cover with cling film, slit twice and reheat at full power for 12 to 14 minutes. Turn 3 or 4 times unless oven has a turntable. Stand 8 minutes before serving.

Beef and Mushroom Kebabs Picture p. 90 Serves 4

Superior in all respects, these choice Kebabs are not for everyday eating but for the small intimate dinner party with special guests and a vintage burgundy!

24 dried bay leaves
6 tblsp water
1½lb (675g) rump steak
6oz (175g) button mushrooms
½ green pepper (2oz or 50g), washed and de-seeded
½ red pepper (2oz or 50g), washed and de-seeded
2oz (50g) butter or margarine, at kitchen temperature
1 level tsp paprika

1. Put bay leaves into a small bowl, add water and cover with a saucer. Heat for 2 minutes at full power to soften, otherwise the leaves will break. (Dried leaves are very brittle.) If you have a bay tree in the garden, use fresh leaves.

2. Trim fat off steak and discard. Cut meat into ¾ inch (about 2cm) cubes. Wash and trim mushrooms and wipe dry.

3. Cut both peppers into smallish squares, put into a dish and only just cover with water. Top with an inverted plate and heat for 1 minute to soften.

4. Drain bay leaves and peppers. Thread steak, mushrooms, pepper squares and bay leaves on to 12 metal skewers (or wooden ones if available), each 4 inch (10cm) long.

5. Arrange, like spokes of a wheel, in a 10 inch (25cm) round and shallow glass or pottery dish.

6. Put butter or margarine into a cup, cover with a saucer and melt for 1½ to 2 minutes at defrost setting. Stir in paprika.

7. Brush over kebabs. Cook, uncovered, for 8 minutes at full power, turning dish twice unless oven has a turntable.

8. Twist kebabs round and brush undersides with rest of butter mixture. Cook a further 4 minutes at full power, turning dish twice.

9. Arrange on a bed of freshly cooked rice (brown is very appetising) and coat with gravy from dish. Allow 3 skewers per person.

Tomato Beef 'Cake' Serves 2 to 3 (F)

Useful for a 'Mum and Toddlers' lunch, this meat loaf takes minutes to prepare and cook. It teams happily with creamy mash and green vegetables to taste.

10oz (275g) raw minced beef, as lean as possible
1oz (25g) plain flour
1 Grade 3 egg
1 level tsp onion salt
¼pt (150ml) tomato juice
1 tsp soy sauce
1 level tsp mixed herbs

1. Well-grease a 1½pt (about 1 litre) oval pie dish.

2. Mix beef with all remaining ingredients and spread smoothly into dish.

3. Cover with cling film, then puncture twice with knife tip.

4. Cook for 7 minutes at full power, turning dish twice unless oven has turntable. Leave to stand 5 minutes inside or outside the oven, whichever is the most convenient.

5. Uncover. Lift out on to a warm plate with 2 spatulas, leaving behind surplus fat in dish which may have seeped out during cooking. Cut loaf into 2 or 3 portions and serve.

VERY GOOD.

Buffet Meat Slice   Picture p. 92   Serves 8 to 10 (F)

Based on a continental idea, this Meat Slice can be served hot or cold and makes an excellent addition to any informal buffet or supper party.

2lb (900g) raw minced beef, as lean as possible
2 Grade 2 eggs, beaten
1 brown gravy cube
2 level tsp onion salt
4 level tblsp plain flour
2 rounded tblsp tomato ketchup
2 level tsp mixed herbs
2 tsp soy sauce

1. Tip meat into a mixing bowl and work in beaten eggs, crumbled gravy cube, onion salt, flour, ketchup and herbs.

2. Spread into a 2pt (1·25 litre) oblong greased dish that resembles a loaf tin.

3. Brush top gently with soy sauce. Cover with cling film, then puncture twice with the tip of a knife.

4. Cook 5 minutes at full power. Leave to stand in the oven for 5 minutes. Continue to cook a further 10 minutes at defrost setting, turning dish 4 times unless oven has a turntable.

5. Stand 5 minutes. Uncover. Carefully drain off surplus fat from container then carefully lift the Meat Slice on to a dish.

6. Garnish with pieces of glacé cherries, black olives and a few mint leaves and serve hot or cold.

Fast Beef Loaf   Serves 6 (F)

Full of flavour and unusually enriched with mayonnaise, this is a speedy dish to put together and can become quite habit-forming! Serve with microwaved jacket potatoes and tomato halves.

1½lb (675g) raw minced beef, as lean as possible
1 slightly rounded tblsp red and green pepper flakes
1 rounded tblsp dried parsley
1 rounded tsp onion salt
2 rounded tblsp plain flour
2oz (50g) thick mayonnaise
1 rounded tsp powder mustard
1 tsp gravy browning

Well-grease a round dish measuring 8 inches (20cm) in diameter by 1 inch (2·5cm) in depth.

2. Mix beef thoroughly with all remaining ingredients. Spread smoothly into dish.

3. Cover with cling film, then puncture twice with the tip of a knife. Alternatively, cover with matching lid.

4. Cook 10 minutes at full power, turning dish 4 times unless oven has a turntable. Leave to stand 5 minutes either inside or outside the oven, whichever is the most convenient.

5. Uncover. Lift loaf out on to a warm plate with 2 spatulas, leaving behind surplus fat in dish which may have seeped out during cooking. Cut loaf into 6 portions and serve.

VERY GOOD

Butter Bean and Beef Stew with Tomatoes
Serves 6 (F)

Practical and economical, this is a good family beef dish and can be put together in next to no time. It is based on convenience foods and fresh meat – often an ideal combination.

1 can (15oz or 425g) butter beans, drained

1 can (10·6oz or 300g) ready-to-serve cream of tomato soup

1 rounded tblsp dried chopped onions

6 slices of feather steak (about 1¼lb or 575g)

salt and pepper to taste

1. Combine butter beans, soup and onions together in an 8 by 2 inch (20 by 5cm) round glass or pottery dish.

2. Cover with a plate. Cook 6 minutes at full power, turning dish 3 times unless oven has a turntable.

3. Uncover and stir to mix. Arrange steak in a border round edge of dish. Cover with cling film, then puncture twice with the tip of a knife. Alternatively, cover with matching lid.

4. Cook 15 minutes at full power, turning dish 4 times as described above under point 2.

5. Leave to stand 10 minutes inside or outside the oven, whichever is the most convenient. Season to taste. Serve with creamed potatoes, Brussels sprouts and microwaved carrots tossed in butter and a hint of nutmeg.

Beef in Wine
Serves 6 (F)

Similar to Bœuf Bourguignonne, this is a simpler version made with what at first sounds very expensive – rump steak. However, because of minimal waste and gristle, because the meat tenderises more readily than stewing steak and because of the short cooking time, the finished dish will serve 6, making the whole thing a fairly economic proposition. For sheer luxury, accompany the beef with Potatoes Savoyard (page 141) and cauliflower, coated with speedy Hollandaise sauce; two more treasures quickly cooked in the microwave oven.

8oz (225) onions, peeled

1 garlic clove, peeled (optional)

4oz (125g) cup mushrooms, trimmed and outsides peeled

1oz (25g) butter or margarine, at kitchen temperature

1lb (450g) rump steak, cut into ½ inch (1·25cm) cubes

1 level tblsp tubed or canned tomato purée

1 rounded tblsp parsley

1 level tblsp cornflour

1 level tsp prepared English or French mustard

½pt (275ml) dry red wine

1 level tsp salt

1. Finely chop onions and garlic. Thinly slice mushrooms. Put butter or margarine in a round glass or pottery dish measuring about 8 by 2 inches (20 by 5cm). Heat, covered, for 1 minute at full power.

2. Stir in prepared vegetables, leave uncovered and cook 5 minutes at full power. Stir in steak then move mixture to edges of dish to form a ring with a hollow in the centre.

3. Cover with a plate and cook 5 minutes at full power. Meanwhile mix together purée, parsley, cornflour and mustard. Blend in the wine. Pour gently into dish over steak and vegetables.

4. Cover with cling film, then puncture twice with the tip of a knife. Alternatively, cover with matching lid.

5. Cook beef 5 minutes at full power, turning dish twice unless oven has a turntable. Leave to stand 5 minutes inside or outside the oven, whichever is the most convenient. Season with salt. Serve hot with suggested accompaniments.

'Braised' Beef *VERY GOOD* Serves 6 (F)

As with the Beef in Wine, I have used rump steak in this 'braise' for a finely-flavoured and rich brown beef dish which serves 6 people adequately. The meat stays tender, there is minimal waste and this top quality cut makes for succulence and speedy cooking. Accompany with microwaved boiled potatoes and broccoli coated with cheese or Hollandaise sauce (page 44).

4oz (125g) onions, peeled
5oz (150g) carrots, peeled
3oz (75g) mushrooms and stalks, trimmed
1oz (25g) butter or margarine, at kitchen temperature
1lb (450g) rump steak, cut into ½ inch (1·25cm) cubes
1 brown gravy cube
1 level tblsp plain flour
½pt (275ml) hot water
1 level tsp salt
pepper to taste

1. Finely chop onions, carrots and mushrooms, either by hand with a sharp knife or in a food processor. A blender goblet may also be used.

2. Put butter or margarine into an 8 by 2 inch (20 by 5cm) round glass or pottery dish. Heat, covered, 1 minute at full power.

3. Add vegetables and steak. Mix round then cook, uncovered, for 3 minutes at full power.

4. Remove from oven. Crumble in gravy cube then stir in flour and hot water. Move mixture to edges of dish to form a hollow in the centre. Cover with cling film, puncturing it twice with the tip of a knife. Alternatively, cover with matching lid.

5. Cook 8 minutes at full power, turning dish 4 times unless oven has a turntable. Leave to stand 5 minutes, uncover then add seasoning. Stir round and serve.

Curried Mince Serves 4 (F)

Curry, traditionally cooked long and lovingly, responds so well to being microwaved that this anglicised Curried Mince is all yours in 20 minutes, excluding preparation time. It is fairly gentle and therefore safe for children. It goes best with rice and curried lentils (Dhal, page 63).

8oz (225g) onions, peeled and chopped
1lb (450g) lean minced beef
1 rounded tblsp plain flour
1 level tblsp mild curry powder
2 level tblsp chutney (I used mango but use any other to suit)
1 level tblsp tomato purée
½pt (275ml) boiling water
1 brown gravy cube
salt and pepper to taste

1. Put onions and meat into an 8 by 2 inch (20 by 5cm) round glass or pottery dish and mash well together.

2. Form into a ring round edge of dish. Cover with a plate and cook 5 minutes at full power.

3. Remove from oven and mix in flour, curry powder, chutney, tomato purée and boiling water. Crumble in gravy cube. Season.

4. Cover with cling film, then puncture twice with the tip of a knife. Alternatively, cover with matching lid.

5. Cook 15 minutes at full power, turning dish 4 times unless oven has a turntable. Leave to stand 5 minutes, stir round and serve.

Artichokes Farci   Serves 4 (F)

Characteristically French and quite delicious, stuffed artichokes make a most adequate main course, tempting, unusual and sustaining teamed with new potatoes cooked in their skins and delicate mange-tout, tossed in melted butter and very lightly seasoned with a trace of basil, chopped fresh for preference, otherwise dried.

4 large globe artichokes
1lb (450g) raw minced beef, as lean as possible
6oz (175g) onions, peeled and finely chopped
1 Grade 2 egg, beaten
1 level tsp mixed dried herbs
1½ level tsp salt
1 tsp Worcestershire sauce
2 tblsp water
¼pt (150ml) tomato or vegetable juice such as V8

1. Cook artichokes as given in recipe for Artichokes in Red Wine with Gribiche Dressing (page 27). Leave upside down in a colander to drain thoroughly.

2. When completely cold, turn right way up. Open out leaves and gently remove central cones. The bristly cores underneath are the 'chokes' and should be plucked out, bit by bit, with fingers. Left behind will be the much prized hearts surrounded by layers of leaves.

3. For stuffing, mix meat with onions, egg, herbs, salt, Worcestershire sauce and water. Spoon into artichoke cavities. Tie round with string. Stand, close together and upright, in a deep glass or pottery dish.

4. Cover with cling film, then puncture twice with the tip of a knife. Alternatively, cover with a matching lid.

5. Cook for 8 minutes at full power, turning dish 4 times unless oven has a turntable. Uncover and add tomato or vegetable juice.

6. Re-cover as before. Cook a further 8 minutes at full power, turning dish 4 times. Serve hot as suggested above or, if preferred, leave until cold then chill in the refrigerator and serve with salad – blissful on a balmy summer day.

Beef in Stroganov Mood   Serves 6

What can I say about this creamy beef concoction, other than to reaffirm its splendour! There are many, many variations on a traditional Stroganov, but this is one version passed on to me by Finnish friends from the east of the country, an area much influenced by the courtly cuisine of old Russia.

1oz (25g) butter
3oz (75g) onions, peeled
1lb (450g) rump steak
4oz (125g) button mushrooms
1oz (25g) chopped gherkins
1 carton (5oz or 142ml) soured cream, at kitchen temperature
salt and pepper to taste

1. Put butter into an 8 by 2 inch (20 by 5cm) round dish. Cover and heat for 1 minute at full power.

2. Grate onions. Cut steak into narrow strips against the grain. Very thinly slice mushrooms.

3. Add onions and steak to butter. Cover with a plate. Cook 4 minutes at full power, turning dish twice unless oven has a turntable.

4. Stir in mushrooms and re-cover with the plate. Cook a further 2 minutes, turning once. Mix in gherkins, cream and seasoning to taste. Cook, uncovered, for 1 more minute at full power. Serve with rice.

Irish Stew   Serves 4 (F)

A fairly workable arrangement in the microwave but do make sure the lamb is fresh from the butcher's and top quality.

2 to 2½lb (900g to just over 1kg) neck of lamb (sold in rounds)
1lb (450g) potatoes, peeled and cut into very thin slices
10oz (275g) onions, peeled and chopped
1 beef gravy cube
½pt (275ml) boiling water
2 heaped tblsp chopped parsley

1. Wash and dry lamb then trim away as much surplus fat as possible.

2. Rest rounds of meat against sides of 10 by 2 inch (25 by 5cm) round glass or pottery dish. Pile vegetables in the centre.

3. Cover with a plate. Cook 10 minutes at full power, turning dish twice.

4. Crumble gravy cube into water and pour into dish. Stir gently to mix all ingredients, incorporating lamb.

5. Cover with cling film, then puncture twice with the tip of a knife. Cook 25 minutes at defrost setting, turning dish 4 times unless oven has a turntable.

6. Uncover, sprinkle with parsley and serve straight away.

Lamb Splits   Serves 4 (F)

A bit Balkanesque, this is one of my favourite ways of preparing neck of lamb fillet, divine with spiced aubergine purée and microwaved Pitta or sesame bread to mop up the juices.

4 pieces of neck of lamb fillets, each 5 to 6 inch (12·5 to 15cm) in length with total weight of 1½lb or 675g
3oz (75g) fresh white bread, cubed with crusts left on
3oz (75g) onions, peeled and cut into biggish pieces
1oz (25g) pine nuts, toasted under the grill or in microwave (see page 225)
1oz (25g) currants
½ level tsp salt
4 heaped tsp thick Greek yogurt
cinnamon
1½oz (40g) button mushrooms, trimmed
½oz (15g) butter or margarine, melted ¾ minute at defrost setting

1. Cut as much fat as possible off lamb fillets, then make a lengthwise slit in each, taking care not to cut right through or filling will fall out.

2. Turn bread into crumbs and very finely grate onions. If you have a food processor or blender, this will save effort.

3. Mix crumbs and onions with nuts, currants and salt. Spoon equal amounts into lamb fillets.

4. Place round the edges of a 10 inch (25cm), fairly shallow round dish to form a square. Smear tops of each with yogurt then sprinkle with a trace of cinnamon. Stud with mushrooms and coat with melted butter or margarine.

5. Cover with cling film, then puncture twice with the tip of a knife. Alternatively, cover with a matching lid.

6. Cook 14 minutes at full power, turning dish 4 times unless oven has a turntable. Leave to stand 5 minutes before serving.

Eastern Mint Kebabs　　　　　　　　　　　Serves 6

When there is a high proportion of meat to metal and provided the metal has no direct contact with the sides of the cooker, metal skewers may be used for the Kebabs without upsetting the action of the microwave. Therefore tackle these Kebabs with confidence and serve them on Saffron Rice (page 144) and a Greek-style salad of mixed vegetables topped with pieces of Feta cheese, tiny black olives and a drizzle of olive oil.

2lb (900g) neck of lamb fillet
12 large fresh mint leaves (or use dried bay leaves, first microwaved in 4 tblsp water for 2 minutes at full power)
3 rounded tblsp thick yogurt
2 rounded tblsp tomato ketchup
1 garlic clove, peeled and crushed
1 tsp Worcestershire sauce

1. Trim fat off lamb fillet then cut meat into 1 inch (2·5cm) slices. Thread on to 6 skewers, each 4 inches (10cm) long, alternately with mint or softened bay leaves.

2. Arrange, like spokes of a wheel, in a 10 inch (25cm) round shallow dish. For baste, beat yogurt with rest of ingredients. Brush about half over kebabs.

3. Cook, uncovered, for 7 minutes at full power, turning dish twice unless oven has a turntable.

4. Remove from oven and turn Kebabs over. Brush with rest of baste. Cook a further 7 minutes at full power, turning as before. Leave to stand 5 minutes then serve as suggested.

Lamb and Vegetable 'Hot Pot'　　　Serves 4 to 5 (F)

If you like a conglomeration of vegetables amid the meat, this will become a favourite in no time. If you cannot abide parsnips, substitute carrots. My pet greenery with this one is deep-toned cabbage, but sprouts serve the same purpose and may be cooked if preferred.

1¼lb (575g) lamb fillet
1lb (450g) potatoes, peeled and washed
8oz (225g) onions, peeled and grated
8oz (225g) parsnips, peeled and grated
2 level tblsp plain flour
3 tblsp cold water
½pt (275ml) boiling water
1 brown gravy cube
1 level tsp salt
chopped parsley

1. Remove surplus fat from lamb then cut meat into ½ inch (1·25cm) thick pieces.

2. Grate potatoes, onions and parsnips. Put into a 10 by 2 inch (20 by 5cm) round glass or pottery dish. Mix in meat and push towards edge of dish to form a ring.

3. Cover with a plate and cook for 7 minutes at full power, turning dish 3 times unless oven has a turntable.

4. Meanwhile, blend flour gradually to a smooth paste with cold water. Stir into meat mixture then add boiling water. Crumble in gravy cube and mix in thoroughly.

5. Cover dish with cling film, then puncture twice with the tip of a knife. Alternatively, cover dish with a matching lid.

6. Cook 10 minutes at full power, turning dish twice unless oven has a turntable. Stand 5 minutes then cook a further 10 minutes at full power, turning as before.

7. Stand a further 5 minutes, stir round, season with salt and serve garnished with parsley.

Luxury Lamb 'Hot Pot'   Serves 4 (F)

An extravagant but well worthwhile lamb casserole, full of flavour and ready in 40 minutes. No additional vegetables are necessary unless you fancy something green to offer contrast of colour and texture.

1½lb (675g) potatoes, peeled and washed

8oz (225g) onions, peeled and washed

4oz (125g) carrots, peeled and washed

4oz (125g) celery, well-scrubbed

8 best end neck of lamb chops (about 2 to 2¼lb or 1kg), surplus fat trimmed off

1 brown gravy cube

½pt (275ml) boiling water

1 level tsp salt

½oz (15g) butter or margarine, melted

1. Very thinly slice potatoes, onions and carrots by hand or in a food processor. Thinly slice celery.

2. Arrange half the prepared vegetables, in layers, in a 4pt (about 2·25 litre) lightly greased casserole. Top with chops. Add remaining vegetables, again in layers, ending with potatoes.

3. Cover with cling film, then puncture twice with the tip of a knife. Alternatively, cover with matching lid. Cook 15 minutes at full power, turning dish 4 times unless oven has a turntable.

4. Remove from oven and uncover. Crumble gravy cube into water then add salt. Pour gently down side of casserole. Drizzle butter or margarine over the top then cover as before.

5. Cook another 15 minutes at full power, turning dish as before. Leave to stand 10 minutes inside or outside the oven, whichever is the most convenient. Spoon out of dish and serve.

Veal Loaf   Serves 4 as a main course, 6 as a starter (F)

Cut the loaf into wedges while still hot and you have a delicious main course with gravy and vegetables. Left to get cold, you can slice the loaf and serve it either as a pâté for starters or use it in sandwiches.

1lb (450g) raw veal, finely minced

1 garlic clove, peeled and crushed

1oz (25g) plain flour

2 Grade 2 eggs, beaten

½ level tsp salt

½ level tsp dried thyme

1 tsp Worcestershire sauce

grated nutmeg

1. Well-grease an oblong dish measuring 5 by 7 by 2 inches in depth (12·5 by 17·5 by 5cm).

2. Mix veal thoroughly with all remaining ingredients, except nutmeg, then spread into prepared dish.

3. Cover with cling film, then puncture twice with the tip of a knife. Alternatively, cover with matching lid.

4. Cook 8 minutes at full power, turning dish 4 times unless oven has a turntable. Remove from oven and take off cling film. Sprinkle Loaf with nutmeg and serve as suggested above.

Instant Meatball Goulash Serves 4 to 6 (F)

I call this 'instant' because the dish combines fresh with convenience products and can be ready and waiting in under half an hour, depending on how quickly you move! Serve with rice or pasta and some microwaved mushrooms.

1lb (450g) raw veal, finely minced

2oz (50g) fresh white breadcrumbs

$\frac{1}{2}$ level tsp onion or garlic salt

1 Grade 2 egg, beaten

$\frac{1}{2}$pt (275ml) boiling water

1 can condensed cream of tomato soup

2 rounded tblsp dried and chopped red and green pepper flakes

2 level tsp paprika

salt and pepper to taste

1 carton (5oz or 142ml) soured cream

1. Mix together veal, crumbs, onion or garlic salt and egg. Shape into 12 balls and arrange round the edge of an 8 by 2 inch (20 by 5cm) round glass or pottery dish.

2. Whisk water into soup then stir in pepper flakes and paprika. Spoon all the mixture into dish, making sure the meatballs have their fair share and are well coated.

3. Cover with cling film, then puncture twice with the tip of a knife. Alternatively, cover dish with matching lid.

4. Cook 15 minutes at full power, turning dish 4 times unless oven has a turntable.

5. Leave to stand 5 minutes then uncover and baste meatballs with tomato mixture. Adjust seasoning to taste and stir in soured cream. Reheat, uncovered, for $1\frac{1}{2}$ minutes at full power.

BUFFET MEATBALL CURRY Serves 8 (F)

Make exactly as above, substituting minced beef for veal and using $1\frac{1}{2}$lb (675g). Shape into 16 balls and arrange round edge of 10 by 2 inch (25 by 5cm) round glass or pottery dish. For sauce, smoothly mix 1 can condensed cream of tomato soup with 1lb (450g) peeled and chopped tomatoes, 2 teaspoons soy sauce, 1 level tablespoon mild curry powder (or more to taste), 1 level tablespoon tubed or canned tomato purée, 1 crumbled brown gravy cube and 3 rounded tablespoons mango chutney. Pour into dish over meatballs. Cover as directed above and cook 18 minutes at full power, turning dish 4 times unless oven has a turntable. Continue as previous recipe but, after basting meatballs with sauce, do *not* mix in soured cream. Serve with rice and salad. Also extra chutney if liked.

Boiled Chicken — Serves 6 to 8

Often useful for making other dishes such as chicken in sauce for vol-au-vents or a quick curry, boiling a bird in the microwave is totally unproblematic and gives you moist and tender meat plus enough liquid to use for the basis of soup (chicken noodle for instance) or an appropriate sauce. If the bird is served as boiled chicken, use the vegetables as accompaniments. Otherwise serve cold with salad.

1 oven ready chicken of about 3lb (1·5kg)

4oz (125g) baby carrots, peeled or thawed if frozen

8oz (225g) onions, peeled and each cut into quarters

1½pt (850ml) boiling water

2 small bay leaves

1 bouquet garni bag

1 level tsp salt

1. Put rinsed bird into a 4pt (2·25 litre) deep glass or pottery dish.

2. Surround with vegetables then add water, bay leaves, bouquet garni bag and salt.

3. Cover with cling film, then puncture twice with the tip of a knife. Cook 30 minutes at full power, turning dish 4 times.

4. Stand 10 minutes inside or outside the oven, whichever is the most convenient. Lift chicken out of liquid and serve hot, cold or in a made-up dish.

5. Strain liquid and reheat for 3 minutes at full power if being served straight away as soup. Otherwise leave until cold, skim off fat and use as required.

Creamy Chicken au Poivre — Serves 6

A fanciful way of preparing chicken or turkey breast fillet. It should appeal to sophisticated palates, is ideal for a dinner party and teams happily with a green salad and microwaved rice, first forked with butter and enough chopped parsley to turn it a pretty green – about 3 heaped tablespoons.

1oz (25g) butter or margarine, at kitchen temperature

5oz (150g) onions, peeled and finely chopped

1lb (450 to 500g) chicken breast fillet (or use turkey if preferred), washed and dried

1 level tblsp cornflour

2 tblsp water

1 level tblsp tubed or canned tomato purée

3 rounded tsp Madagascan green peppercorns, available in cans or glass jars from speciality food shops

1 carton (5oz or 142ml) soured cream

1 level tsp salt

1. Put butter or margarine into an 8 by 2 inch (20 by 5cm) round glass or pottery dish. Melt, uncovered, 1 to 1½ minutes at defrost setting.

2. Stir in onions. Cook, also uncovered at full power, allowing 2 minutes. Leave to stand while preparing chicken. Cut, across the grain, into 1 inch wide (2·5cm) strips.

3. Mix well with onions and butter. Cover with a plate or matching lid. Cook 6 minutes at full power.

4. Meanwhile, mix cornflour smoothly with water then add purée, green peppercorns, soured cream and salt.

5. Stir into chicken and onions then move mixture to edges of dish to form a hollow in the centre.

6. Cover with cling film (more secure than a plate) then puncture twice with the tip of a knife. Alternatively, cover with matching lid. Cook 8 minutes at full power, turning dish 4 times unless oven has a turntable.

7. Leave to stand 5 minutes, uncover and stir round before serving.

Chicken and Vegetable Paprika Cream   Serves 4 (F)

Shades of Hungary here in the use of paprika and soured cream with chicken and vegetables. It provides a quietly subtle main course, delicately pink and perfect with small pastini – small bows or shells or even short cut macaroni.

1oz (25g) butter or margarine, at kitchen temperature

8oz (225g) onions, peeled and chopped

1 small green pepper (2oz or 50g), washed and dried then de-seeded and chopped

1 small red pepper (2oz or 50g), washed and dried then de-seeded and chopped

6oz (175g) washed and dried courgettes, very thinly sliced

12oz (350g) chicken breast fillet, diced

1 level tblsp paprika

3 level tblsp tubed or canned tomato purée

1 carton (5oz or 142ml) soured cream

1 level tsp salt

1. Put butter or margarine in an 8 by 2 inch (20 by 5cm) round dish and melt, uncovered, 1 to 1½ minutes at defrost setting.

2. Stir in onions, leave uncovered and cook 3 minutes at full power.

3. Mix in peppers, courgettes, chicken breast, paprika and tomato purée. Cover with cling film, then puncture twice with the tip of a knife. Alternatively, cover with a matching lid.

4. Cook 5 minutes at full power, turning dish twice unless oven has a turntable. Uncover. Mix in soured cream and salt thoroughly. Re-cover.

5. Cook a further 8 minutes at full power, turning dish 4 times if no turntable. Again stir round, adjust seasoning to taste and serve straight away with pasta. A lettuce salad, tossed in a mild French dressing, makes a worthy accompaniment.

Peanut Chicken   Serves 4 (F)

With shades of the Orient, I seem to have found one way of enlivening rather mundane chicken joints. The mild, spicy topping is very easy to prepare and the dish teams well with those Chinese-style noodles available from most supermarkets. By way of an accompaniment, why not microwaved Chinese leaves?

2lb (900g) chicken joints

4oz (125g) smooth peanut butter

½ level tsp ground ginger

½ level tsp onion salt

1 rounded tsp medium strength Madras curry powder

Chinese barbecue sauce (Hoi Sin)

1. Arrange joints, in a single layer, around the edge of a 10 inch (25cm) round dish which is fairly shallow.

2. Put peanut butter into a small dish. Leave uncovered and heat 1 minute at defrost setting.

3. Stir in ginger, onion salt and curry powder. Spread over joints.

4. Top each with a little barbecue sauce (Hoi Sin). Cover with cling film, then puncture twice with the tip of a knife.

5. Cook 16 minutes at full power, turning dish 4 times unless oven has a turntable. Stand 5 minutes before serving.

Normandy Apple Chicken — Serves 4 (F)

Stylishly-flavoured and in the traditions of French family cooking, this chicken dish is different from the usual run, slightly rustic, perfect with boiled potatoes tossed in butter and a full blown mixed salad.

2oz (50g) butter or margarine, at kitchen temperature
2lb (900g) chicken joints, thawed completely if frozen
6oz (175g) onions, peeled and chopped
8oz (225g) cooking apples, peeled and finely chopped (cores removed)
1 garlic clove, peeled and chopped (optional)
2 level tblsp flour
$\frac{1}{2}$pt (275ml) medium cider
2 brown gravy cubes
1 level tsp dried thyme
salt and pepper to taste
1 rounded tblsp chopped parsley

1. Put butter or margarine into a 10 by 2 inch (25 by 5cm) glass or pottery dish. Leave uncovered and melt 1$\frac{1}{2}$ to 2 minutes at defrost setting.

2. Add chicken joints and toss round in the butter or margarine. Cover with cling film then puncture twice with the tip of a knife. Alternatively, cover with a matching lid.

3. Cook 15 minutes at full power, turning dish 4 times unless oven has a turntable.

4. Uncover then sprinkle onions, apples and garlic (if used) over chicken. Mix flour smoothly with some of the measured cider. Add remainder.

5. Crumble in the 2 gravy cubes then add thyme. Spoon liquid into dish over chicken and vegetables etc. Cover as directed above. Cook 15 minutes at full power, turning dish 4 times unless oven has a turntable. Leave to stand 10 minutes.

6. Uncover and gently stir round. Adjust seasoning to taste and sprinkle with parsley.

Chestnut Chicken — Serves 4 generously (F)

A beauty, this one, with a classic flavour. It is most acceptable with brown rice and cooked peas, mixed together while hot with butter or margarine and a tablespoon of fresh coriander, finely chopped.

2oz (50g) butter or margarine
8oz (225g) onions, peeled and finely chopped or grated
1 can (about 15oz or 430g) natural chestnut purée
$\frac{1}{2}$ level tsp salt
4 chicken breasts (1lb or 450g), washed and dried
8oz (225g) blanched tomatoes, skinned and sliced
2 level tblsp chopped parsley

1. Put butter or margarine into a 10 inch (25cm) round, shallow dish. Melt, uncovered, for 1$\frac{1}{2}$ to 2 minutes at defrost setting.

2. Mix in onions and cook, also uncovered, for 4 minutes at full power. Stir in chestnut purée smoothly then season with salt.

3. Flatten into an even layer and arrange chicken breasts on top round edge of dish. Top with tomato slices and sprinkle with parsley.

4. Cover with cling film, then puncture twice with the tip of a knife. Alternatively, cover with matching lid.

5. Cook 10 minutes at full power, turning dish 4 times unless oven has a turntable.

6. Leave to stand 5 minutes inside or outside the oven, whichever is the most convenient. Spoon out on to 4 warm plates to serve.

Chicken with Chinese Gold Sauce   Picture p. 93   Serves 4 (F)

Gently sweet-sour and delicately spiced, this Chinese-style chicken speciality goes best with saffron or plain rice, cooked bean sprouts and Chinese leaves.

2lb (900g) chicken joints, washed and dried then dusted with plain flour

2oz (50g) onion, peeled and grated

2 garlic cloves, peeled and crushed

2 tblsp soy sauce

2 tblsp medium sherry

2 tblsp salad oil

4 tblsp lemon juice

2 level tblsp light brown soft sugar

2 slightly rounded tblsp melted apricot jam minus large pieces of fruit

1 level tsp coriander

3 drops Tabasco

1. Arrange chicken joints in a fairly shallow, 10 inch (25cm) round glass or pottery dish with skin sides facing. Slash through to flesh in several places with a sharp knife.

2. Beat rest of ingredients well together and pour over chicken. Cover loosely and leave to stand at kitchen temperature for 2 hours ($1\frac{1}{2}$ hours in the height of summer), turning chicken joints over 3 times.

3. Finally turn the chicken joints so that skin sides are again facing. Cover dish with cling film, then puncture twice with the tip of a knife.

4. Cook 22 minutes at full power, turning dish 4 times unless oven has a turntable. Serve coated with pan juices, and the accompaniments suggested above.

Chicken from the Forest   Picture p. 94   Serves 4 (F)

A warm-hearted way of serving chicken drumsticks and a feast of a family dinner with freshly microwaved noodles or rice and a selection of vegetables.

2½lb (just over 1kg) chicken drumsticks

2 tblsp salad oil or the same amount of melted butter or margarine

6oz (175g) streaky bacon, chopped

4oz (125g) onions, peeled and chopped

4oz (125g) button mushrooms, washed then dried and sliced

10oz (275g) jar or can tomato sauce for spaghetti

1 tblsp malt vinegar

1 tblsp lemon juice

2 level tblsp light brown soft sugar

1 level tsp prepared Continental mustard

2 tblsp Worcestershire sauce

chopped parsley for garnishing

1. Skin drumsticks and leave on one side temporarily.

2. Pour oil or fat into an oblong glass dish measuring about 14 by 9 inches (35 by 22·5cm). Heat I minute at full power, leaving uncovered.

3. Add bacon and onions. Stir well to mix. Cook, uncovered, for 5 minutes at full power.

4. Add drumsticks, turning over and over in the bacon and onion mixture. Finally arrange with the thickest parts towards the edge of the dish.

5. Sprinkle with mushrooms. Beat tomato sauce with vinegar, lemon juice, sugar, mustard and Worcestershire sauce. Spoon over chicken.

6. Cover with cling film, then puncture twice with the tip of a knife. Cook 15 minutes at full power. Uncover, turn drumsticks over and re-cover with film. Puncture.

7. Continue to cook for a further 15 minutes at full power. Remove from oven, leave to stand 5 minutes, uncover and sprinkle with parsley.

Pineapple Chicken Loaf   Picture p. 95   Serves 8 (F)

A fantasy of a loaf, with the subtle tang of pineapple and an elusive sweet-sour taste that makes it seem almost Chinese in character. Serve it cold, cut into slices, and accompany with salad vegetables as shown in the photograph.

1lb (450g) cold cooked chicken, finely minced

3oz (75g) onions, peeled and finely minced

1 can crushed pineapple in syrup (about 1lb or 450g in size with a drained weight of between 8 to 9oz or 225 to 250g)

2 packets (each 26·5g or just under the official ounce) bread sauce mix

$\frac{1}{2}$ level tsp salt

2 Grade 3 eggs, beaten

1oz (25g) flaked and toasted almonds (page 224)

1. Line a 1½pt (850ml) oblong, glass pie dish smoothly with cling film.

2. Put chicken and onions into a bowl. Fork in pineapple with its syrup, bread sauce mix, salt and eggs. Mix thoroughly.

3. Spread smoothly into prepared dish. Sprinkle with flaked almonds.

4. Leave uncovered and cook 30 minutes at defrost setting, turning dish 3 or 4 times unless oven has a turntable.

5. Remove from oven. Lift out of dish when lukewarm and stand on a wire cooling rack. Peel away cling film when loaf is completely cold. Wrap leftovers and store in the refrigerator.

Spanish Chicken   Picture p. 96   Serves 4 generously (F)

Note quite a Paella but still related, here is a chicken dish that is vividly-coloured and tantalisingly-flavoured – a delightful weekender for a family group or small dinner party.

1oz (25g) butter or margarine
4oz (125g) streaky bacon, chopped
1 garlic clove, peeled and crushed
8oz (225g) onions, peeled and very finely chopped
1 can (about 6½oz or 185g) red pimientos, drained and fairly finely chopped
1 can (14oz or 400g) tomatoes
8oz (225g) easy-cook, long-grain rice
1 level tsp paprika
2 rounded tsp turmeric
6oz (175g) frozen peas
2lb (900g) chicken joints, thawed if frozen
soy sauce
1 cut-up fresh tomato for garnishing

1. Put butter or margarine into a fairly shallow 10 inch (25cm) round glass or pottery dish and melt 1 to 1½ minutes at defrost setting. Leave uncovered.

2. Stir in bacon, garlic and onions. Cover with a plate and cook for 5 minutes at full power.

3. Stir in pimientos, canned tomatoes (taking care not to break them up too much), rice, paprika, turmeric and peas.

4. Stand chicken joints on top then brush lightly with soy sauce.

5. Cover dish with cling film, then puncture twice with the tip of a knife. Alternatively, cover with matching lid. Cook 35 minutes at full power, turning dish 4 times unless oven has a turntable.

6. Remove from oven, uncover and serve.

QUICKIE PAELLA   Serves 4 generously
After cooking and uncovering, stud with 4oz (125g) peeled prawns, thawed if frozen.

Roast Turkey   Picture p. 146
Allow 12oz (350g) raw weight per person

When dealing with such a large and important bird, correct defrosting times are necessary for success and I am very grateful to the Home Economics staff at Bejam for their advice and guidance on this score.

Keep the size of turkey to be defrosted and microwaved around 10lb or 4·5 to 5kg. It can be accommodated comfortably in most ovens (except small ones) and works better than a weightier bird. Remove metal ties but keep bird in its original wrapper. Put into microwave, set control to defrost and leave the turkey to thaw partially for 45 minutes. Take out of oven, remove giblet bag if it is loose enough, then leave turkey to continue thawing overnight in the kitchen. On this basis, it makes sense to carry out the 45 minute defrost the evening before the turkey is to be cooked.

Remove giblet bag if this has not already been done, then make sure *inside* of turkey is totally free of ice crystals. If not, leave in a sink of cold water until bird has completely and thoroughly thawed. Rinse inside and out with fresh water then wipe dry with paper towels.

Alternate Method of Defrosting

If you have been unable to leave the turkey overnight to thaw, following its 45 minutes defrost in the microwave as described above, try this technique:

1. Microwave bird for 45 minutes at defrost setting. Leave to stand 45 minutes. Check to see if giblet bag has loosened and can be removed. If not leave bag where it is. Turn bird over.

2. Microwave bird for 30 minutes at defrost setting. Leave to stand 30 minutes and check giblet bag. Remove if possible. Turn turkey over.

3. Repeat No. 2 above, removing giblet bag if it has not already been taken out.

4. Check for ice crystals and if any are still in body cavity, leave bird in a sink of cold water up to 1 hour or until completely and thoroughly defrosted.

TO COOK TURKEY

Cover wing tips and ends of legs with foil to prevent overcooking. Stand turkey, breast side down, in a dish large enough to hold the bird comfortably, even if its body domes up above the rim. Cover with cling film, then puncture 4 times with the tip of a knife. Cook at full power, allowing 8 minutes per lb (450g). Remove from oven and carefully turn over so that breast of turkey is now uppermost. Brush thickly with baste (page 43), choosing a fat-based one if bird is plain, or a non-fat one if bird is self-basting* and impregnated with fat or oil. This browns the skin and makes turkey look as though it had been roasted conventionally. Re-cover as before and finish cooking at full power. Leave to stand 15 minutes inside or outside the oven, whichever is the most convenient. Carve. Serve with gravy (page 46) made from $\frac{1}{2}$pt (275ml) pan juices and microwaved vegetables with trimmings to taste. Alternatively, cook turkey in a giant roasting bag, secured with an elastic band at the top. Basting will be unnecessary.

*It is not essential to brush the self-basting turkey with extra baste.

WHOLE TURKEY BREAST ON THE BONE (bought ready-prepared)

This might weigh from 2 to $2\frac{1}{4}$lb (about 1kg). Defrost if frozen then remove wrapping. Put on to a plate, skin side uppermost. Brush with baste, cover as 'roast' turkey and cook at full power, allowing 8 minutes per lb (450g). Standing time should be about 7 minutes.

BONED TURKEY ROAST WITH STUFFING (bought ready-prepared)

A 'roast' of this nature, which is fairly dense, should be thoroughly defrosted and then cooked at full power for 15 minutes per lb (450g) with a 10 minute rest period between and at the end. It should be unwrapped, put on to a dish and covered as roast turkey. The stringy casing should be removed before slicing. If the slices look slightly undercooked, they can be put on to individual plates, covered as for 'roast' turkey with film or with an inverted plate, and cooked at full power for about 1 to $1\frac{1}{2}$ extra minutes. When choosing a joint of this kind, ensure the weight does not exceed 2lb (1kg).

NOTE: If turkey or joint has been taken straight from the refrigerator, allow 1 extra minute cooking time per lb (450g).

Mild Turkey Curry   Picture p. 145   Serves 4 (F)

For all those times when you wonder how to perk up the remains of a large family turkey, here is a recipe to set the taste buds tingling! If a hotter curry is preferred, add cayenne pepper to taste, allowing from an eighth of a teaspoon to one level – or use a few drops of Tabasco. Chicken may be substituted for turkey.

1oz (25g) butter or margarine, at kitchen temperature

5oz (150g) onions, peeled and very thinly sliced

1 garlic clove, peeled and crushed

1oz (25g) raisins

1oz (25g) desiccated coconut

1oz (25g) flour

3 rounded tsp Madras curry powder

$\frac{1}{2}$pt (275ml) boiling water

2 tblsp milk

$\frac{1}{2}$ level tsp salt

3 tsp fresh lemon juice

12oz (350g) cooked turkey, removed from bones and diced

1. Put butter or margarine into an 8 by 2 inch (20 by 5cm) round dish. Melt, uncovered, for about 1 to $1\frac{1}{2}$ minutes at defrost setting.

2. Stir in onions, garlic, raisins and coconut. Leave uncovered and cook 2 minutes at full power.

3. Mix in flour, curry powder, water, milk, salt, lemon juice and turkey. Cover with cling film then puncture twice with the tip of a knife. Alternatively, cover with a matching lid.

4. Cook 6 minutes at full power, turning dish 4 times unless oven has a turntable. Leave to stand 5 minutes inside or outside the oven, whichever is the most convenient.

5. Uncover, stir round, transfer to a warm dish and serve with freshly cooked rice, mango chutney and a salad of sliced onions, separated into rings, with thinly sliced red or green pepper. If liked, also serve a dish of plain yogurt sprinkled with chopped preserved ginger.

Sweet-Sour Duckling   Serves 4

A remarkably easy way of giving a microwaved duck a warm, golden glow and Chinese flavour. It goes well with freshly cooked noodles tossed with peas and strips of omelet. Another appetising accompaniment – bean sprouts microwaved as described on page 132.

1 × $4\frac{1}{2}$lb (2kg) duckling, thawed and weighed *after* giblets have been removed

2 slightly rounded tblsp mango chutney

1. Keep giblets from duckling and use for conventionally-cooked soup such as vegetable broth or Minestrone.

2. Wash bird inside and out under cold, running water.

3. Place a plastic rack or 2 inverted saucers into an oblong dish measuring about 12 by $7\frac{1}{2}$ inches (30 by 19cm). Stand duck on top, breast side down.

4. Cover with cling film, then puncture twice with the tip of a knife.

5. Cook 20 minutes at full power, turning dish 4 times unless oven has a turntable.

6. Uncover. Turn duckling over carefully, using 2 wooden spoons, so that breast side is now uppermost.

7. Spread thickly with the chutney then re-cover with cling film as before. Cook a further 20 minutes, turning as above.

8. Leave to stand 10 minutes inside or outside the oven, whichever is the most convenient. Cut into 4 portions with poultry shears and serve.

TIP: Keep duck juices in the refrigerator overnight. Next day, remove fat and discard, then use remaining semi-jellied stock for soups, stews or sauces.

Turkey Flan   Serves 6 to 8

Hot or cold, this is an appetising flan and especially useful at Christmas or Easter when leftover turkey can become a burden. It responds well to an accompaniment of salad or cauliflower cheese.

BASE
shortcrust pastry made with 6oz (175g) plain flour, 3oz (75g) fat etc.

FILLING
12oz (350g) cold cooked turkey, cut into large cubes or strips

4oz (125g) onion, peeled and cut into eighths

2 Grade 3 eggs, beaten

5 tblsp cold milk

1 scant level tsp salt

white pepper to taste

GARNISH
sliced onion, separated into rings

chopped parsley

1. Roll out pastry on floured surface and use to line a greased, round pie plate with rim. It should be about $7\frac{1}{2}$ inches in diameter at the top, sloping downwards to $6\frac{1}{2}$ inches (about 19 to 16cm). The depth should be about $1\frac{1}{2}$ inches (4cm).

2. Prick well all over, especially where base of pastry meets sides. Bake, uncovered, for 6 minutes at full power, turning 4 times unless oven has a turntable. Remove from oven and gently press down any bulges with hand protected by oven glove.

3. For filling, finely mince turkey and onion. Transfer to mixing bowl then add eggs, milk, salt and pepper. Mix thoroughly and spread smoothly into pastry case.

4. Cook, uncovered, $7\frac{1}{2}$ to 8 minutes (or until filling is firm and set), at full power, turning dish 4 times unless oven has a turntable.

5. Leave to stand 5 minutes inside or outside the oven, whichever is the most convenient. Garnish with a border of onion rings then sprinkle with parsley. Cut into wedges and serve hot or cold.

French Country Liver
Serves 4 to 6 (F)

An absolute winner for those who enjoy offal, and liver in particular. Rice is the best partner, while buttered carrots and Casseroled Leeks (see Vegetable Section) are also admirable accompaniments.

1oz (25g) butter or margarine
6oz (175g) onions, peeled and finely chopped or grated
1lb (450g) lambs liver, cut into strips measuring 4 by 1 inch (10 by 2·5cm)
1 rounded tblsp plain flour
½pt (275ml) dry red wine
2 rounded tsp dark brown sugar
1 brown gravy cube, crumbled
1 rounded tblsp parsley
seasoning to taste

1. Put butter or margarine into a 10 inch (25cm) fairly shallow round dish and melt 1 to 1½ minutes at defrost setting. Leave uncovered.

2. Stir in onions and liver. Cover with a plate and cook 5 minutes at full power.

3. Mix in all remaining ingredients except seasoning. Cover with a plate as before and cook 6 minutes at full power, stirring mixture twice.

4. Leave to stand 3 minutes then uncover, stir round and season to taste. Serve as suggested above.

Liver and Bacon
Serves 6 (F)

A special attraction main course made from those tubs of frozen chicken livers now readily available from supermarket chains. Diced pork or lamb liver may be used instead, soaked first for 1 hour in milk to eliminate bitterness.

6oz (175g) onions, peeled and sliced
8oz (225g) streaky bacon, de-rinded and chopped
1lb (450g) chicken livers (2 tubs), de-frosted if frozen then rinsed and well-drained
3 level tblsp cornflour
4 tblsp cold water
¼pt (150ml) boiling water
1 to 1½ level tsp salt (care here as bacon may be very salty)
pepper to taste

1. Put onions and chopped bacon into a 3pt (1·75 litre) glass or pottery dish. Leave uncovered and cook 7 minutes at full power, stirring 3 times.

2. Mix in livers, each of which should first be punctured with the tip of knife to prevent popping. Cover with a plate and cook 8 minutes at full power, stirring 2 or 3 times. Leave to stand in oven for 5 minutes.

3. Mix cornflour smoothly with cold water. Add boiling water and salt then add to livers. Stir thoroughly.

4. Cover with a plate and cook 6 minutes at full power, turning dish 3 times unless oven has a turntable.

5. Stir round, season to taste with pepper then serve with creamed potatoes or freshly cooked rice and a selection of vegetables to taste.

Vegetables

If you refer to the charts, you will see how easy it is to cook a wide selection of both fresh and frozen vegetables in the microwave without loss of colour, flavour and texture. And because the amount of cooking water is, in most instances, minimal, valuable nutrients are retained instead of being drained away at the end.

Imagination as far as flavourings and additions are concerned has been left to you but cooked vegetables can be served with sauces chosen from the Sauce Section on pages 39–48, tossed or coated with melted butter or margarine, flavoured and garnished with a shower of chopped parsley or chives (or other fresh herbs or spices to taste), and even sprinkled with chopped nuts, grated lemon peel or a dusting of paprika or nutmeg.

You will notice I have recommended cooking vegetables in dishes while some other books suggest using roasting bags. My reasons for this are many. It is easier to turn a dish round than to move a bag of vegetables swishing about in very hot or boiling water; one can stir vegetables that need stirring (peas for instance) easily by lifting up the cover; in some cases the cooking dish may also be used for serving which reduces washing up; juices are liable to leak out of a bag more readily than from a dish; even when draining after cooking, a coolish dish is easier to handle and less likely to cause steam burns than a pack of hot vegetables; there is no additional cost incurred through the use of bags. The value of roasting bags, tied loosely at the top with elastic bands, is that no liquid need be added at all and 2 or even 3 bags may either be cooked together or individually in quick succession, depending on the capacity of the oven.

The choice is yours but take care, when dealing with bags of vegetables, to avoid scalds. *Always* put the bag into a dish for cooking and lift out with your hand protected by an oven glove. With the top of the bag pointing downwards into the sink, carefully remove the elastic band and gently tip vegetables out into a colander to drain.

For simplicity when cooking smallish packs of frozen vegetables, leave in their original bags. Puncture each bag 2 or 3 times with the tip of a knife and stand in a dish. Cook for the length of time given in the charts, or on the bag itself, then drain and serve as previously suggested. If cooking a block of frozen vegetables, open out and put into a dish with the ice side facing. Cook as directed.

A short selection of vegetable dishes follows, ranging from Gratin Dauphinoise and Danish-Style Red Cabbage to a Spiced Aubergine Purée and Ratatouille. Even creamed potatoes, with their hundred and one uses, have been included.

Frozen Vegetables (to cook from frozen)

	COOK/HEAT (100%)	COMMENTS
ASPARAGUS SPEARS 8oz (225g)	6 minutes	Put into an oblong dish. Add 1 tablespoon boiling water and $\frac{1}{2}$ level teaspoon salt. Cover with plate or lid. Half way through cooking, separate spears and arrange in the dish with the thick ends pointing outwards. Drain before serving.
1lb (450g)	10 minutes	As above, adding 3 tablespoons boiling water and 1 level teaspoon salt.
BEANS, broad 8oz (225g)	5 minutes	Put into bowl or dish. Add 1 tablespoon boiling water and $\frac{1}{2}$ level teaspoon salt. Cover with plate or lid. Stir half way through cooking. Drain before serving.
1lb (450g)	9 minutes	As above, adding 3 tablespoons boiling water and 1 level teaspoon salt.
BEANS, green, cut or whole 8oz (225g)	6 minutes	Put into bowl or dish. Add 1 tablespoon boiling water and $\frac{1}{2}$ level teaspoon salt. Cover with plate or lid. Stir half way through cooking. Drain before serving.
1lb (450g)	10 minutes	As above, adding 3 tablespoons boiling water and 1 level teaspoon salt.
BEANS, green, sliced 8oz (225g)	5 minutes	Put into dish or bowl. Add 1 tablespoon boiling water and $\frac{1}{2}$ level teaspoon salt. Cover with plate or lid. Stir half way through cooking. Drain before serving.
1lb (450g)	9 minutes	As above, adding 3 tablespoons boiling water and 1 level teaspoon salt.
BROCCOLI SPEARS 14oz (400g) pack	8 minutes	Put into oblong dish. Add 2 tablespoons boiling water and 1 level teaspoon salt. Cover with plate or lid. Separate half way through cooking. Drain before serving.
2 × 14oz (400g) packs	14 minutes	As above, adding 4 tablespoons boiling water and 2 level teaspoons salt.
BRUSSELS SPROUTS 8oz (225g)	5 minutes	Put into bowl or dish. Add 1 tablespoon boiling water and $\frac{1}{2}$ level teaspoon salt. Cover with plate or lid. Stir half way through cooking. Drain before serving.
1lb (450g)	9 minutes	As above, adding 3 tablespoons boiling water and 1 level teaspoon salt.
CARROTS, baby 8oz (225g)	8 minutes	Put into bowl or dish. Add 1 tablespoon boiling water and $\frac{1}{2}$ level teaspoon salt. Cover with plate or lid. Drain before serving.
1lb (450g)	15 minutes	As above, adding 3 tablespoons boiling water and 1 level teaspoon salt.

	COOK/HEAT (100%)	COMMENTS
CARROTS, sliced 8oz (225g)	5 minutes	Put into bowl or dish. Add 1 tablespoon boiling water and $\frac{1}{2}$ level teaspoon salt. Cover with plate or lid. Stir half way through cooking. Drain before serving.
1lb (450g)	9 minutes	As above, adding 3 tablespoons boiling water and 1 level teaspoon salt.
CAULIFLOWER FLORETS 8oz (225g)	6 minutes	Put into bowl or dish. Add 1 tablespoon boiling water and $\frac{1}{2}$ level teaspoon salt. Cover with plate or lid. Stir half way through cooking. Drain before serving.
1lb (450g)	10 minutes	As above, adding 3 tablespoons boiling water and 1 level teaspoon salt.
CORN-ON-THE-COB 1 head	6 minutes	Put on to plate. Cover with kitchen paper. Turn over twice during cooking.
2 heads	8 to 9 minutes	As above, turning corn over 3 times during cooking.
COURGETTES, sliced 8oz (225g)	5 minutes	Put into bowl or dish. Add 1 tablespoon boiling water and $\frac{1}{2}$ level teaspoon salt. Cover with plate or lid. Stir half way through cooking. Drain before serving.
1lb (450g)	9 minutes	As above, adding 3 tablespoons boiling water and 1 level teaspoon salt.
MACEDOINE 8oz (225g)	5 minutes	Put into bowl or dish. Add 1 tablespoon boiling water and $\frac{1}{2}$ level teaspoon salt. Cover with plate or lid. Stir half way through cooking. Drain before serving or using in Russian salad etc.
1lb (450g)	9 minutes	As above, adding 3 tablespoons boiling water and 1 level teaspoon salt.
MANGE TOUT 8oz (225g)	5 minutes	Put into bowl or dish. And 1 tablespoon boiling water and $\frac{1}{2}$ level teaspoon salt. Cover with lid or plate. Stir half way through cooking. Drain before serving.
1lb (450g)	9 minutes	As above, adding 3 tablespoons boiling water and 1 level teaspoon salt.
MEXICAN MIX 8oz (225g)	5 minutes	Put into bowl or dish. Add 1 tablespoon boiling water and $\frac{1}{2}$ level teaspoon salt. Cover with plate or lid. Stir half way through cooking. Drain before serving.
1lb (450g)	9 minutes	As above, adding 3 tablespoons boiling water and 1 level teaspoon salt.
MIXED VEGETABLES, Farmhouse Style 8oz (225g)	5 minutes	Put into bowl or dish. Add 1 tablespoon boiling water and $\frac{1}{2}$ level teaspoon salt. Cover with plate or lid. Stir half way through cooking. Drain before serving.
1lb (450g)	9 minutes	As above, adding 3 tablespoons boiling water and 1 level teaspoon salt.

	COOK/HEAT (100%)	COMMENTS
ONIONS, sliced 8oz (225g)	3 to 4 minutes	Put into bowl or dish. Add no liquid. Cover with plate or lid. Stir half way through cooking. Drain before serving.
PEAS, garden 8oz (225g)	5 minutes	Put into bowl or dish. Add 1 tablespoon boiling water and $\frac{1}{2}$ level teaspoon salt. Cover with plate or lid. Stir half way through cooking. Drain before serving.
1lb (450g)	9 minutes	As above, adding 3 tablespoons boiling water and 1 level teaspoon salt.
PEPPERS, mixed/sliced 8oz (225g)	2 to 3 minutes	Put into bowl or dish. Add $\frac{1}{2}$ level teaspoon salt with $\frac{1}{2}$oz (15g) butter or margarine but no liquid. Cover with plate or lid. Stir half way through cooking. Do not drain.
RATATOUILLE 8oz (225g)	5 minutes	Put into bowl or dish. Add $\frac{1}{2}$ level teaspoon salt with $\frac{1}{2}$oz (15g) butter or margarine but no liquid. Cover with plate or lid. Stir half way through cooking. Do not drain.
1lb (450g)	9 minutes	As above, increasing salt to 1 level teaspoon and butter or margarine to 1oz (25g).
SPINACH, chopped 8oz (225g)	5 minutes	Put into bowl or dish. Add 1 tablespoon boiling water and $\frac{1}{2}$ level teaspoon salt. Cover with plate or lid. Stir half way through cooking. Drain very thoroughly before serving.
1lb (450g)	9 minutes	As above, adding 3 tablespoons boiling water and 1 level teaspoon salt.
SWEETCORN 8oz (225g)	5 minutes	Put into bowl or dish. Add 2 tablespoons boiling water and $\frac{1}{2}$ level teaspoon salt. Stir half way through cooking. Drain well before serving.
1lb (450g)	9 minutes	As above, adding 3 tablespoons boiling water and 1 level teaspoon salt.

Tips on Cooking Fresh Vegetables

Microwaved vegetables should be cooked either in a mixing bowl or, for convenience, a dish suitable for serving. The bowl or dish should be covered with cling film and slit twice. Alternatively, a matching lid or plate may be used for covering if stirring or rearranging is required during cooking.

Weights given are for vegetables *before* trimming, peeling etc. It is advisable to leave firm vegetables to stand for 2 to 3 minutes after cooking but soft vegetables, such as sliced cabbage, tomato halves or mushrooms, may be served straight away.

BLANCHING IN THE MICROWAVE PRIOR TO FREEZING VEGETABLES

When carrying out this operation, allow $\frac{1}{4}$ pint (150ml) water to every 1lb (450g) prepared vegetables. Put both together into a dish, cover with film as directed above and allow *only half* the amount of cooking time given in the charts. Afterwards drain vegetables and rinse under cold, running water. Pack as directed in your own freezer instruction book or manual.

Cooking Fresh Vegetables

	COOK/HEAT (100%)	COMMENTS
ARTICHOKES, globe 4	25 to 35 minutes, depending on size	Cut off stems and tips of leaves. Soak in a large bowl of cold water for 1 hour with leaves pointing downwards. Drain. Stand upright in a large glass or pottery dish, add 1 inch (2·5cm) boiling water and 1 level teaspoon salt. Cover with film and slit twice. Turn dish twice or three times. Drain before serving.
ARTICHOKES, Jerusalem 1lb (450g)	12 to 14 minutes	Peel artichokes and wash. Put into dish or bowl with 1 tablespoon lemon juice, 6 tablespoons boiling water and $\frac{1}{2}$ level teaspoon salt. Cover with film and slit twice. Turn dish twice. Drain before serving.
ASPARAGUS, medium to thin spears 8oz (225g)	10 minutes	Wash, leave whole and put into dish. Add 2 tablespoons water and $\frac{1}{2}$ to 1 level teaspoon salt. Cover with film and slit twice. Turn dish twice. Drain before serving.
thick spears 8oz (225g)	12 minutes	As above. *TIP: Cut a thin sliver off the root end of each asparagus spear before washing and cooking. If spears are thick, scrape downwards from tips to remove a thin layer from outside of each. This applies particularly to white asparagus from north Europe.*
AUBERGINES 1lb (450g)	6 minutes	Cut tops (stem ends) off unpeeled aubergines and slice. Put into dish or bowl with 4 tablespoons water, 2 teaspoons lemon juice and $\frac{1}{2}$ to 1 level teaspoon salt. Cover with plate or matching lid. Stir half way through cooking. Drain before serving.

	COOK/HEAT (100%)	COMMENTS
BEANS, broad, French or runner 1lb (450g)	8 to 10 minutes	Prepare according to type of bean. Put into shallow dish with 2 tablespoons water (4 for broad beans) and $\frac{1}{2}$ to 1 level teaspoon salt. Cover with plate or matching lid. Stir half way through cooking. Drain before serving.
BROCCOLI SPEARS 3 to 4	11 minutes	Wash and shake dry. Split the spears lengthwise if thick. Put in shallow dish with 4 tablespoons water and $\frac{1}{2}$ to 1 level teaspoon salt. Cover with film and slit twice. Turn dish twice. Drain before serving.
BRUSSELS SPROUTS 8oz (225g)	10 minutes	Wash sprouts and remove outer leaves if bruised. Make a cross cut in stem end of each. Put into shallow dish with 2 tablespoons water and $\frac{1}{2}$ to 1 level teaspoon salt. Cover with plate or matching lid. Stir half way through cooking. Drain before serving.
CABBAGE 1lb (450g)	10 minutes	Remove any outer leaves that may be damaged or bruised. Wash cabbage and shred. Put into dish or bowl with 2 tablespoons water and $\frac{1}{2}$ to 1 level teaspoon salt. Cover with plate or matching lid. Stir half way through cooking. Drain before serving.
CARROTS, new 8oz (225g)	12 to 14 minutes	Scrape carrots and leave whole. Put into shallow dish with 4 tablespoons boiling water and $\frac{1}{2}$ to 1 level teaspoon salt. Cover with film and slit twice. Turn dish half way through cooking. Drain before serving.
CARROTS, old, 8oz (225g)	12 to 14 minutes	Peel and slice carrots. Put into shallow dish with 4 tablespoons boiling water and $\frac{1}{2}$ to 1 level teaspoon salt. Cover with plate or matching lid. Stir half way through cooking. Drain before serving.
CAULIFLOWER 1$\frac{1}{2}$lb (675g)	10 to 12 minutes	Wash cauliflower and cut head into small florets. Put into dish or bowl with 4 tablespoons water and $\frac{1}{2}$ to 1 level teaspoon salt. Cover with plate or matching lid. Stir half way through cooking. Drain before serving.
CELERY 12oz (350g)	10 minutes	Wash and scrub celery then slice. Put into shallow dish with 2 tablespoons water and $\frac{1}{2}$ to 1 level teaspoon salt. Cover with film and slit twice. Turn dish half way through cooking. Drain before serving.
CHICORY 8oz (225g)	8 minutes	Remove a cone-shaped bitter core from the base of each head of chicory. Wash heads gently, removing any damaged outer leaves. Put into dish with 1 tablespoon lemon juice and 3 tablespoons water. Cover with film and slit twice. Turn dish half way through cooking. Drain before serving.

	COOK/HEAT (100%)	COMMENTS
CORN-ON-THE-COB		Cook in own husk and silk for maximum flavour and moistness. Otherwise wrap each in film, slitting in 2 or 3 places. Leave corn to stand 3 to 5 minutes before unwrapping and serving.
1 medium	2 minutes	
2 medium	4 to 5 minutes	
3 medium	6 to 7 minutes	
4 medium	8 to 10 minutes	
COURGETTES 1lb (450g)	8 to 9 minutes	Top and tail courgettes. Wash. Slice unpeeled and put into shallow dish. Add *no* water. Sprinkle with $\frac{1}{2}$ to 1 level teaspoon salt. Cover with plate or matching lid. Stir half way through cooking.
CUCUMBER 8oz (225g)	4 minutes	Peel cucumber and cut into dice. Put into shallow dish with 1 tablespoon water and $\frac{1}{2}$ level teaspoon salt. Cover with plate or matching lid. Stir half way through cooking. Drain before serving.
LEEKS 1lb (450g)	10 minutes	Slit leeks and wash thoroughly. Trim and slice. Put into dish or bowl with 2 tablespoons water and $\frac{1}{2}$ to 1 level teaspoon salt. Cover with plate or matching lid. Stir half way through cooking. Drain before serving.
MARROW 1lb (450g)	8 to 9 minutes	Peel. Slice into rings and remove centre 'cores' of seeds and fibres. Cut each empty ring into small cubes. Put into shallow dish and sprinkle with $\frac{1}{2}$ to 1 level teaspoon salt. Add *no* water. Cover with plate or matching lid. Stir half way through cooking. If necessary, drain before serving.
MUSHROOMS 8oz (225g)	6 minutes	Peel mushrooms. Wash if necessary. Put into shallow dish with 1 tablespoon water and $\frac{1}{2}$ level teaspoon salt. Cover with plate or matching lid. Stir half way through cooking. Drain before serving. If preferred, omit water and cook in 1 tablespoon melted butter or margarine. Do *not* drain after cooking but serve with juices.
OKRA 1lb (450g)	7 to 8 minutes	Top and tail washed okra. Put into shallow dish with 2 tablespoons melted butter or margarine. Cover with plate or matching lid. Stir gently half way through cooking. Do *not* drain before serving.
ONIONS 1lb (450g)	8 to 10 minutes	Peel onions and halve or quarter if large. Put into a dish or bowl and sprinkle with $\frac{1}{2}$ to 1 level teaspoon salt. Add 2 tablespoons water. Cover with film and slit twice. Turn dish half way through cooking. Drain, if necessary, before serving.
PARSNIPS 1lb (450g)	8 to 10 minutes	Peel and dice parsnips. Put into a shallow dish with 3 tablespoons water and $\frac{1}{2}$ to 1 level teaspoon salt. Cover with plate or matching lid. Stir halfway through cooking. Drain before serving.

	COOK/HEAT (100%)	COMMENTS
PEAS 1lb (450g)	9 minutes	Shell peas. Put into shallow dish with 2 tablespoons water. Add $\frac{1}{2}$ to 1 level teaspoon salt and sugar. Cover with plate or matching lid. Stir half way through cooking. Drain before serving.
POTATOES new small, in their skins 1lb (450g)	11 minutes	Wash and scrub potatoes well. Put into shallow dish with 2 tablespoons water and $\frac{1}{2}$ to 1 level teaspoon salt. Cover with plate or matching lid. Stir half way through cooking. Drain before serving.
POTATOES, old, in their jackets 1 medium potato (4oz or 125g)	5 to 6 minutes Stand 5 minutes wrapped in tea towel	Wash and dry potatoes thoroughly. Slit or prick skins in several places. Stand on plate or kitchen paper. Cover with more kitchen paper. Turn over twice or three times during cooking. When cooking more than one potato, leave 1 inch (2·5cm) space between each. Arrange 3 potatoes in triangle; 4 in square; 5 to 8 round edge of plate or paper.
2 medium potatoes	$6\frac{1}{2}$ to 8 minutes Stand 5 minutes as above	
3 medium potatoes	9 to 11 minutes Stand 5 minutes as above	
4 medium potatoes	12 to 14 minutes Stand 5 minutes as above	
5 medium potatoes	15 to 17 minutes Stand 5 minutes as above	
6 medium potatoes	18 to 20 minutes Stand 5 minutes as above	
7 medium potatoes	20 to 22 minutes Stand 5 minutes as above	
8 medium potatoes	23 to 25 minutes Stand 5 minutes as above	

	COOK/HEAT (100%)	COMMENTS
SPINACH	7 to 8 minutes	Wash very thoroughly to remove grit. Tear leaves into small pieces. Put into dish with $\frac{1}{2}$ level teaspoon salt but *no* water. Cover with plate or matching lid. Stir half way through cooking. Drain if necessary.
SPRING GREENS 1lb (450g)	7 to 9 minutes	Tear leaves off stalks, wash and shake dry. Shred coarsely and put into shallow dish. Sprinkle with $\frac{1}{2}$ to 1 level teaspoon salt. Cover with plate or matching lid. Stir half way through cooking. Drain before serving.
SWEDES 1lb (450g)	10 minutes	Peel swedes and dice. Put into shallow dish with 4 tablespoons water and $\frac{1}{2}$ to 1 level teaspoon salt. Cover with plate or matching lid. Stir half way through cooking. Drain before serving.
SWEET PEPPERS 1lb (450g)	8 minutes	Halve peppers and remove inside fibres and seeds. Slice or chop. Put into bowl with 2 tablespoons water and $\frac{1}{2}$ to 1 level teaspoon salt. Cover with film and slit twice. Turn bowl half way through cooking. Drain before serving.
TOMATOES 1lb (450g)	6 to 7 minutes	Wash tomatoes and halve. Put into shallow dish, cut sides facing, then sprinkle with $\frac{1}{2}$ to 1 level teaspoon salt and sugar. Add *no* water. Cover with film and slit twice. Turn dish half way through cooking. If liked, brush cut sides with melted butter or margarine before sprinkling with salt and sugar.
TURNIPS 1lb (450g)	10 to 12 minutes	Peel turnips and dice. Put into shallow dish with 4 tablespoons water and $\frac{1}{2}$ to 1 level teaspoon salt. Cover with plate or matching lid. Stir half way through cooking. Drain before serving.

Spiced Aubergine Purée   Serves 4

An unusual accompaniment which is a simple variation of the dip given on page 30.

Cook aubergines as directed. Drain and work to a purée with the lemon juice. Scrape into a dish and add ½oz (15g) melted butter or margarine, 1 rounded tablespoon finely chopped fresh coriander, ½ to 1 level teaspoon salt, ⅛ teaspoon mixed spice and ¼ level teaspoon paprika. Put into a dish, cover with a plate and reheat 2½ to 3 minutes at full power. Stand 1 or 2 minutes before eating.

TIP: The purée may be made ahead of time and left, covered, in the refrigerator before using. Either bring to kitchen temperature before mixing with rest of ingredients, or allow an extra ½ to 1 minute cooking time.

Bean Sprouts in Chinese-Style Sauce   Serves 4

Well worth a try as an accompaniment to omelets or Chinese dishes, be they homemade or take-away. The sprouts are also appetising with chicken.

1lb (450g) fresh bean sprouts	1. Toss all ingredients well together in a bowl. Transfer to an 8 inch (20cm) round glass or pottery dish that is fairly deep.
2 tsp soy sauce	
1 tsp Worcestershire sauce	2. Cover with cling film, then puncture twice with the tip of a knife.
1 level tsp onion salt	
	3. Cook 5 minutes at full power, turning dish twice unless oven has a turntable. Uncover, stir round and serve.

Orange Beets   Serves 4 to 6

Hot beetroots in orange juice may sound unusual, but they make a lively accompaniment to pork, ham, duck and goose; certainly worth trying in the winter as a change from the more predictable run-of-the-mill sprouts, cabbage and cauliflower.

1lb (450g) cooked beetroots, peeled and sliced	1. Put beetroot slices into a fairly shallow, 7 inch (17·5cm) round glass or pottery dish.
5 tblsp fresh orange juice (reconstituted frozen is ideal)	2. Beat together rest of ingredients. Pour over beetroot. Cover with cling film, then puncture twice with the tip of a knife.
1 tblsp malt vinegar	
½ level tsp salt	3. Cook 6 minutes at full power, turning dish twice unless oven has a turntable. Stand one minute then serve hot.
1 garlic clove, peeled and crushed	

Danish-Style Red Cabbage　　　　Serves 6 to 8 (F)

I've said Danish, but cooked red cabbage is eaten throughout Scandinavia and Northern Europe. It is a winter speciality, a treat with pork or goose or even sausages, and bliss to cook in the microwave where it remains slightly crisp and bright-coloured – cooked conventionally, it dulls down and looks a bit like mahogany. One warning. The cabbage tends to stain the hands when shredding so use a food processor if you have one or alternatively the shredding attachment of a mixer. The flavour will be more mature if cooked a day in advance.

2lb (900g) red cabbage

$\frac{3}{4}$pt (425ml) boiling water

$1\frac{1}{2}$ level tsp salt

8oz (225g) onions, peeled and finely chopped

8oz (225g) peeled cooking apples, cored and chopped

2 level tblsp light brown soft sugar

$\frac{1}{4}$ level tsp caraway seeds

2 level tblsp cornflour

3 tblsp malt vinegar

1 extra tblsp cold water

1. Wash cabbage, taking off any outer damaged and/or bruised leaves. Cut cabbage into pieces, minus stalks, and shred as finely as possible.

2. Put into a 4pt (2·25 litre) glass or pottery dish with $\frac{1}{2}$pt (275ml) boiling water and 1 teaspoon salt. Mix thoroughly. Cover with a plate and cook 10 minutes at full power.

3. Stir round then add rest of water, salt, onions, apples, sugar and caraway seeds. Mix thoroughly. Cover with cling film then puncture twice with the tip of a knife.

4. Cook 20 minutes at full power, turning dish 4 times unless oven has a turntable. Remove from oven. Blend cornflour smoothly with vinegar and tablespoon of water.

5. Add to cabbage and stir well to mix. Leave uncovered and cook 10 minutes at full power. Stir 4 times. Remove from oven and cover. Leave until cold then refrigerate overnight as this helps to mature the flavour. Reheat, covered, 5 to 6 minutes before serving.

Sour Cabbage　　　　Serves 8 to 10 (F)

I first found this tucked away in the depths of Norway's countryside, teamed with a hearty cafeteria meal of sausages and mash! It takes a while to cook conventionally – about $1\frac{1}{2}$ to 2 hours – but the microwave does a magnificent job in about half that time at defrost setting. Like the red cabbage from Denmark, this one is also best cooked one day for the next and is not unlike mild sauerkraut. You will find the cabbage takes on a creamy gold colour and stays very slightly crisp.

2lb (900g) white cabbage

6 tblsp water

4 tblsp malt vinegar

2 rounded tblsp granulated sugar

2 level tsp caraway seeds

$1\frac{1}{2}$ level tsp salt

1. Wash cabbage, taking off any outer damaged and/or bruised leaves. Cut cabbage into pieces, minus stalk, and shred as finely as possible.

2. Put into a 4pt (2·25 litre) dish with all remaining ingredients. Stir well to mix. Cover with cling film, then puncture twice with the tip of a knife.

3. Cook $\frac{3}{4}$ hour at defrost setting, turning dish 4 times unless oven has a turntable. Cool and leave out at kitchen temperature overnight.

4. Before serving, reheat individual portions on side plates, covering with kitchen paper and allowing about 1 minute each at full power.

Scalloped Celeriac

Serves 6

Easier and quicker to cope with in the microwave than when cooked conventionally, this large, swede-shaped vegetable tasting of celery makes a grand accompaniment to meat, poultry, egg and fish dishes and is worth a try in the winter months when it is most readily available.

2lb (900g) celeriac
½pt (275ml) hot water
1 tblsp lemon juice (added to prevent browning)
2 level tsp salt
2oz (50g) lean bacon, chopped and microwaved for 1½ minutes at full power
½pt (275ml) single cream
1oz (25g) potato crisps, crushed

1. Peel celeriac thickly, wash well and cut each head into eighths. Put into 4pt (2·25 litre) dish with hot water, lemon juice and half the salt.

2. Cover with cling film then puncture twice with the tip of a knife. Cook 20 minutes at full power, turning dish twice unless oven has a turntable.

3. Drain then cut celeriac into cubes. Return to dish in which it was cooked. Gently mix in rest of salt, bacon and cream.

4. Sprinkle with potato crisps and cook, uncovered, 4 minutes at full power, turning dish 3 times unless oven has a turntable.

Buttered Lime Carrots

Serves 4 to 6 (F)

An all-occasion carrot dish, unusually brightened with lime cordial. Try it with veal, turkey, game dishes or offal.

2oz (50g) butter or margarine
1lb (450g) carrots, peeled and grated
4oz (125g) onions, peeled and grated
1 tblsp lime cordial
1 level tsp salt

1. Put butter or margarine into an 8 inch (20cm) round glass or pottery dish. Melt for 1½ to 2 minutes at defrost setting. Leave uncovered.

2. Stir in carrots, onions, lime cordial and salt. Mix well and cover with cling film. Puncture twice with the tip of a knife.

3. Cook 15 minutes at full power, turning dish 3 times unless oven has a turntable. Leave to stand 2 or 3 minutes before serving.

Buttered Cucumber   Serves 4

Cooked cucumber, with its delicate crunch and pale green colour, is a tantalising and unusual accompaniment for fish and chicken. A dinner party winner!

1 medium cucumber (about 1lb or 450g), peeled
1oz (25g) butter or margarine, at kitchen temperature
½ level tsp salt
1 rounded tblsp finely chopped parsley

1. Very thinly slice cucumber and wring dry in a tea towel.

2. Put butter into a fairly shallow glass or pottery dish measuring about 8 by 8 inches (20 by 20cm). Or use any other shaped dish of about 2pt (1·25 litre) capacity. Melt, uncovered, for 1 to 1½ minutes at defrost setting.

3. Stir in cucumber and salt. Cover with an inverted plate, matching lid or cling film. If using film, puncture twice with tip of knife.

4. Cook 6 minutes at full power, turning dish 4 times unless oven has a turntable. Uncover and stir in parsley. Serve straight away.

Cauliflower Camelia   Serves 4

Imagine a superior version of cauliflower cheese, the head of this flowery vegetable nestling under a coating of a fine, full-flavoured sauce laced with soured cream or Crème Frâiche (page 226). Serve it as a vegetable with beef, lamb, chicken, turkey, gammon or microwaved fish.

1½lb (675g) head of cauliflower, weighed *after* leaves and most of the woody centre stalk have been cut off
4 tblsp hot water
1 carton (5oz or 142ml) soured cream (or use homemade Crème Frâiche page 226)
1 Grade 2 egg
1 round tsp cornflour
2 tsp cold water
5oz (150g) Cheshire cheese, grated
salt and pepper to taste
paprika

1. Stand cauliflower upright in deepish glass or pottery dish. Add hot water and cover with cling film. Puncture twice with the tip of a knife. Alternatively, cover with a matching lid.

2. Cook for 10 minutes at full power, turning dish 4 times unless oven has a turntable.

3. Uncover and drain off water. Beat soured cream and egg well together then stir in cornflour, first smoothly mixed with cold water.

4. Stir in cheese then season to taste with salt and pepper. Spoon over cauliflower and sprinkle with paprika. Cover as before.

5. Cook a further 3 minutes at full power, turning dish at the end of every minute unless oven has a turntable. Stand 2 minutes. Serve as suggested.

Chicory Braise

Serves 4

Chicory has a distinctive taste with a very slight bitterness which people either love or hate and this recipe is essentially for the former group! It goes well with egg and poultry dishes.

4 heads of chicory (about 1½lb or 675g)
1oz (25g) butter or margarine
1 chicken stock cube
1 tblsp boiling water
½ level tsp onion salt
2 tsp lemon juice

1. Trim chicory, removing any outside leaves which are bruised or damaged. Remove a cone-shaped core from base of each, as this helps to eliminate bitterness.

2. Coarsely chop chicory and put into a 2pt (1·25 litre) dish. Melt butter or margarine for 1 to 1½ minutes at defrost setting. Keep covered. Pour over chicory.

3. Crumble chicken stock cube into the water and stir until smooth. Blend in onion salt and lemon juice.

4. Mix well, pour into dish then cover with cling film. Puncture twice with the tip of a knife. Alternatively, cover with matching lid.

5. Cook 9 minutes at full power, turning dish 3 times unless oven has a turntable. Stand 1 minute then serve coated with juices from dish.

Chicory Ham Wraps in Cheese Sauce   Picture p. 147

Serves 4 generously

A Belgian classic main course which adapts happily to microwave cooking. In traditional fashion serve with chips or boiled potatoes.

8 heads of chicory (about 2¼lb or 1kg)
¼pt (150ml) boiling water mixed with
1 tblsp lemon juice
8 slices ham (7 to 8oz or 200 to 225g)
1pt (575ml) milk, taken from the refrigerator
2oz (50g) butter or margarine
1½oz (40g) plain flour
4oz (125g) Gouda cheese, grated
2oz (50g) Double Gloucester cheese, grated

1. Trim chicory, removing any outer leaves that are either bruised or damaged. Cut out a cone-shaped core from base of each chicory head as this is very often bitter and can spoil the flavour.

2. Arrange in a 14 inch (35cm) oval glass dish or in an oblong dish measuring about 12 by 7½ inches (30 by 19cm). Coat with water and lemon juice.

3. Cover with cling film, then puncture twice with the tip of a knife. Cook 14 minutes at full power, turning dish twice.

4. Stand outside the microwave oven 5 minutes. Lift into a colander, drain thoroughly and leave until lukewarm. Wrap a slice of ham round each then return to washed and dried dish in which chicory were originally cooked.

5. Heat milk in an uncovered jug for 3 minutes at full power. Leave to stand outside oven. Put butter or margarine into a 2pt (1·25 litre) bowl and melt, uncovered, 2 to 2½ minutes at defrost setting. Stir in flour then gradually whisk in hot milk until mixture is very smooth.

6. Cook for 5 to 6 minutes at full power or until sauce just comes up to the boil. Beat hard at the end of every minute. Mix in cheese.

7. Pour over wrapped chicory in dish then cover with cling film as directed above. Reheat for 3 minutes at full power and stand 5 minutes before serving.

Juniper Courgettes   Serves 4 to 5

The inclusion of juniper berries adds a gin-like and unexpected note of subtlety to the courgettes, a most pleasing accompaniment to poultry and fish dishes.

1oz (25g) butter or margarine
1lb (450g) topped and tailed courgettes, washed and thinly sliced
6 juniper berries, lightly crushed with the back of a spoon
$\frac{1}{2}$ level tsp salt
1 heaped tblsp finely chopped parsley

1. Put butter or margarine in an 8 inch (20cm) round glass or pottery dish and melt, uncovered, 1 to $1\frac{1}{2}$ minutes at defrost setting.

2. Stir in courgettes, juniper berries and salt and spread evenly into a layer that covers base of dish.

3. Cover with cling film then puncture twice with the tip of a knife. Cook 10 minutes at full power, turning dish 4 times unless oven has a turntable.

4. Stand 2 minutes before uncovering and sprinkling with parsley.

Buttered Chinese Leaves with Pernod   Picture p. 148   Serves 4

A cross in texture and flavour between white cabbage and firm lettuce, Chinese leaves make a very presentable cooked vegetable and are greatly enhanced by the addition of Pernod which adds a delicate and subtle note of aniseed.

$1\frac{1}{2}$lb (675g) Chinese leaves, well-washed and shredded
2oz (50g) butter or margarine, melted in microwave for $1\frac{1}{2}$ to 2 minutes
3 tsp Pernod
$\frac{1}{2}$ level tsp salt

1. Mix all ingredients well together in a 3pt (1·75 litre) glass or pottery dish.

2. Cover with cling film, then puncture twice with the tip of a knife. Alternatively, cover with matching lid.

3. Cook 12 minutes at full power, turning dish 4 times unless oven has a turntable. Leave to stand 5 minutes then serve.

Wine-Braised Leeks with Ham

Serves 4

An interesting accompaniment to poultry and lamb; a perfect winter vegetable dish when made with small and elegant leeks.

4 to 5 narrow leeks (1lb or 450 to 500g)

1oz (25g) butter or margarine, at kitchen temperature

8oz (225g) mild and lean ham, fairly finely chopped

4 tblsp red wine

black pepper to taste

1. Trim away fuzzy tops from leeks then cut off all but 4 inches (10cm) of green 'skirt' from each. Slit leeks carefully in half lengthwise, almost to top.

2. Wash gently under cold, running water, making sure earth and grit have been thoroughly removed.

3. Melt butter or margarine, uncovered, in an oblong dish measuring 10 by 8 inches (25 by 30cm). Allow about 1 to $1\frac{1}{2}$ minutes at defrost setting, then rotate dish until base is completely covered with fat.

4. Add leeks, arranging them in a single layer. Sprinkle with ham and wine. Season to taste with freshly ground black pepper.

5. Cover with film, then puncture twice with the tip of a knife. Alternatively, cover with matching lid.

6. Remove turntable (if oven has one) or place turntable upside down, if model permits, to prevent it from rotating. This will stop the dish banging against the sides of the oven and causing damage.

7. Cook leeks 15 minutes at full power, turning dish twice. Uncover and serve straight away.

CASSEROLED LEEKS

Serves 4

Chop slit leeks and put into a 3pt (1·75 litre) dish. Add 1oz (25g) melted butter or margarine mixed with 4 tablespoons chicken stock and salt and pepper to taste. Cover as directed above. Cook 10 minutes at full power.

Fennel with Tarragon   Serves 4

A sophisticated vegetable with a mild aniseed flavour, fennel is companionable with fish or chicken and is quite special cooked as suggested below.

2lb (900g) fennel
2oz (50g) butter or margarine
$\frac{1}{2}$ level tsp salt
1 rounded tsp Bordeaux mustard
2 tblsp medium sherry
$\frac{1}{2}$ level tsp tarragon

1. Wash and dry fennel. Cut off any bruised or damaged pieces but leave on 'fingers' and 'fronds'.

2. Melt butter or margarine, uncovered in cup, for $1\frac{1}{2}$ to 2 minutes at defrost setting. Gently beat in salt, mustard, sherry and tarragon.

3. Cut each head of fennel into quarters, working from top to bottom and retaining 'fingers' and 'fronds'.

4. Arrange in a 10 inch (25cm) round and fairly shallow glass or pottery dish. Coat with the butter or margarine mixture.

5. Cover with cling film, then puncture twice with the tip of a knife.

6. Cook for 20 minutes at full power, turning dish twice unless oven has a turntable. Leave to stand for 7 minutes inside or outside the oven, whichever is the most convenient. Serve as suggested.

Creamed Mushrooms   Serves 6 to 8

The last time I ate anything like these luxurious creamed mushrooms was in Poland where the people pride themselves not only on the quality of their fungi, but also the way they are cooked.

1oz (25g) butter or margarine
1lb (450g) button mushrooms, washed and dried
2 level tblsp cornflour
2 tblsp cold water
1 large carton (10oz or 284ml) soured cream
2 level tsp salt

1. Put butter or margarine into a 4pt (2·25 litre) dish and melt 1 to $1\frac{1}{2}$ minutes at defrost setting. Leave uncovered.

2. Mix in mushrooms, cover with a plate and cook 5 minutes at full power, stirring twice.

3. Remove from oven and uncover. Blend cornflour smoothly with water then beat into soured cream. Add to mushrooms then combine thoroughly with the help of a wooden spoon.

4. Cover as a above and cook 7 minutes at full power, stirring 3 or 4 times. Season with salt. Serve straight away.

Boiled Potatoes　　　　　　　　　　Serves 2 to 3

Potatoes boiled in the microwave never fall to pieces, retain their flavour and colour, and have an excellent texture. Nutrients are conserved because the amount of water used for boiling is minimal, fuel is saved and there is no pan to wash – you can cook the potatoes in the serving dish.

1lb (450g) old potatoes (4 medium or 2 large)

4 tblsp boiling water

$\frac{1}{2}$oz (15g) butter or margarine (optional)

1 level tblsp chopped parsley (optional)

1. Wash potatoes then peel thinly. Cut each medium potato into 8 chunks; large ones into 16.

2. Put into 2pt (1·25 litre) glass or pottery dish with the water. Cover with cling film, then puncture twice with the tip of a knife. Alternatively, cover with matching lid.

3. Cook 10 minutes at full power, turning dish 4 times unless oven has a turntable. Leave to stand 3 minutes, uncover and pour off any leftover water.

4. Add butter or margarine and the parsley (if used), toss gently to mix and serve hot.

CREAMED POTATOES

After draining potatoes, mash finely in the dish. Add $\frac{1}{2}$oz (15g) butter or margarine, seasoning to taste, then beat in 4 to 5 tablespoons milk. When potatoes are light and creamy, 'rough up' with a fork then reheat, uncovered, 1 to $1\frac{1}{2}$ minutes at full power.

BOILED POTATOES　　　　　　　　For 3 to 5

Boil potatoes as previously directed, using 2lb (900g), and 6 tablespoons boiling water. Allow 15 to 16 minutes at full power.

Stuffed Jacket Potatoes　　Allow 2 halves per person (F)

First cook as many jacket potatoes as are required for stuffing, following instructions given in the chart on page 130.

CHEESE POTATOES　　　　Allow 2 halves per person (F)

Cut each potato in half horizontally and scoop insides into a bowl. Mash finely then cream until light with butter or margarine, cold milk and seasoning to taste. Mix in 1oz (25g) grated Cheddar cheese and $\frac{1}{2}$ level teaspoon mustard to every potato. Return mixture to potato shells put on to a plate, cover with kitchen paper and reheat as follows:

2 halves, $1\frac{1}{2}$ to $1\frac{3}{4}$ minutes
3 halves, 2 to $2\frac{1}{2}$ minutes
4 halves, $2\frac{3}{4}$ to $3\frac{1}{4}$ minutes

BACON AND CHEESE POTATOES
Allow 2 halves per person (F)

Make as Cheese Potatoes, but allow 2oz (50g) chopped and microwaved cooked bacon to every 2 potatoes in addition to the cheese.

BLUE CHEESE POTATOES
Allow 2 halves per person (F)

Make as Cheese Potatoes, but substitute mashed or crumbled blue cheese for Cheddar.

TOPPING

If desired, sprinkle potatoes with chopped parsley, chives or paprika before reheating.

Savoyard Potatoes
Serves 6 (F)

A wonderful potato dish from the French, Swiss, Italian borders, memorably appetising as a meal on its own with pickles and salad, or as an accompaniment to any number of meat and poultry dishes. If you are able to slice the potatoes in a food processor, so much the better. If not, use a grater or cut into hair-thin wafers with a very sharp knife.

2lb (900g) potatoes, peeled and cut into wafer thin slices

1 garlic clove, peeled and crushed, mixed with 3oz (75g) butter or margarine, melted

6oz (175g) grated cheese – Gruyère or Emmental are ideal but for greater economy, use Cheddar or Edam

1 level tsp salt

pepper to taste

½pt (275ml) chicken stock, made with cube and water or white wine

paprika

1. Grease a 10 inch (25cm) round glass or pottery dish, of about 2 inches (5cm) in depth, with butter or margarine.

2. Fill with alternate layers of potatoes, two-thirds of the garlic and butter or margarine mixture, and the same amount of cheese. Begin and end with potatoes and sprinkle salt and pepper between layers.

3. Gently pour stock or wine down side of dish. Trickle rest of butter over the top then sprinkle with remaining cheese. Add a light dusting of paprika.

4. Cover with cling film, then puncture twice with the tip of a knife. Alternatively, cover with a matching lid.

5. Cook for 20 minutes at full power, turning dish 4 times unless oven has a turntable. Leave to stand 5 minutes in the oven, uncover and serve.

DAUPHINOISE POTATOES
Serves 6 (F)

Make as the Savoyard Potatoes, substituting long life milk for the stock or wine. Garlic may be omitted if preferred and the top sprinkled with a small amount of nutmeg either with, or instead of, the paprika. It, too, may be served with similar dishes to the Savoyard Potatoes.

CHATEAU POTATOES
Serves 6 (F)

Make exactly as Savoyard Potatoes but use medium cider instead of stock or wine.

142

Ratatouille   Serves 6 to 8 (F)

Temperamentally Mediterranean, Ratatouille is a warmly-flavoured pot-pourri of semi-exotic vegetables, melded together by gentle cooking. Again very much at home in the microwave, serve Ratatouille with meat, egg and poultry dishes or, for vegetarian tastes, spoon over rice, pasta or bulgar. The flavour is improved if Ratatouille is cooked one day for the next and reheated, covered, for about 7 minutes at full power. It may also be reheated on individual plates.

4 tblsp salad oil

6oz (175g) onions, peeled and chopped

1 garlic clove, peeled and crushed

8oz (225g) courgettes, topped and tailed then washed and thinly sliced

12oz (350g) aubergines, stem ends removed then washed and cubed without peeling

4oz (125g) washed red or green pepper, deseeded and chopped

½ can (7oz or 200g) tomatoes

1 rounded tblsp tomato purée

3 rounded tsp brown sugar

2 level tsp salt

2 heaped tblsp chopped parsley

1. Pour oil into a 4pt (2·25 litre) glass or pottery dish. Heat 1 minute at full power. Leave uncovered.

2. Add onions and garlic. Mix in well then cook, uncovered, for 4 minutes at full power.

3. Stir in courgettes, aubergines, red or green pepper, tomatoes, purée, sugar, half the salt and half the parsley. Cover with cling film, then puncture twice with the tip of a knife.

4. Cook for 20 minutes at full power, turning dish 4 times unless oven has a turntable. Uncover and stir. Add rest of salt and parsley.

5. Leave uncovered and continue to cook 8 to 10 minutes at full power or until most of the liquid has evaporated. Stir at least 4 times. Cool and cover.

Boiled Sweet Potatoes   Serves 4 (F)

Becoming increasingly more available in the UK via supermarket chains and some greengrocers, these yellowy-orange fleshed vegetables are packed with Vitamin A. Their own natural sweetness enables them to be used as an ingredient in sweet dishes and surprisingly they also make a subtle accompaniment to poultry, ham and game. In North America, sweet potatoes are cubed then fried with sugar and fat to give them a candied appearance. They are then eaten with the Thanksgiving Day roast turkey. Yams are another 'breed' of sweet potato but are moister, deeper-toned and with a higher sugar content. But the two are virtually interchangeable.

1lb (450g) sweet potatoes or yams

4 tblsp boiling water

1. Peel and dice potatoes and put into a 1¾pt (1 litre) dish. Add water. Cover with cling film, then puncture twice with the tip of a knife. Alternatively, cover with matching lid.

2. Cook 10 minutes at full power, turning dish 4 times unless oven has a turntable. Leave to stand 2 or 3 minutes, drain and serve.

BUTTERED SWEET POTATOES	Serves 4

After draining potatoes, toss with butter.

CREAMED SWEET POTATOES	Serves 4

Boil sweet potatoes as directed above. Drain and mash finely. Cream with $\frac{1}{2}$ to 1oz (15 to 25g) butter or margarine and 3 to 4 tablespoons warm milk. Season to taste and put into serving dish. Reheat 1 to $1\frac{1}{2}$ minutes at full power. Covering is unnecessary.

Herb Garden Mosaic   Serves 6 to 8

A lovely frozen vegetable mix for those occasions when you are short of time and grateful for the bounty in the freezer. I tend to make this in the summer, when my potted fresh herbs are at their most abundant and fragrant.

Ingredients	Method
8oz (225g) frozen broad beans	1. Put all vegetables, used from frozen, into a 3 to $3\frac{1}{2}$pt (2 litre) glass or pottery dish, stirring well to mix.

8oz (225g) frozen broad beans

8oz (225g) frozen sliced courgettes

8oz (225g) frozen sweetcorn

3oz (75g) frozen mixed diced red and green peppers

4oz (125g) frozen sliced onions

4 leaves of basil, chopped

2 leaves of mint, chopped

2 inch (5cm) sprig of rosemary, 'needles' taken off stalks

2 inch (5cm) sprig of savory, leaves taken off stalks

3 inch (7·5cm) sprig of thyme, left as a sprig

1 to 2oz (25 to 50g) butter or margarine

$1\frac{1}{2}$ to 2 level tsp salt

1. Put all vegetables, used from frozen, into a 3 to $3\frac{1}{2}$pt (2 litre) glass or pottery dish, stirring well to mix.

2. Cover with cling film, then puncture twice with the tip of a knife. Alternatively, cover with a matching lid.

3. Cook 16 minutes at full power, turning dish twice unless oven has a turntable.

4. Leave to stand 5 minutes inside or outside the oven, whichever is the most convenient. Uncover. Drain off liquid then stir in the fresh herbs and butter or margarine. Season to taste with salt and serve hot.

Vegetables with Hollandaise Sauce

The vegetables most enhanced by Hollandaise sauce are cauliflower, broccoli, asparagus and globe artichokes. Therefore cook vegetables as directed in the charts on pages 127–131, then serve with Hollandaise sauce (page 44). It is usual to coat cauliflower and broccoli with the sauce but serve the Hollandaise separately as an accompaniment to hot asparagus and artichokes.

Rice and Pasta

Cooking rice and pasta in a microwave is not necessarily speedier in time, but fuel costs are reduced by at least half, minimal involvement is required of the cook, there are no sticky saucepans to clean up afterwards and the kitchen stays steam-free and fresh – important considerations, particularly in summer when one tries to keep the room cool and comfortable, and in winter when getting rid of steam and condensation often involves a blast of cold air from an open window or back door.

There are other advantages to be gained as well. Rice grains retain their shape and do not disintegrate into a mush, they absorb all or most of the liquid as good rice should and are independent of each other, remaining dry, firm, separate and, once forked through, light and fluffy into the bargain. And this applies equally to the most popular types: easy-cook, American long grain, easy-cook, Italian short grain, slender Indian Basmati and round grain pudding rice.

Pasta reacts as favourably as rice and whether it be broken spaghetti or any of the small varieties such as macaroni or shells, it rarely overcooks and, almost without exception, stays firmly 'al dente' in texture, true to Italian tradition.

One tip is worth remembering. Rice should be covered while cooking, pasta on its own uncovered unless the recipe states otherwise.

Easy-Cook, Long Grain or Basmati Rice (F)

Put 8oz (225g) rice into a fairly large glass or pottery dish. Add 1 pint (575 ml) boiling water and 1 level teaspoon of salt. Stir round. Cover with cling film, then puncture twice with the tip of a knife. Cook 16 minutes at full power, turning dish 4 times unless oven has a turntable. Leave to stand 8 minutes inside or outside the oven, whichever is the most convenient, so that rice grains absorb all the liquid. Remove film, fluff up with a fork, adding $\frac{1}{2}$ to 1oz (15 to 25g) butter or margarine if desired.

SAFFRON RICE (F)
Microwave as easy-cook, long grain, adding 6 or 8 saffron strands at the same time as the salt. The addition of $\frac{1}{2}$ level teaspoon turmeric gives the rice a vibrant golden colour and means less costly saffron need be used.

CHICKEN OR BEEF RICE (F)
Microwave as easy-cook, long grain, adding boiling chicken or beef stock instead of water. Reduce salt to $\frac{1}{2}$ level teaspoon.

TOMATO RICE (F)
Microwave as easy-cook, long grain, adding half boiling water and half boiling tomato juice.

Mild Turkey Curry. Metal dish for serving only. See page 120.

Chicory Ham Wraps in Cheese Sauce. See page 136.

*Left: Roast
Turkey.
See page 118.*

Chinese Leaves. See recipe page 137.

Right:
Pineapple Rice.
See page 153.

Pasta Ham Casserole. See page 157.

Sweetcorn and Chicken Rice.
Metal dish for serving only.
See page 153.

Top: *Spaghetti Carbonara. See page 157.* Centre: *Macaroni Chicken Curry. See page 159.*
Bottom: *Spaghetti with Sweet-Sour Sauce. See page 158.*

HERB RICE   (F)

Microwave as easy-cook, long grain, adding 1 level teaspoon mixed herbs with the salt.

PARSLEY RICE   (F)

Microwave as easy-cook, long grain, adding 2 heaped tablespoons of parsley at the very end when forking through.

PINEAPPLE RICE   (Picture p. 149)   (F)

Microwave as easy-cook, long grain, then fork in 6oz (175g) cut up fresh pineapple at the end. Arrange on plates and garnish with rolls of ham.

SWEETCORN AND CHICKEN RICE   (Picture p. 150)   (F)

Microwave as easy-cook, long grain, adding 4oz (125g) frozen sweetcorn, 2oz (50g) chopped-up red pepper and 6oz (175g) cut-up cooked chicken with the water and salt. Allow 18 minutes cooking time then stand 8 or 9 minutes. Sprinkle with paprika before serving.

Brown Rice   Serves 3 to 4 (F)

Nutty-flavoured and nutritional, brown rice makes a pleasant change from white, although it needs a longish time in the microwave to tenderise. The advantage over conventional cooking is a saving of about 15 minutes, no attention, and a kitchen that remains completely cool and fresh. Brown rice is delicious with almost everything, but is especially appetising with poultry, veal, lamb, offal and scrambled eggs or omelets.

1 level tsp salt

4oz (125g) brown rice

2pts (1·2l) boiling water

1. Put all ingredients into a $3\frac{1}{2}$pt (2 litre) glass or pottery dish and stand on a plate in case water boils over.

2. Stir round to mix. Cover with cling film, then puncture twice with the tip of a knife. Alternatively, cover with matching lid.

3. Cook 35 minutes at full power, turning 4 times unless oven has a turntable. Leave to stand 10 minutes inside or outside the oven, whichever is the most convenient.

4. Uncover, drain and fluff up by stirring with a fork.

Pilau Rice   Serves 4 (F)

Middle Eastern in origin, Pilau Rice (also called Pilav, Pilaf or Pilaff) has many facets, but this version is one of the simplest and enhanced with raisins and toasted pine nuts. Partner it with microwaved roast lamb or chicken joints though vegetarians may well settle for omelets or scrambled eggs.

2 tblsp salad oil
6oz (175g) onions, peeled and grated
8oz (225g) easy-cook, long grain rice
1pt (575ml) boiling chicken or vegetable stock
2oz (50g) seedless raisins
1oz (25g) toasted pine nuts (page 225)
½ level tsp salt

1. Pour oil into an 8 inch (20cm) fairly deep and round glass or pottery dish and heat 1 minute at full power. Leave uncovered.

2. Stir in onions and rice. Leave uncovered and cook 4 minutes at full power.

3. Mix in remaining ingredients. Cover with cling film then puncture twice with the tip of a knife.

4. Cook 17 minutes at full power, turning dish 4 times unless oven has a turntable.

5. Leave to stand 8 minutes inside or outside the oven, whichever is the most convenient, so that rice grains absorb all the liquid.

6. Uncover, fluff up with a fork and serve.

Mild Curry Rice   Serves 6 to 8 (F)

Attractively flavoured and coloured, this Mild Curry Rice makes an amiable accompaniment to fish, egg and poultry dishes and should please all those who enjoy oriental food.

1oz (25g) butter or margarine
10oz (275g) onion, peeled and grated
8oz (225g) Basmati rice
1 large bay leaf
2 cloves
seeds from 4 opened-out cardamom pods
2 rounded tblsp mild curry powder
1 level tsp salt
1pt (575ml) boiling chicken or vegetable stock
2 rounded tblsp mango chutney

1. Melt butter or margarine in a 4pt (2·25 litre) glass or pottery dish for 1 to 1½ minutes at defrost setting. Leave uncovered. Add onion. Cook, uncovered, for 5 minutes at full power.

2. Stir in all remaining ingredients. Cover dish with cling film, then puncture twice with the tip of a knife.

3. Cook 18 minutes at full power, turning dish 4 times unless oven has a turntable.

4. Leave to stand 8 minutes inside or outside the oven, whichever is the most convenient, so that rice grains absorb all the liquid. Uncover.

5. Fluff up with a fork and serve.

Peanut Rice   Serves 6 to 8 (F)

An attractive accompaniment – serve it with poultry or fish, even hardboiled eggs for a vegetarian-style main course.

8oz (225g) easy-cook, long grain rice

2oz (50g) toasted peanuts (page 226), skins rubbed off then nuts coarsely chopped

1 pint (575ml) meat or vegetable stock

1 level tsp dried dill weed

½ to 1 level tsp salt

½oz (15g) butter or margarine, at kitchen temperature

1. Sprinkle rice into a large and fairly shallow glass or pottery dish. A comfortable size is one measuring about 10 inches (25cm) in diameter by 2 inches (5cm) in depth.

2. Stir in rest of ingredients. Cover with an inverted plate or cling film. If using the latter, puncture twice with the tip of a knife. Alternatively, cover with matching lid.

3. Cook 15 minutes at full power, turning dish 4 times unless oven has a turntable. Leave to stand 5 minutes inside or outside the oven, whichever is the most convenient.

4. Uncover and fluff up rice by tossing gently with a fork. Serve hot.

BRAZIL NUT RICE   Serves 6 to 8 (F)

If you have a food processor, thinly slice 2 to 3oz (50 to 75g) brazils. Toast under the grill. Add to the rice instead of peanuts.

Eastern Gold Rice   Serves 6 (F)

A fluff of brilliant colour and a warm flavour reminiscent of the Middle East. A lovely accompaniment to kebabs or lamb roasts.

2oz (50g) dried apricots

hot water

1oz (25g) pine nuts

8oz (225g) easy-cook, long grain rice

1 chicken stock cube

1pt (575ml) boiling water

1 level tsp salt

½ level tsp saffron strands, crushed in a mortar with pestle

1. Wash apricots thoroughly and put into a cup. Add hot water to cover. Top with a saucer. Microwave for 2 minutes at full power. Drain. Snip into small pieces with scissors.

2. Toast pine nuts under the grill until deep gold, or follow microwave directions on page 225.

3. Tip rice into a deep dish. Crumble over stock cube then mix in water, salt and saffron. Add prepared apricots and nuts.

4. Stir round. Cover with cling film, then puncture twice with the tip of a knife. Alternatively, cover with matching lid.

5. Cook for 15 minutes at full power, turning dish 4 times unless oven has a turntable.

6. Uncover then fluff up with a fork. Serve hot.

Italian-Style Risotto   Serves 4 to 6 (F)

Classic, as only an Italian dish can be, this Risotto contains the marrow from a beef bone, its fair share of wine and one of the country's most renowned cheeses – Parmesan – for sprinkling over the top.

2oz (50g) butter
4oz (125g) onions, peeled and chopped
1oz (25g) beef bone marrow, sliced or diced
8oz (225g) easy-cook, Italian round grain rice
¾pt (425ml) boiling chicken stock
½pt (275ml) dry white wine
4 saffron strands soaked in an egg cup of water
½ level tsp salt
grated Parmesan cheese (about 2oz or 50g)

1. Put half the butter into a 3pt (1·75 litre) glass or pottery dish and melt for 1 to 1½ minutes at defrost setting. Leave uncovered.

2. Stir in onions and bone marrow. Cook, uncovered, 5 minutes at full power, stirring twice.

3. Mix in rice, boiling stock and the wine. Cover with a plate or matching lid and cook 14 minutes at full power, stirring twice with a fork.

4. Uncover. Add rest of butter, saffron strands and liquid, salt and 1oz (25g) Parmesan cheese.

5. Cook, uncovered, until rice grains have absorbed all the mixture; depending on the rice, this could take from 4 to 8 minutes. Fork-stir at the end of every 2 minutes, working gently to prevent breaking up the rice.

6. Spoon out on to plates and sprinkle each portion with rest of Parmesan chese.

Dry Pasta – to cook   Serves 4 (F)

Choose spaghetti (broken into thirds to ensure even cooking), macaroni, shells, bows, wheels or any other fancy shapes. Allow 8oz (225g) for 4 people. Put into a large glass or pottery dish. Add 1½pt (850ml) boiling water, 1 level teaspoon salt and two of salad oil as it helps to prevent the pasta from sticking together. Leave uncovered. Cook 12 to 15 minutes at full power, stirring gently 4 times. Remove from oven, cover and leave to stand for another 6 to 8 minutes or until pasta swells and absorbs most of the liquid. Drain and use as required. For very small pasta (pastini) and vermicelli, cook at full power for 10 minutes only.

FRESH PASTA – TO COOK   Serves 4

Follow directions above but allow only 1 pint (575ml) boiling water to 8oz (225g) fresh pasta. Cook, uncovered, for half the time of dry pasta. Cover. Stand 5 minutes then drain and serve.

TIP: All pasta is improved if, after draining, it is tossed with a little butter or margarine for extra glisten.

SPAGHETTI BOLOGNESE   Serves 4

Cook dry or fresh pasta as above. Drain. Transfer to 4 plates. Coat with about two-thirds of the Bolognese sauce, given on page 42. Sprinkle each serving with grated Parmesan cheese.

Pasta Ham Casserole   Picture p. 151   Serves 4

Fast food from home makes appetising sense and this carefree casserole is both filling and nutritious, a good companion to salad or cooked vegetables such as beans, peas, sprouts or even a mixture.

8oz (225g) pasta shells

1½pt (850ml) boiling water

1 rounded tsp salt

2 tsp salad oil

1 can condensed cream of mushroom soup

4oz (125g) lean ham, chopped

4oz (125g) button mushrooms, sliced

1 level tsp prepared mustard

seasoning to taste

4oz (125g) Cheddar cheese, finely grated

1. Put pasta shells into a large glass or pottery dish. Add boiling water, salt and oil. Cook, uncovered, for 10 minutes at full power. Stir 3 times with spoon, taking care not to break up shells.

2. Remove from oven, cover with a plate and leave to stand for 10 minutes. Drain and return to dish.

3. Stir in soup, ham, mushrooms and mustard. Season to taste with salt and pepper. Sprinkle with cheese.

4. Leave uncovered and re-heat 5 minutes at full power, turning dish 3 times unless oven has a turntable.

Spaghetti Carbonara   Picture p. 152   Serves 6

A classic from Italy, delightfully simple to make and with an element of chic. Serve it with a green salad tossed in a mild dressing and garnish with black olives, capers and rolls of anchovy fillets.

8oz (225g) spaghetti, snapped into thirds

1½pt (850ml) boiling water

1 rounded tsp salt

2 tsp salad oil

7oz (200g) lean bacon, chopped

2 tblsp milk + 2 Grade 2 eggs beaten together

4oz (125g) Cheddar or Gruyére cheese, finely grated

4 tblsp double cream

salt and pepper to taste

paprika

1. Put spaghetti into a 3pt (1·75 litre) glass or pottery dish. Add boiling water, salt and oil. Cook, uncovered, for 15 minutes at full power. Stir at least 3 times. Remove from oven.

2. Cover with a plate and leave to stand a further 5 minutes when spaghetti should be more swollen and a little bit softer. Drain and return to dish. Re-cover with a plate to keep hot.

3. Put chopped bacon into a separate small dish. Cover with a plate and cook 4 minutes at full power, stirring once.

4. Add to spaghetti with beaten milk and eggs, cheese, cream and seasoning to taste. Toss with 2 spoons. Cover with plate again then reheat 5 minutes at full power to give egg and milk mixture a chance to scramble.

5. Uncover. Toss gently to mix and sprinkle with paprika. Serve straight away, while still very hot.

Spaghetti with Sweet-Sour Sauce   Picture p. 152   Serves 4

Appetising and colourful, I can see this easy-style main course becoming a firm family favourite with its colourful appearance and oriental overtones.

8oz (225g) spaghetti, snapped into thirds

1½pt (850ml) boiling water

1 rounded tsp salt

2 tsp salad oil

1oz (50g) butter or margarine

8oz (225g) onion, peeled and chopped

12oz (350g) pork fillet, cut into thin strips

¼tsp dried minced garlic

1 rounded tblsp tubed or canned tomato purée

1 level tblsp cornflour

1 can (12oz or 340g) pineapple chunks

3oz (75g) red pepper, de-seeded and chopped

3oz (75g) green pepper, de-seeded and chopped

¼ level tsp ginger

1 tblsp soy sauce

salt and pepper to taste

1. Put spaghetti into a 4pt (2·25 litre) glass or pottery dish. Add boiling water, salt and oil. Cook, uncovered, for 10 minutes at full power. Stir at least 3 times. Remove from oven.

2. Cover with a plate and leave to stand while preparing sweet-sour mixture. Put butter or margarine into 3pt (1·75 litre) glass or pottery dish and melt 1 to 1½ minutes at defrost setting. Add onions. Cover dish with plate and cook 2 minutes at full power.

3. Gently stir in all remaining ingredients. Cover with a plate or matching lid. Cook 15 minutes, stirring 3 times.

4. Reheat spaghetti for 2 minutes. Drain. Spoon into a serving dish and top with sweet-sour pork mixture. Serve straight away.

Macaroni Chicken Curry   Picture p. 152   Serves 6

A useful and imaginative way of using up cold chicken, though any other kind of cooked meat may be used. Worth keeping on hand for Christmas and Easter!

8oz (225g) elbow macaroni
1½pt (850ml) boiling water
1 rounded tsp salt
2 tsp salad oil
1½oz (40g) butter or margarine
6oz (175g) onions, peeled and chopped
3oz (75g) red or green pepper, de-seeded and cut into small dice
1oz (25g) plain flour
2 rounded tsp curry powder (mild or hot, depending on taste)
2 level tblsp tubed or canned tomato purée
8oz (225g) cold cooked chicken, cut into small cubes
¾pt (425ml) chicken stock
½ level tsp garlic salt
1 level tsp salt
1 level tsp turmeric
3 rounded tblsp apple purée

1. Put macaroni into a 3pt (1·75 litre) glass or pottery dish. Add boiling water, salt and oil. Cook, uncovered, for 15 minutes at full power. Stir 3 times. Remove from oven. Stir again.

2. Cover with a plate and leave to stand while preparing chicken mixture. Put butter or margarine into a 3pt (1·75 litre) glass or pottery dish. Melt, uncovered, 1½ to 2 minutes at defrost setting.

3. Mix in onions and pepper. Cover with a plate. Cook 3 minutes at full power.

4. Gradually blend in rest of ingredients. Again cover with a plate and cook until very hot and thickened; 8 to 9 minutes at full power, stirring 3 times.

5. Drain macaroni and transfer to serving dish. Spoon chicken mixture over the top. Accompany with chutney. If liked, garnish with lemon slices and parsley.

Family Pasta Pot   Serves 4 generously

A useful dish if you happen to have leftover meat to use up such as boiled bacon, cooked smoked gammon, even sausages. It's an economical meal for midweek with plenty of colour and flavour. Serve it with Brussels sprouts and carrots, or even cooked red cabbage for novelty.

1oz (25g) butter or margarine, at kitchen temperature

6oz (175g) onions, peeled and chopped

8oz (225g) pasta bows or shells (uncooked)

8oz (225g) tomatoes, blanched and skinned then chopped

12oz (350g) boiled bacon, gammon or cold cooked sausages, cubed

1¼pt (725ml) hot stock, made with cubes and water

1 level tsp salt

1 level tsp mixed herbs

1 level tblsp tubed or canned tomato purée

1. Put butter or margarine into a 3 to 3½pt (1.75 to 2 litre) round glass or pottery dish. Leave uncovered and melt for 1 to 1½ minutes at defrost setting. Stir in onions. Continue to cook, still uncovered, for 2 minutes at full power.

2. Mix in pasta bows or shells and tomatoes then add either the bacon, gammon or cold cooked sausages.

3. Combine stock with rest of ingredients, pour into dish of pasta and mix well. Cover with cling film, then puncture twice with the tip of a knife. Alternatively, cover with a matching lid.

4. Cook 25 minutes at full power, turning dish 4 times unless oven has a turntable. Leave to stand 5 minutes inside or outside the oven, whichever is the most convenient.

5. Uncover. Stir round and serve with accompaniments as suggested above.

Tortellini Verdi   Serves 3 to 4 as a main course; 8 as a starter in soup

Compact little cases of fresh pasta, enclosing a cheese or meat filling, are becoming increasingly available from supermarket chains and speciality food shops. Cooking them in the microwave poses no problems at all and in fact they work beautifully, retaining a pale green colour and 'al dente' or firm texture which all Italian cooks recommend. Whether green or white, toss with butter or margarine and serve with a dusting of grated Parmesan cheese. Or add to clear soup as a starter.

8 to 9oz (225 to 250g) fresh tortellini (green or white)

1pt (575ml) boiling water

1 level tsp salt

1. Put all ingredients into a 3pt (1·75 litre) glass or pottery dish.

2. Cook, uncovered, for 10 minutes at full power. Stir 4 times.

3. Continue to cook a further 3 to 5 minutes when tortellini should be plump and almost double in size.

4. Drain and serve as suggested above.

Lasagne

Serves 4 to 6 (F)

Microwave 6oz (175g) lasagne leaves as previously directed for dry or fresh pasta but cook *only 3 or 4 leaves at a time* so that lasagne can move about in the liquid. Lift out on to a clean tea towel and leave to drain. When all the lasagne has been cooked, assemble the layers. Grease an 8 inch (20cm) square glass or pottery dish and fill with alternate layers of cooked lasagne, Bolognese sauce (page 42) and Cheese sauce (page 40). Begin with lasagne and end with a layer of Cheese sauce. Sprinkle top with 1oz (25g) grated Parmesan cheese, 1oz (25g) melted butter or margarine and paprika. Reheat, uncovered, for 10 to 15 minutes at full power. The time will vary depending on whether the sauces were hot, warm or cold.

TIP: Watch the level of the water as each batch of lasagne is cooked and top up with extra boiling water if necessary.

LASAGNE VERDI   **Serves 4 to 6 (F)**

Use green lasagne instead of white.

BROWN LASAGNE   **Serves 4 to 6 (F)**

Use wholewheat (brown) lasagne instead of white.

Fruit

Defrosting Frozen Fruit

	DEFROST (50%)	COMMENTS
APPLES 1lb (450g)	7 minutes Stand 8 minutes	Put into dish or bowl. Cover with plate or matching lid. Stir gently when partially thawed, bringing softer fruit from edge of dish to centre.
BLACKBERRIES	8 minutes Stand 7 minutes	As above.
BLACKCURRANTS	5 minutes Stand 6 minutes	As above.
CHERRIES	4 minutes Stand 5 minutes	As above.
GOOSEBERRIES	7 to 8 minutes Stand 7 minutes	As above.
RHUBARB	8 minutes Stand 8 minutes	As above.
STRAWBERRIES	6 minutes Stand 6 minutes	As above.

Cooking Fresh Fruit

	COOK/HEAT (100%)	COMMENTS
APPLES, 1lb (450g)	7 to 8 minutes	Peel, core and slice apples. Put into dish or bowl with 2 tablespoons boiling water. Sprinkle with 4oz (125g) caster sugar. Cover with plate or matching lid. Stir during cooking. For pulpy fruit, allow 1 minute *less* cooking time than suggested, beat fruit to purée then stir in sugar. Cover. Reheat $1\frac{1}{2}$ minutes when sugar should have melted completely. Remove from oven and stir round.
APRICOTS 1lb (450g)	8 to 9 minutes	Halve, stone and wash apricots. Put into dish or bowl with 4 tablespoons boiling water. Sprinkle with 4oz (125g) caster sugar. Cover with plate or matching lid. Stir during cooking. For pulpy fruit, see apples.
BLACKBERRIES 1lb (450g)	5 to 7 minutes	Hull the berries and wash well. Put into dish or bowl with 2 tablespoons boiling water. Sprinkle with 4oz (125g) caster sugar. Cover with plate or matching lid. Stir during cooking. For pulpy fruit, see apples.

	COOK/HEAT (100%)	COMMENTS
BLACKCURRANTS 1lb (450g)	8 to 10 minutes	Remove currants from stalks and wash well. Put into dish or bowl with 4 tablespoons boiling water. Sprinkle with 4oz (125g) caster sugar. Cover with plate or matching lid. Stir during cooking. If skins remain tough, cook for an extra $\frac{1}{2}$ to 1 minute. For pulpy fruit, see apples then blend currant and sugar mixture to smooth purée in food processor or blender goblet.
DAMSONS 1lb (450g)	8 to 10 minutes	Wash damsons and slit each with sharp knife. Put into dish or bowl with 4 tablespoons boiling water. Sprinkle with 5 to 6oz (150 to 175g) caster sugar. Cover with plate or matching lid. Stir during cooking. Do not pulp because of stones.
GOOSEBERRIES 1lb (450g)	6 to 7 minutes	Top and tail gooseberries. Wash and put into dish or bowl with 4 tablespoons boiling water. Sprinkle with 5 to 6oz (150 to 175g) caster sugar. Cover with plate or matching lid. Stir during cooking. For pulpy fruit, see apples.
PEACHES 1lb (450g)	5 to 7 minutes	Halve, stone and wash the peaches. Put into dish or bowl with 2 tablespoons boiling water and 1 tablespoon lemon juice. Sprinkle with 4oz (125g) caster sugar. Cover with plate or matching lid. Stir during cooking. For pulpy fruit, see apples.
PEARS 1lb (450g)	8 to 10 minutes	Peel, halve and core the pears. Arrange in dish or bowl. Put 3 tablespoons boiling water into jug. Partially dissolve 3oz (75g) caster sugar in the water and add 3 or 4 cloves. Pour over fruit and cover bowl with plate or matching lid. Stir during cooking but take care not to break up the pear halves. Do not pulp.
PLUMS and GREENGAGES 1LB (450g)	5 to 7 minutes	Stone and wash the fruit. Put into dish or bowl with 4 tablespoons boiling water. Sprinkle with 4oz (125g) caster sugar and the grated peel or half a lemon. Cover with plate or matching lid. Stir during cooking. For pulpy fruit, see apples.
RHUBARB 1lb (450g)	7 to 9 minutes	Trim and wash the rhubarb and cut into small pieces. Put into dish or bowl with 2 tablespoons boiling water. Sprinkle with 5oz (150g) caster sugar and the grated peel of one lemon or small orange. Cover with plate or matching lid. Stir during cooking. For pulpy fruit, see apples.

Puddings and Desserts

Puddings and desserts, the treat of the nation, are represented here in all their glory and if you are astonished at a baked apple taking only 5 minutes to cook in the microwave, you will be even more surprised to learn that a steamed suet pudding takes even less!

Speed, economy of fuel and almost instant success characterise this collection of old and new favourites but, for more detailed guidelines, I would ask you please to read the introduction to the cake section as part of it is applicable to this section as well.

Tipsy Cake   Picture p. 185   Serves 6 to 8

Tipsy Cake, in up-to-date terminology, is a trifle but this one is much, much better than average and closer to the grand affairs of yesteryear which our elders would have us believe were infinitely superior to modern copies! And maybe it's true. In my version of edible Victoriana, real Egg Custard sauce (page 47) is the base, apricots the fruit, rum the flavour, cream and chocolate the decorations. It's rich and lavish, a pretty party piece to show off with and lovely as a festive sweet for Christmas or Easter – or both.

2 chocolate Swiss rolls, cream filled and thinly sliced

1 can (14½oz or 420g) apricot halves, drained

2 tblsp dark rum

Egg Custard sauce (page 47), freshly made with 1pt (575ml) milk etc

¼pt (150ml) double cream

1 rounded tblsp caster sugar

about 2oz (50g) plain chocolate (left as a bar and *not* broken up)

1. Press 6 slices of Swiss roll against the sides of a round, glass serving bowl about 8 inches (20cm) in diameter and no taller than 3 inches (7½cm).

2. Reserve 6 apricot halves for decoration. Coarsely chop remainder. Almost fill centre of bowl with broken-up Swiss roll slices and apricots. Soak with rum and 4 tablespoons apricot syrup.

3. Pour just over half the hot custard into the bowl, making sure it coats the sides as shown in the picture and also the cake and fruit. Spoon rest of custard over the top. Cover and cool.

4. Chill 3 to 4 hours in the refrigerator. Before serving, decorate top edge with reserved apricot halves. Whip cream until thick, sweeten with sugar then pipe or spoon whirls or mounds in between the fruit.

5. Decorate middle with chocolate curls, made by standing chocolate on one long edge and running a vegetable peeler towards you along the opposite edge. Hold bar securely.

TIP: For total convenience, use 2 cans (each 15oz or 425ml) canned custard. Tip contents into a dish, cover with a plate and heat 2½ to 3 minutes at full power. Stir round and use.

SHERRY TRIFLE   Serves 8 to 10

If preferred, follow recipe for Tipsy Cake but use 2 jam-filled Swiss rolls and flavour with sweet sherry instead of rum.

Chocolate Roulade Cuts into about 10 slices (F)

Grand, stylish and heaven to eat is the only way I can describe this very rich and sumptuous chocolate roll, filled with plain or flavoured whipped cream. For me, personally, it works better in the microwave than it does when baked conventionally and is a marvellous centrepiece at dinner parties or luncheons, though rather too sophisticated for the teatable. It does need a large capacity oven.

5 Grade 2 eggs
$\frac{1}{8}$ tsp lemon juice
5oz (150g) caster sugar
2oz (50g) cocoa powder + $\frac{1}{2}$oz (15g) cornflour sifted together twice onto a plate
1 tblsp boiling water
icing sugar

FILLING
$\frac{1}{2}$pt (275ml) double cream
2 level tblsp caster sugar
2 tblsp cold milk

1. Lightly grease a 12 inch (30cm) square plastic tray with shallow sides. Line with non-stick parchment paper, allowing it to protrude 1 inch (2½cm) above top edge of tray all the way round to support mixture as it rises.

2. Separate eggs, putting whites into one bowl and yolks into another. Beat whites to a stiff snow with the lemon juice, using electric beaters for speed.

3. Add sugar to yolks and beat until very thick and pale in colour. Stir in cocoa and cornflour mixture, thinning down with the boiling water.

4. When smooth and evenly combined, gently beat in one-third of the egg whites. Finally fold in remaining whites with a large metal spoon or spatula, cutting smartly across base of bowl then flipping mixture over and over on itself.

5. Spread evenly into prepared tray and cook, uncovered, 7½ to 8 minutes at full power, turning once. Remove from oven and inspect. If cake is very tacky along the edges, cook a further ½ to 1 minute.

6. Take out of oven and leave, in the tray, until completely cold. Turn out on to a piece of greaseproof paper or foil *thickly* dusted with sifted icing sugar. Carefully and gently peel away lining paper.

7. To complete, whip cream until thick then stir in sugar and milk. Re-whip *briefly* then spread over Roulade. Roll up with the help of the paper on which it is standing.

8. The Roulade will crack but this is quite in order. Dredge thickly with more sifted icing sugar then, using two fish slices or large spatulas, transfer to a dish. Serve cut in slices.

CHOCOLATE CRUNCH ROULADE Cuts into about 10 slices

Add a crumbled chocolate flake bar to the cream filling.

BLACK FOREST CHERRY ROULADE Cuts into 10 slices

Flavour cream with 1 tablespoon Kirsch or cherry brandy instead of milk then add 1 large crushed milk flake bar and 2 heaped tablespoons canned cherry pie filling.

BRANDY ROULADE   Cuts into 10 slices

Flavour cream with 2 tablespoons brandy instead of milk.

NUT ROULADE   Cuts into 10 slices

Make as first Roulade but add 1 teaspoon vanilla to cream in addition to sugar and milk. Just before using, fold in 1oz (25g) finely chopped walnuts or toasted hazelnuts.

YULE LOG

Make Roulade as directed in first recipe. Cut a 2 inch (5cm) slice diagonally off one end and stand on top of Roulade to look like a baby log. Dredge with sifted icing sugar and add Christmas decorations to taste.

Coffee Roulade   Cuts into about 10 slices (F)

Another stunning dessert, as easy to make as the Chocolate Roulade and just as much a party piece. I have filled the roll with coffee cream but it would work just as well with lemon or orange, as you can see from the directions below.

5 Grade 2 eggs

$\frac{1}{8}$ tsp lemon juice

5oz (150g) caster sugar

$2\frac{1}{2}$oz (65g) cornflour

1 tsp vanilla essence

1 tblsp boiling water

icing sugar

FILLING

2 rounded tsp instant coffee powder or granules

3 tsp hot water

$\frac{1}{2}$pt (275ml) double cream, taken from the refrigerator

2 rounded tblsp caster sugar

1. Lightly grease a 12 inch (30cm) plastic tray with shallow sides. Line with non-stick parchment paper, allowing it to protrude 1 inch ($2\frac{1}{2}$cm) above top edge of tray all the way round to support mixture as it rises.

2. Separate eggs, putting whites into one bowl and yolks into another. Beat whites to a stiff snow with the lemon juice, using electric beaters for speed.

3. Add sugar to yolks and beat until very thick and pale in colour. Stir in cornflour, thinning down with vanilla essence and the boiling water.

4. When smooth and evenly-combined, gently beat in one-third of the egg whites. Finally fold in remaining whites with a large metal spoon or spatula, cutting smartly across base of bowl then flipping mixture over and over on itself.

5. Spread evenly into prepared tray and cook, uncovered, $7\frac{1}{2}$ to 8 minutes at full power, turning once. Remove from oven and inspect. If cake is very tacky along the edges, cook a further $\frac{1}{2}$ to 1 minute.

6. Take out of oven and leave, in the tray, until completely cold. Turn out on to a piece of greaseproof paper or foil *thickly* dusted with sifted icing sugar. Carefully and gently peel away lining paper.

7. To complete, mix coffee with water and leave until almost cold. Whip cream until thick then gently stir in coffee and sugar. Re-whip *briefly* then spread over roulade. Roll up with the help of the paper on which it is standing.

8. Roulade will crack but this is quite in order. Dredge thickly with more sifted icing sugar then, using two fish slices or large spatulas, transfer to a dish. Serve cut in slices.

LEMON ROULADE   Cuts into 10 slices

Make as Coffee Roulade but add 2 level teaspoons finely grated lemon peel to the cake mixture just before the cornflour. Omit vanilla and thin down with water only. Flavour cream with 1 level teaspoon finely grated lemon peel instead of coffee.

ORANGE ROULADE   Cuts into 10 slices

Make as above but use orange peel instead of lemon.

Louisiana Spice Pie   Serves 8

A dream of a pie if ever there was one, remarkable for its beautiful flavour and texture, an ideal dinner party show-piece. It is made with a filling of spicy sweet potatoes and is a variation of a dessert I tried out when visiting the deep south of the USA.

shortcrust pastry made with 6oz (175g) plain flour and 3oz (75g) fat etc
1 egg yolk, beaten

FILLING
1lb (450g) sweet potatoes, freshly cooked as directed on page 142.
3oz (75g) caster sugar
1 rounded tsp mixed spice
3 Grade 2 eggs
$\frac{1}{4}$pt (150ml) cold milk
1oz (25g) melted butter

1. Roll out pastry fairly thinly and use to line a 20cm (8 inch) glass or pottery fluted flan dish. Prick well all over, especially where sides join base.

2. Cook, uncovered, for 6 minutes at full power, turning dish 4 times unless oven has a turntable. If pastry has bulged in places, press down very gently with fingers protected by oven gloves.

3. Brush all over with yolk to seal up holes then cook, uncovered, a further minute at full power. Remove from oven and leave to stand temporarily while preparing filling.

4. Drain sweet potatoes and mash finely or, for smoother texture, work to a purée in blender goblet or food processor.

5. Tip into bowl and leave until cold. Add remaining ingredients and beat well until smoothly mixed. Spoon into pastry case, leave uncovered.

6. Cook for 22 to 25 minutes at defrost setting, when filling should be set, turning 4 times unless oven has a turntable. Leave until just warm then cut into portions and serve topped with lightly whipped cream or vanilla ice cream.

Chilled Cheesecake   Serves 8 to 10

A joy to eat, this is a melt-in-the-mouth cheesecake that 'cooks' quietly in the refrigerator.

BASE

2oz (50g) butter or margarine

4oz (125g) digestive biscuits, finely crushed

2oz (50g) caster sugar

FILLING

4 level tsp gelatine (that means 1 envelope of 0·40oz or 11g plus 1 extra tsp from second envelope)

3 tblsp cold water

2 Grade 3 eggs

1lb (450g) curd cheese

$\frac{1}{4}$pt (150ml) double cream

4oz (125g) caster sugar

finely grated peel and strained juice of 1 medium lemon

1 tsp vanilla essence

1. Put butter or margarine into a basin and melt $1\frac{1}{2}$ to 2 minutes at defrost setting. Stir in crumbs and caster sugar then spread over base and sides of a buttered, 8 inch (20cm) spring clip tin. Tilt tin so that a thin coating of crumb mixture coats the sides.

2. For filling, put gelatine into a cup with 2 tablespoons water. Cover with a saucer and heat $1\frac{3}{4}$ to 2 minutes at defrost setting when gelatine should have melted. Add rest of water and stir briskly until mixture is clear.

3. Put all remaining ingredients into a food processor or blender goblet. Add gelatine and run machine until smooth, wiping down sides twice.

4. Pour into tin over crumbs. Refrigerate until set. To serve, dip a knife into hot water and run round sides of cake two or three times to loosen. Unclip tin and remove hinged sides. Stand cake, still on its metal base, on to a doyley-lined plate.

5. Cut into portions with a knife dipped in cold water. Keep any leftovers in the refrigerator.

Raspberry Cream Crescent   Serves 6

A dream of a sweet, this would be impossible to make in a conventional oven, so the microwave triumphs yet again! It consists of a walnut 'omelet' based on egg whites, folded round double cream and raspberries. I keep this one for New Year's Eve, using frozen raspberries, as it somehow teams admirably with 'bubbly' at the end of the party meal and brings with it the promise of summer skies and holidays to come.

3 egg whites from Grade 2 eggs

$\frac{1}{8}$ tsp lemon juice

6oz (175g) caster sugar

3oz (75g) walnuts, finely ground in blender or food processor

$\frac{1}{4}$pt (150ml) double cream

8oz (225g) raspberries, thawed if frozen and crushed

icing sugar

1. Line the base of an 8 inch (20cm) round glass or pottery dish, no taller than 2 or 3 inches (5 to 7·5cm), with non-stick parchment paper. For safety and to prevent sticking, lightly grease the inside of the dish first.

2. Whisk egg whites and lemon juice together until very stiff. Gradually beat in sugar and continue beating until meringue is thick and heavy in texture. Fold in walnuts with a metal spoon.

3. Spread smoothly into the prepared dish. Leave uncovered and cook 5 minutes at full power, turning dish once. Remove from microwave, leave until lukewarm then invert on to a piece of foil or greaseproof paper sprinkled thickly with sifted icing sugar.

4. When completely cold, remove lining paper. Whip cream until thick and gently fold in raspberries. Pile over one half of the walnut 'omelet'. Fold over so that the filling shows, dust with extra icing sugar and transfer to a serving dish. Chill lightly in the refrigerator before serving.

TIP: If making in the summer, use fresh raspberries.

Chocolate Pear Advocaat Mousse   Serves 6

A heady confection for special occasions, a dream over canned pears.

2 level tsp gelatine

2 tblsp cold water

1 bar (3$\frac{1}{2}$oz or 100g) plain chocolate

2 Grade 3 eggs, separated

$\frac{1}{4}$pt (150ml) advocaat

1 can (15oz or 425g) pear halves in juice or syrup, drained

2 level tblsp chopped walnuts

1. Shower gelatine into a small glass bowl. Add water. Stir round and cover with a saucer. Heat 1$\frac{1}{2}$ to 1$\frac{3}{4}$ minutes at defrost setting.

2. Remove from oven and stir round to ensure gelatine has dissolved. Leave aside temporarily.

3. Break up chocolate and put into a bowl. Leave uncovered and heat for 3 to 3$\frac{1}{2}$ minutes at defrost setting, stirring once. Add gelatine, egg yolks and advocaat then beat in well.

4. Cover and refrigerate until just beginning to thicken and set. Beat egg whites to a stiff snow. With a large metal spoon, gently fold into chocolate mixture.

5. Divide drained pears between 6 sundae dishes then top with chocolate mousse. Sprinkle with nuts and refrigerate until set.

Chocolate Mousse   Serves 4

The now famous Chocolate Mousse that has made such a noteworthy contribution to gracious living. It is child's play with a microwave.

1 bar (3½oz or 100g) plain chocolate, broken into pieces

½oz (15g) butter

4 Grade 3 eggs, at kitchen temperature and separated

1. Put chocolate into a glass or pottery bowl or basin. Add butter.

2. Leave uncovered and heat for 3½ to 3¾ minutes at defrost setting or until both have melted. Stir once.

3. Beat in egg yolks. Whip egg whites to a stiff foam and fold smoothly into chocolate mixture with a large metal spoon.

4. Divide equally between 4 wine-type glasses and chill in the refrigerator until firm.

CHOCOLATE MOCHA MOUSSE   Serves 4

Make as Chocolate Mousse but heat in 2 level teaspoons instant coffee powder with the egg yolks.

CHOCOLATE RUM, SHERRY OR PEPPERMINT MOUSSE   Serves 4

Make as Chocolate Mousse but beat in 1 teaspoon rum, sherry or peppermint essence with the egg yolks.

CHOCOLATE ORANGE MOUSSE   Serves 4

Make as Chocolate mousse but beat in 1 rounded teaspoon very finely grated orange peel with the egg yolks.

CHOCOLATE CREAM MOUSSE   Serves 4

Make as Chocolate Mousse. When set, decorate top with softly whipped cream.

Bread and Butter Pudding   Serves 4 to 6

Very few can resist the temptation of one of Britain's best loved puddings and although the microwave version lacks the traditional golden brown and crispy top, it passes muster all the same and is much appreciated by men of all ages.

6 medium or 4 large slices of white bread (4 to 4½oz or 125 to 140g)
2oz (50g) butter, softened
2oz (50g) currants
2oz (50g) caster sugar
1pt (575ml) cold milk
3 Grade 3 eggs
1oz (25g) demerara sugar
nutmeg

1. Leave crusts on bread then spread slices with butter, taking it right to the edges. Cut each slice into 4 squares.

2. Well-butter a 3pt (1·75 litre) deepish glass or pottery dish. Arrange half the bread squares over the base, buttered sides facing.

3. Sprinkle with currants and caster sugar then top with remaining bread squares, also buttered sides facing.

4. Pour milk into a bowl, leave uncovered and warm for 3 minutes at full power. Beat in eggs then pour gently over bread and butter in dish.

5. Sprinkle with the demerara sugar and nutmeg. Leave uncovered and cook 30 minutes at defrost setting, turning dish 3 times unless oven has a turntable. Stand for 5 minutes before serving.

Baked Egg Custard   Serves 3 to 4

Well-liked by almost everyone, Egg Custard responds happily to microwave treatment and shows no signs of separating out or behaving in a temperamental fashion. Just follow the directions. . .

½pt (275ml) evaporated milk or single cream (for extra richness)
3 Grade 3 eggs
1 extra Grade 3 egg yolk
4oz (125g) caster sugar
1 tsp vanilla essence
½ level tsp nutmeg

1. Pour milk or cream into a jug. Leave uncovered and warm 1½ to 2 minutes at full power.

2. Whisk in eggs, egg yolk, sugar and vanilla essence. Strain into a 1¾pt (1 litre) buttered glass or pottery dish then stand in a second dish, capacity 3½ pints or 2 litres.

3. Pour sufficient boiling water into the large dish until it reaches the level of custard in the smaller dish.

4. Sprinkle top of custard with nutmeg then cook for 6 to 8 minutes at full power when custard should be only just set.

5. Take smaller dish of custard out of the larger dish and wipe the sides dry. Leave to stand until centre has set. Serve warm or cold.

Semolina Milk Pudding   VERY GOOD   Serves 4

Satiny-smooth and easily and cleanly made in the microwave, the Semolina Pudding can cook in its own serving dish.

2oz (50g) semolina
2oz (50g) caster sugar
1pt (575ml) cold milk
½oz (15g) butter or margarine

1. Tip semolina into a serving dish. Mix in sugar and milk. Cook, uncovered, for 7 to 8 minutes at full power when pudding should have come to the boil and thickened.

2. Whisk hard at the end of every minute. Finally mix in the butter or margarine. Spoon into dishes and serve while hot.

FLAVOURED SEMOLINA MILK PUDDING   Serves 4

Flavour to taste with essence or grated lemon peel, adding it at the same time as the butter or margarine.

Blackberry and Lemon Pudding   Serves 6

Fragrant and slightly gungy, this is one of the best autumnal puddings I have ever made in the microwave. It's a treat with double cream or custard.

½lb (225g) blackberries, washed and drained
finely grated peel and juice of 1 medium lemon (approximate weight, 4oz or 125g)
8oz (225g) self-raising flour
4oz (125g) butter or block margarine, at kitchen temperature
4oz (125g) dark brown soft sugar
2 Grade 3 eggs, beaten
4 tblsp cold milk

1. Well-grease a dish measuring 7 inches (17·5cm) in diameter by 3 inches (7·5cm) in depth.

2. Crush blackberries. Combine with grated lemon peel and juice. Leave aside temporarily.

3. Sift flour into a bowl. Rub in butter or margarine finely. Toss in sugar.

4. Using a fork, stir to a softish consistency with the fruit mixture, eggs and milk.

5. Spread into prepared dish and cook, uncovered, for 7 to 8 minutes at full power, turning dish 4 times unless oven has turntable. Pudding is ready when it rises to top of dish and *just* loses its shiny top.

6. Leave to stand 5 minutes. Loosen edges then turn out on to a warm dish. Note that pudding will drop slightly but this is perfectly satisfactory.

TIP: Sometimes soft brown sugar develops lumps, so check carefully and break down any that have formed by pressing against the sides of a bowl with the back of a wooden spoon. Alternatively, rub between fingertips.

Nectarine and Blueberry Crumble   Serves 6 (F)

Summer madness, maybe, but just for a brief spell, when nectarines abound and your greengrocer is ambitious enough to stock blueberries, try this exquisite crumble with its vibrant colour, perfumed flavour and enticing crown of spicy sweetness. Cosseted in a blanket of cream, there is little to better such a stunning sweet.

1lb (450g) nectarines

8oz (225g) blueberries, washed

4 tblsp cold water

3oz (75g) caster sugar

TOPPING

6oz (175g) wholewheat flour

3oz (75g) butter or margarine, at kitchen temperature

2 level tsp cinnamon

3oz (75g) demerara sugar

1. Puncture skin of nectarines by nicking once or twice with a knife. Put into bowl and cover with boiling water. Leave 2 minutes. Drain and cover with cold water. Drain again and remove skins.

2. Cut each nectarine in half then twist to separate. Remove stones and cut flesh into slices. Put into a buttered glass or pottery soufflé-type dish, about 3pt (1·75 litre).

3. Mix in blueberries and water. Cover with cling film, then puncture twice with the tip of a knife. Alternatively, cover with a matching lid.

4. Cook 5 minutes at full power, turning dish 3 times unless oven has a turntable. Uncover, add sugar and stir until melted.

5. For crumble, put flour into a bowl. Rub in butter or margarine finely. Toss in cinnamon and sugar. Sprinkle thickly over fruit mixture. Leave uncovered.

6. Cook 4 minutes at full power, turning 4 times unless oven has a turntable. Remove from oven, stand 2 minutes then spoon on to plates.

Cherry Orchard Pudding   Serves 6

Cascading with cherries and sauce, flavoured with lemon and light as a feather, here is a stupendous pudding which cooks in 9 minutes.

1 can (about 14oz or 200g) cherry pie filling

8oz (225g) self-raising flour

4oz (125g) butter or margarine, at kitchen temperature

4oz (125g) caster sugar

finely grated peel of 1 medium washed and dried lemon

2 Grade 2 eggs beaten with 5 tblsp cold milk

1. Well-grease a 3pt (about 1·75 litre) round soufflé-type glass or pottery dish. Cover base with whole can of cherry pie filling.

2. Sift flour into a bowl. Rub in butter or margarine finely with fingertips. Toss in sugar and lemon peel.

3. Using a fork, mix to a soft consistency with the eggs and milk.

4. Spoon gently and evenly over cherries. Leave uncovered and cook 9 minutes at full power, turning dish 3 times unless oven has a turntable.

5. Leave to stand 3 minutes then turn out into a dish (*not* a plate as the cherries and liquid will flow over the sides). Spoon portions on to plates and serve either as it is, or accompany with cream, ice cream or custard.

Jamaican Pudding   Serves 6

An exotic harmony of flavours characterise this very slightly stodgy pudding – the sort of thing men drool over! It is at its best served with single cream or very rich chocolate ice cream.

1 can (13¼oz or 376g) crushed pineapple
8oz (225g) self-raising flour
4oz (125g) butter or block margarine, at kitchen temperature
4oz (125g) light brown soft sugar
2 Grade 3 eggs
3 tblsp cold milk
2 tblsp dark rum
1 rounded tblsp demerara sugar

1. Well-grease a round dish measuring 7 inches (17·5cm) in diameter by 3 inches (7·5cm) in depth.

2. Cover base of dish with half the pineapple and liquid from can. Leave remainder on one side temporarily.

3. Sift flour into bowl. Rub in fat finely then toss in sugar. If sugar seems at all lumpy, continue to rub in until mixture looks like a mass of small breadcrumbs.

4. Add unbeaten eggs, milk, rum and rest of pineapple with liquid from can. Fork-stir to a soft consistency.

5. Spread over pineapple in dish. Cook, uncovered, for 9 minutes at full power, turning dish 4 times unless oven has a turntable.

6. Leave to stand 10 minutes inside or outside the oven, whichever is the most convenient. Invert carefully on to a warm plate then sprinkle with the demerara sugar. Serve while still hot.

Blackcurrant Stodge Pudding   VERY GOOD   Serves 6

I am including this recipe at the special request of my husband and son who regard stodgy, sticky puddings as one of life's ultimate delights! I do not subscribe to that view but as men seem to dote on schoolboy desserts, who am I to argue?

10oz (275g) self-raising flour
5oz (150g) butter or margarine, at kitchen temperature
4oz (125g) soft brown sugar
2 Grade 3 eggs, beaten
1 can (about 14oz or 200g) blackcurrant pie filling*
3 tblsp cold milk

1. Well-grease a 3 pt (about 1·75 litre) round soufflé-type glass or pottery dish.

2. Sift flour into a bowl. Rub in butter or margarine finely. Toss in sugar.

3. Mix to a soft consistency with eggs, pie filling and cold milk, stirring briskly with a fork.

4. Spoon into prepared dish. Leave uncovered and cook 9 minutes at full power, turning dish 3 times unless oven has a turntable.

5. Stand 5 minutes, turn out on to a warm dish and spoon into portions. Good with thick cream.

* OR ANY PIE FILLING

Steamed Suet Syrup Pudding   Serves 4

Unbelievably light in texture and beautifully spongy, this pudding cooks in under five minutes and looks and tastes as though it had been steamed for hours. No mean achievement.

3 level tblsp golden syrup, melted
4oz (125g) self-raising flour
pinch of salt
2oz (50g) finely shredded packeted suet
2oz (50g) caster sugar
1 Grade 3 egg beaten with 6 tblsp cold milk and 1 tsp vanilla essence

1. Well-grease a 2pt (just over 1 litre) pudding basin. Pour syrup into base.

2. Sift flour and salt into a bowl. Toss in suet and sugar.

3. Add beaten egg, milk and essence *all at once* and stir briskly with a fork to mix.

4. Spoon into basin, cover with cling film, then puncture twice with the tip of a knife.

5. Cook 4 to 4½ minutes at full power or until mixture reaches top of basin and just meets the film.

6. Remove from oven, leave to stand 2 minutes then uncover. Turn out on to a plate and serve portions with cream, custard or one of the sweet sauces from the Sauce Section.

STEAMED SUET HONEY PUDDING   Serves 4

Make as Steamed Suet Syrup Pudding, using honey instead of syrup.

STEAMED SUET JAM OR MARMALADE PUDDING   Serves 4

Make as Steamed Suet Syrup Pudding, using jam or marmalade instead of syrup.

Jam Sponge Pudding

Serves 4 to 6

As light as a puff of wind with a fluffy texture and high-rise finish. Wickedly inviting!

3 level tblsp red jam
6oz (175g) self-raising flour
pinch of salt
3oz (75g) butter or margarine, at kitchen temperature
3oz (75g) caster sugar
2 Grade 3 eggs beaten with 3 tblsp milk

1. Spoon jam into a 2½pt (1·5 litre) well-greased pudding basin.

2. Sift flour and salt into a bowl. Rub in butter or margarine finely then toss in caster sugar.

3. Using a fork, stir to a soft consistency with beaten eggs and milk. Spoon into the prepared basin and leave uncovered.

4. Cook 7 to 8 minutes, turning basin twice unless oven has a turntable. Leave to stand 3 or 4 minutes then invert on to a plate. Serve with cream or custard.

ORANGE JAM SPONGE PUDDING (Picture p. 186)

Serves 4 to 6

Make as above, but add the finely grated peel of 1 medium washed and dried orange with the sugar. Add about ½ teaspoon orange colouring essence with eggs and milk.

ALTERNATIVE FLAVOURS

Use 1 teaspoon of any essence to taste, adding it with the eggs and milk. Syrup or honey may also be used instead of the jam.

Spirited Christmas Puddings   Picture p. 187
Makes 2, each enough for 10 servings

Make up Spirited Christmas Cake mixture as directed on page 200. Divide remaining half of mixture between 2 well-greased glass or pottery pudding basins, each 1½pt capacity or 850ml. Leave uncovered. Cook individually, allowing 5 minutes at full power, a rest period of 5 minutes then 2 further minutes cooking at full power.

The puddings may be flamed with alcohol and eaten straight away or left until cold, wrapped in greaseproof paper, overwrapped with foil and left to mature for several weeks. For reheating instructions, see Convenience Food Chart on page 21.

Special Plum Pudding
Makes 2 × 1½pt (just under 1 litre) Puddings (F)

Fabulous. Every year requests pour in for these rich and fruity Christmas puddings which, until now, I have always steamed conventionally. But they work just as well in the microwave and take 14 to 15 minutes each to cook! The inclusion of cherry pie filling gives them instant maturity so they can be made shortly before Christmas and still taste luscious flamed with rum or brandy.

8oz (225g) soft white breadcrumbs, freshly made
4oz (125g) plain flour
1 level tsp mixed spice
1 level tsp cinnamon
¼ level tsp ginger
¼ level tsp nutmeg
6oz (175g) dark brown soft sugar
10oz (275g) finely shredded suet
1¼lb (675g) mixed dried fruit
3 Grade 3 eggs, beaten
1 can (13·6oz or 383g) cherry pie filling (dark fruit)
2 tblsp black treacle

1. Well-grease 2 × 1½pt (850ml) basins.

2. Tip crumbs into a bowl. Sift in flour, spice, cinnamon, ginger and nutmeg.

3. Add sugar, suet and dried fruit then mix to a softish mixture by stirring in the eggs, cherry pie filling and black treacle.

4. When evenly combined, spread smoothly into prepared basins. Leave uncovered then cook each pudding for 6 minutes at full power, turning 4 times unless oven has a turntable.

5. Stand 5 minutes then cook a further 3 minutes, turning twice. Remove from oven and leave to stand in the basins until lukewarm.

6. Turn out on to greaseproof paper and wrap when cold. Overwrap with foil and store in the cool until required. Reheat as directed in the chart on page 21. Decorate. Flame with alcohol.

Calypso Pudding
Serves 4 to 5

One of those soft and comforting puddings, always welcome in the depths of winter with an overcoat of hot custard. It cooks in around 8 minutes.

8oz (225g) self-raising flour
4oz (125g) butter or margarine (or mixture), at room temperature
4oz (125g) caster sugar
2 Grade 2 eggs, well-beaten
5 rounded tblsp crushed pineapple with syrup
1 tblsp liquid coffee and chicory essence

1. Well-grease a 3pt (1·75 litre) straight-sided round dish. A glass or pottery soufflé dish is ideal.

2. Sift flour into a bowl. Rub in fats finely. Toss in sugar.

3. Using a fork, stir to a soft consistency with the eggs, pineapple and coffee.

4. Spread smoothly into prepared dish. Leave uncovered and cook 6½ minutes at full power, turning dish 3 times unless oven has a turntable.

5. Invert on to a plate and if centre looks tacky, return to oven and cook an extra 1 to 1¼ minutes.

6. Spoon into bowls and coat with hot custard.

Lime Floss
Serves 4 generously

Not for haute cuisiners but certainly for Mum, Dad and the children who all look forward to something light and refreshing at the end of a filling meal. It's nourishing too.

1 lime flavour jelly ($4\frac{3}{4}$oz or 135g)

hot water

$\frac{1}{2}$pt (275ml) cold Egg Custard sauce (page 47) or the same amount of canned custard

2 Grade 2 eggs, separated

$\frac{1}{2}$ tsp lemon juice

hundreds and thousands for decoration

1. Divide jelly up into cubes and put into a measuring jug. Cover with a saucer. Melt for 2 to $2\frac{1}{2}$ minutes at defrost setting.

2. Make up to $\frac{1}{2}$pt (275ml) with hot water then whisk into the Egg Custard sauce or canned custard. Follow by beating in yolks.

3. Cover. Leave until cold then refrigerate until just beginning to thicken and set.

4. Whisk egg whites and lemon juice to a stiff snow. Beat one-third into jelly mixture then fold in remainder.

5. Divide equally between 4 dishes and set in the refrigerator. Sprinkle with hundreds and thousands before serving.

LEMON FLOSS — Serves 4 GENEROUSLY

Just as cooling and tangy, make as above but use a lemon jelly instead of lime.

Orchard Fruit Crush
Serves 4

What a blissful flavour this sweet has, yet it's the easiest thing in the world to put together and, with its glowing colour, contributes admirably to autumnal mellowness. It is quite splendid with a topping of whipped cream, dusted prudently with very finely grated lemon peel and cinnamon.

1 tangerine flavour packet jelly ($4\frac{3}{4}$oz or 135g)

hot water

8oz (225g) blackberries, washed and crushed with a fork

apple juice (I use Copella, available from some supermarkets and health food shops)

4 rounded tblsp whipped cream

1 rounded tsp grated lemon peel

$\frac{1}{2}$ level tsp cinnamon

1. Divide jelly up into cubes and put into a measuring jug. Cover with a saucer. Melt for 2 to $2\frac{1}{2}$ minutes at defrost setting.

2. Stir in hot water and blackberries then make up to 1 pint (575ml) with apple juice. Leave until cold.

3. Refrigerate, covered, until just beginning to thicken and set. Spoon into 4 dishes and leave in the refrigerator until firm.

4. Top with cream then sprinkle with the lemon peel and cinnamon.

Wine-Spiced Peaches   Serves 6 to 8

For sophisticates, I present a heady and sweet-smelling dessert to savour with pleasure. Serve it with pieces of bought or homemade sponge cake, crisp biscuits or wedges of gingerbread.

8 large peaches
lemon juice
½pt (275ml) dry red wine
6oz (175g) caster sugar
1 by 2 inch (5cm) piece of cinnamon stick
4 cloves
2 medium oranges, peeled and thinly sliced

1. Puncture skin of peaches by nicking once or twice with a knife. Put into a bowl and cover with boiling water. Leave 2 minutes. Drain and cover with cold water. Drain again and remove skins.

2. Cut each peach in half and twist to separate. Remove stones. Brush halves all over with lemon juice.

3. Put wine, sugar, cinnamon stick and cloves into an 8 by 2 inch (20 by 5cm) round dish. Cover with an inverted plate and heat 4 minutes at full power.

4. Stir round, add peaches (cut sides down) and baste with wine mixture. Stud here and there with orange slices and cover with cling film, puncturing it twice with the tip of a knife. Alternatively, cover with a matching lid.

5. Cook 10 minutes at full power, turning dish 4 times unless oven has a turntable. Leave to cool then refrigerate until well-chilled before serving.

Festive Apple Snow   Picture p. 189   Serves 4

As a change from the abundant foods of Christmas, this lighter dessert should be well-received, flavoured as it is with apple purée and the ever popular vanilla.

1 packet (1·1oz or 31g) vanilla blancmange powder
¾pt (425ml) cold milk
3 level tblsp caster sugar
4oz (125g) apple purée
2 egg whites (Grade 2 eggs)
2 to 3 drops lemon juice

1. Tip blancmange powder into a 2pt (1·75 litre) bowl and mix smoothly with 4 tablespoons of the measured milk.

2. Heat rest of milk, uncovered, for 4 minutes at full power. Blend with blancmange mixture then stir in the sugar.

3. Return to oven and cook, uncovered, at full power until mixture boils and thickens; about 2½ minutes. Beat at the end of every ½ minute to ensure smoothness.

4. Remove from oven and whisk in the apple purée. Cool to lukewarm. Beat egg whites to a stiff snow with lemon juice. Fold into blancmange mixture gently and smoothly with a large metal spoon.

5. Spread evenly into a bowl then cover and chill several hours in the refrigerator. Add seasonal decorations just before serving.

Cranberry Parfait   Serves 6

A luscious dessert which I learned how to make in Finland from locally grown berries; smaller than the ones we import from America but with a wonderful wild and woodland taste and aroma. And so easy.

Make up any of the Cranberry sauces given on page 46. Leave until completely cold. Whip ½pt (275ml) double cream and 2 tablespoons milk until thick. Fold in the Cranberry sauce then divide mixture between 6 dishes. Refrigerate at least 2 hours before serving.

Compote of Arabian Nights   Serves 6

The subtle tones of this sweet are reminiscent of magic carpets and mosques, sand dunes and palm trees, gardens and orchards! It's mystical hot and even more so cold as the flavours intensify and the whole thing becomes perfumed with roses and apricots. A 7-minute wonder.

1 lb (450g) *fresh* dates, at their best during the winter months

1 lb (450g) bananas, just ripe but not bruised

juice of ½ medium lemon

3 tblsp apricot brandy

½ tsp rose flavouring essence

1 rounded tblsp demerara sugar

1. Skin dates, slit each in half and remove stones. Put into a 3pt (1·75 litre) serving dish.

2. Peel bananas and slice directly on top of dates. Sprinkle with lemon juice then add apricot brandy and rose essence.

3. Toss gently together and sprinkle with the sugar. Cover with cling film, then puncture twice with the tip of a knife.

4. Cook 7 minutes at full power, turning dish 3 times unless oven has a turntable. Serve as suggested above.

Honeyed Raspberry Marshmallow Dream   Serves 6

I make this in the winter with frozen raspberries and think of summer! This rather grand sweet can be put together in under 10 minutes and then served hot or cold with sponge cake and cream. It has a wonderful fragrance, is a delight to eat and eminently suitable for entertaining.

1lb (450g) raspberries, thawed if frozen
3 slightly rounded tblsp clear honey
1 packet (about 4½oz or 240g) pink and white marshmallows

1. Put raspberries and honey into a 3pt (1·75 litre) dish. Cover with a plate and cook 5 minutes at full power, turning twice.

2. Remove from oven and uncover. Arrange marshmallows close together on top, forming a wide border.

3. Leave uncovered and cook a further 3 minutes at full power. If serving cold, cool off in the kitchen, cover and refrigerate about 8 hours. If serving hot, spoon out on to plates and serve straight away.

'Mulled' Pineapple   Serves 8 to 10

A wonderful way with fresh, ripe pineapple. It has a unique fragrance and needs no accompaniments at all, just appreciative diners.

8oz (225g) caster sugar
¼pt (150ml) cold water
1 whole pineapple, about 4lb or 2kg
6 cloves
2 inch (5cm) piece of cinnamon stick
⅛ tsp nutmeg
4 tblsp ruby port
1 tblsp brandy

1. Put sugar and water into a 4pt (2·25 litre) dish. Stir round and cover with a plate. Cook 8 minutes at full power.

2. Meanwhile, peel pineapple and cut flesh into wedges. Removal of centre core is a matter of personal choice but is not necessary.

3. Add to dish with rest of ingredients. Stir well to mix. Cover with cling film, then puncture twice with the tip of a knife.

4. Cook 10 minutes at full power, turning dish 3 or 4 times unless oven has a turntable.

5. Remove from microwave, leave until cold then refrigerate overnight. Before serving, bring back to room temperature and spoon into dishes.

TIP: The pineapple may be served hot but is not as flavoursome.

Lemon Spiced Pears   Picture p. 188   Serves 6

A palate tingler this one, with autumnal dessert pears coated in a spicy lemon sauce.

3oz (75g) light brown soft sugar

½pt (275ml) water

4 tblsp dry white wine

2 inch (5cm) piece of cinnamon stick

3 cloves

6 medium-sized dessert pears (not over-soft)

2½oz (71g) packet lemon meringue pie filling mix

¼pt (150ml) milk, at kitchen temperature

2 level tsp finely grated lemon peel

extra shreds of lemon peel for decoration

1. Put sugar, water, wine, cinnamon stick and cloves into a 3pt (1·75 litre) dish. Heat 3 minutes, uncovered, at full power.

2. Remove from oven. Peel pears, leaving in stalks. Stand upright in dish. Baste with syrup mixture. Slide dish into a roasting bag and loosely seal top with a non-metal tie.

3. Cook 6 to 8 minutes at full power, turning dish 4 times unless oven has a turntable.

4. Remove from microwave and carefully strain syrup from pears directly into a jug. Stir in lemon filling mix. Cover with a saucer. Cook 2 minutes at full power or until mixture comes to the boil. Whisk every ½ minute.

5. Cool slightly then beat in milk and lemon peel. Refrigerate pears and lemon sauce until well-chilled. Pour some sauce over pears before serving and decorate with strips of lemon peel. Hand extra sauce separately.

Baked Apples   Allow 1 per person

As though by magic these puff up like soufflés in minutes, and may be cooked individually or in a group. The flavour is very fresh and more fruity than if baked conventionally.

Wash and dry as many cooking apples as are required, up to a maximum of 4. Remove cores from stalk ends then score a line round each apple with a sharp knife, about one-third of the way down from the top. Fill with sugar and/or dried fruit, honey, jam or even lemon curd. Top each with a teaspoon of butter or margarine.

For 1 apple: Stand on a plate and leave uncovered. Cook 3 to 4 minutes at full power.

For 2 apples: Arrange in a small dish. Cook 5 minutes.

For 3 apples: Arrange in a dish like a triangle. Cook 6 to 7 minutes.

For 4 apples: Arrange in a dish to form a square. Cook 8 to 10 minutes.

Cakes and Biscuits

'Surely not cakes?' has been a comment thrust at me often enough by those who assume a microwave cooker is unable to cope with the complexities of sponges, Victoria sandwiches, Christmas cakes and even shortbread, and I call them sceptics, one and all!

Cakes in a microwave, contrary to misguided belief, work like a charm and what they sometimes lack in colour, they make up for in texture and flavour. I have to admit a microwave will never give you that traditional golden brown, crusty finish associated with conventional baking but a dusting of icing or caster sugar, a topping of glacé icing, a casing of butter cream or a whoosh of whipped cream all serve to cover, camouflage if you like, the pale tops and sides of light-by-nature cakes although chocolate, spice or even coffee ones can stand on their own feet with no disguises.

And the speed is incredible. A sponge in 4 minutes, a Christmas cake in 30, shortbread in 20 and cheesecake in 12. Plus, of course, a cool kitchen and no tins to clean. Cakes of all kinds can be made in glass, china, pottery or firm plastic dishes; indeed anything non-metallic that resembles cake tins in shape. For total cleanliness and ease of removal, the dishes may be base and side-lined smoothly with cling film, or greased and the bases lined with greaseproof or non-stick parchment paper. The advantage of film is that the cakes can be lifted out of the dishes without being inverted; useful if the texture is fragile as in the case of sponges.

One trick is essential for success. The cake mixture itself (with the exception of fatless sponges) should be made wetter than usual to prevent dryness and, for the same reason, some cakes should be covered with film while cooking.

When the cake is ready, based on the timings given in individual recipes, it may still look fractionally damp on top. This is quite in order. As it cools in the dish, the heat will spread from the outside through to the centre and after about 15 minutes or so standing time, the cake should be completely cooked. If not, give it an extra half to one minute, checking every 15 seconds. Even after a cake has been turned out, seemingly cooked, the base may be runny. All that is then necessary is to return the cake, on its plate, to the microwave for a brief spell of cooking, again checking about 4 times every minute. The thing to avoid is overcooking, otherwise the cake will dry out, harden and in some cases become inedible.

Sponge Cake Serves 6 (F)

Here is the traditional fatless sponge which turns out like a dream in 4 minutes flat.

3oz (75g) caster sugar

3 Grade 3 eggs, at kitchen temperature

3oz (75g) plain flour, sifted twice for maximum aeration

1. Line a 7 by 4 inch (17·5 by 10cm) round glass dish smoothly with cling film. Make sure the dish is the same diameter top and bottom.

2. Tip sugar into a bowl and warm 2 minutes at defrost setting. Add eggs and whisk steadily until mixture bulks up to almost 1 pint (575ml) and is as thick as whipped cream. It should also be very pale in colour.

3. Cut and fold in flour with a metal spoon, cutting side edge of spoon along base of bowl and flipping mixture over and over on itself until smoothly and evenly combined.

4. Spoon into prepared dish, leave uncovered and cook 4 minutes at full power.

5. Remove from oven and leave to stand 10 minutes before lifting out of dish (by holding edges of cling film) and transferring to a wire rack.

6. Peel film away when cake is completely cold. Afterwards dust with caster sugar, cut into wedges and eat the same day; fatless sponges go stale quickly and are best made and consumed within hours.

NOTE: *Cake rises up to the top of the dish during the initial stages of cooking and falls to a depth of 2 to 3 inches (5 to 7·5cm). This is quite in order.*

JAM AND CREAM SPONGE Serves 6 (F)

Make Sponge Cake as directed. When completely cold, split in half horizontally and sandwich together with jam and whipped cream.

CHOCOLATE NUT GATEAU Serves 8 (F)

Make Sponge Cake as directed then split in half horizontally when completely cold. For Chocolate Cream, melt 1 bar ($3\frac{1}{2}$oz or 100g) plain chocolate as directed in the chart on page 22. Leave until cool but still liquid. Whip $\frac{1}{2}$ pint (275ml) double cream until thick. Gently whisk in melted chocolate alternately with 2 tablespoons of milk. Sandwich cake together with just under half the Chocolate Cream. Pile remainder thickly over the top then stud with hazelnuts or walnuts. Chill lightly before serving. To ring the changes, fill split cake with a little apricot jam. Spread Chocolate Cream over top and sides then dust with a sifting of drinking chocolate powder. Decorate with nuts. Chill lightly before serving.

185

Tipsy Cake. See page 164.

Orange Jam Sponge Pudding. See page 176.

Right: *Spirited Christmas Pudding. See page 176.*

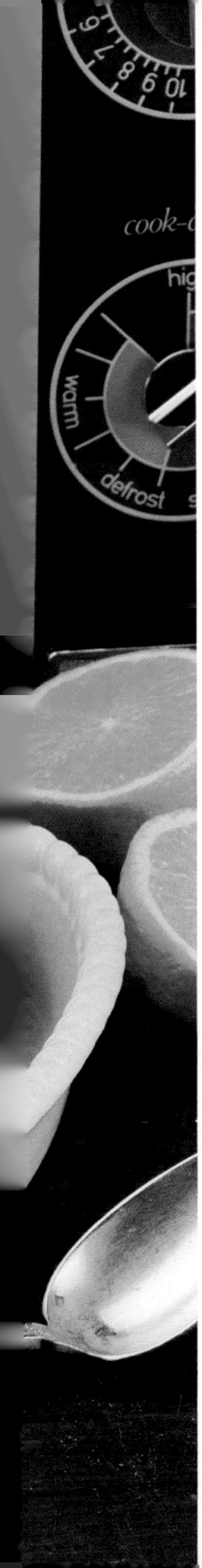

Festive Apple Snow. See page 179.

Left: *Lemon Spiced Pears. See page 182.*

Chocolate Christmas Cake. See page 197.

Coffee Apricot Gateau. See page 201.

Coffee Truffles. See page 215.

Genoese Cake   Serves 6 (F)

This is an enriched version of the Sponge Cake and much favoured by chefs. It, too, lends itself to variations and creative fantasies.

Make exactly as Sponge Cake on page 184 but increase sugar by 1oz (25g) and eggs to 4 instead of 3. *Gently and lightly* cut and fold in 2oz (50g) melted unsalted butter alternately with 4oz (125g) plain flour. Leave uncovered and cook $5\frac{1}{2}$ to 6 minutes at full power. Stand for 7 minutes, remove from dish and cool as directed for the Sponge Cake. Dust with caster sugar before serving.

CITRUS CREAM TORTE   Serves 8 (F)

Split Genoese Cake in half horizontally when completely cold. Sandwich together with fine shred orange marmalade. Coat top and sides with $\frac{1}{2}$pt (275ml) whipped double cream, sweetened to taste with sifted icing sugar and flavoured with the finely grated peel of 1 medium lemon. Dust with a light dusting of instant coffee powder. Chill lightly before serving.

ORANGE CREAM RUM TORTE   Serves 8 (F)

Make as above but flavour sweetened whipped cream with 2 level teaspoons finely grated orange peel and 2 tablespoons rum. Sprinkle with chocolate flake bar, first finely crushed. Chill lightly before serving.

STRAWBERRY AND CREAM CAKE   Serves 8 (F)

Make as Genoese Cake. Split in half horizontally and fill with 8oz (225g) sliced strawberries mixed with $\frac{1}{4}$pt (150ml) sweetened whipped cream. Mound top with a further $\frac{1}{4}$pt (150ml) whipped cream and stud with whole berries.

Victoria Sandwich Cake

Serves 8 (F)

A fine-textured cake, Britain's favourite, and a joy to make in the microwave.

6oz (175g) self-raising flour

pinch of salt

6oz (175g) butter or margarine, at kitchen temperature

6oz (175g) caster sugar

3 Grade 3 eggs, at kitchen temperature

3 tblsp cold milk

v.6.

1. Well-grease 2 × 8 inch (20cm) round glass Pyrex dishes of about 2 inches (5cm) in depth. Line bases with rounds of greaseproof paper.

2. Sift flour and salt on to a plate. Put butter or margarine and sugar into a bowl and cream until very light and fluffy in consistency; also much paler than its original colour.

3. Beat in eggs, one at a time, adding 1 tablespoon sifted flour with each.

4. Lastly fold in rest of flour alternately with milk. When evenly combined, spread smoothly into prepared dishes. Cover each with cling film, then puncture twice with the tip of a knife.

5. Cook cakes individually for 4 minutes at full power, turning once unless oven has a turntable.

6. Remove from oven and uncover. Leave until lukewarm then invert on to greaseproof or parchment paper sprinkled with caster sugar.

7. Sandwich together, when completely cold, with jam or lemon curd. Store leftovers in an airtight tin.

VANILLA (F)
Add 1 level teaspoon vanilla essence to fat and sugar before creaming.

OTHER FLAVOURING ESSENCES (F)
As above.

FRESH LEMON OR ORANGE (F)
Add 2 level teaspoons finely grated lemon or orange peel to fat and sugar before creaming.

NUT (F)
Add 2oz (50g) finely chopped walnuts to mixture after beating in eggs. Allow an extra $\frac{1}{2}$ minute cooking time.

CUP CAKES   Makes 18 (F)

Make up Victoria Sandwich Cake recipe or any of the listed variations. Spoon into 18 paper cake cases. Stand, 6 at a time, on floor of oven in a ring. Allow plenty of space between each then bake 2 to 2½ minutes or until well-risen. Decorate when cold with a dusting of icing sugar or by coating tops with glacé icing, made by sifting 8oz (225g) icing sugar into a bowl and mixing to a fairly stiff icing with fruit juice, cold coffee or alcohol. Decorate with nuts, glacé cherries, chocolate drops etc.

FAIRY CAKES   Makes 18 (F)

Add 2oz (50g) currants after beating in eggs. Allow an extra ½ minute cooking time.

SEED CAKES   Makes 18(F)

Add 2 level teaspoons caraway seeds and 1 teaspoon vanilla essence to the creamed fat and sugar.

FRUIT AND NUT CUP CAKES   Makes 18 (F)

Add 1oz (25g) sultanas or raisins and 1oz (25g) chopped walnuts or hazelnuts after beating in eggs.

HASTY MADELEINES   Makes 18 (F)

Make Cup Cakes as directed. When just cold, spread tops of each with red jam and sprinkle with desiccated coconut. Top each with ½ a glacé cherry and 2 leaves cut from green angelica.

TIP FOR FANCY GATEAU

Make up the Victoria Sandwich Cake as directed, then turn into Gateaux by following any of the ideas given in the recipes for Sponge and Genoese Cakes. Instead of cream, use Butter Cream made by creaming 6oz (175g) softened butter (unsalted for preference) with 8oz (225g) sifted icing sugar, 1 tablespoon milk and flavourings to taste. Colour, if liked, with a few drops of edible food colouring.

Family Fruit Cake *Excellent*   Serves 8 (F)

The sort of cut-and-come-again cake that is close to the heart of all families. It cooks in an amazing 7 minutes and keeps perfectly in an airtight container.

8oz (225g) self-raising flour
pinch of salt
1½ level tsp mixed spice
4oz (125g) butter or margarine, at kitchen temperature
4oz (125g) light brown soft sugar
6oz (175g) mixed dried fruit
2 Grade 3 eggs beaten with 5 tblsp cold milk
icing sugar

1. Sift flour, salt and spice into a bowl. Rub in butter or margarine finely. Toss in sugar and fruit.

2. Add eggs and milk in one go, then stir to a soft consistency with a fork.

3. Spread evenly into an 8 inch (20cm) round glass dish (deep and straight-sided), closely lined with cling film. Leave uncovered.

4. Cook 6½ to 7 minutes at full power when cake should be well-risen and beginning to pull away from sides.

5. Remove from microwave and leave to stand ¼ hour. Lift out on to a wire cooling rack and carefully peel away film.

6. When completely cold, dust top with sifted icing sugar.

DATE AND WALNUT CAKE   Serves 8 (F)

Make as Family Fruit Cake, but use 3oz (75g) *each*, chopped dates and walnuts instead of mixed dried fruit.

CHOCOLATE DOT CAKE   Serves 8 (F)

Make as Family Fruit Cake, but use 4oz (125g) chocolate dots instead of fruit.

GINGER AND LEMON CAKE   Serves 8 (F)

Make as Family Fruit Cake, but use 4oz (125g) chopped preserved ginger instead of the fruit, and toss in the finely grated peel of 1 washed and dried lemon at the same time.

Chocolate Christmas Cake   Picture p. 190 *EXCELLENT*   Serves 10

Unusual, to say the least, is this deeply dark chocolate Christmas cake filled with vanilla butter cream and snow-iced in traditional style.

2 level tblsp cocoa powder

4 tblsp boiling water

6oz (175g) butter or block margarine, at kitchen temperature and soft

6oz (175g) dark brown soft sugar

1 tsp vanilla essence

3 Grade 3 eggs, at room temperature

6oz (175g) self-raising flour

1 tblsp black treacle

FILLING

3oz (75g) butter, softened

6oz (175g) icing sugar, sifted

2 tsp cold milk

1 tsp vanilla essence

ROYAL ICING

2 egg whites from Grade 4 or 5 eggs

12oz (350g) icing sugar, sifted

$\frac{1}{2}$ tsp lemon juice

2 or 3 drops glycerine (to prevent icing from hardening too much)

1. Line an 8 inch (20cm) straight-sided, soufflé type dish with cling film, making sure it is as smooth as possible and pressed well into the edges where sides meet base.

2. Mix cocoa powder smoothly with boiling water and leave aside temporarily.

3. Cream butter, sugar and essence together until light and fluffy. Beat in eggs singly, adding a tablespoon of flour with each. *BEAT IN COCOA* Fold in rest of flour with black treacle.

4. When smooth and evenly combined, transfer to prepared dish. Leave uncovered and cook 6 to $6\frac{1}{2}$ minutes at full power, turning 4 times unless oven has a turntable. Cake is ready when well-risen and no longer damp-looking on top. *Do not overcook or cake will toughen and shrink.*

5. Remove from oven and leave to stand until lukewarm. Lift out of dish and place on a wire cooling rack.

6. Peel back film and leave cake until cold. Remove film altogether and cut cake into 3 layers.

7. To make butter cream filling, beat butter until light then gradually whisk in sugar. Add milk and essence and mix in well. Use to sandwich layers together.

8. For icing, whip whites to a light foam (but *not* to a stiff snow) then gradually beat in sugar. When icing forms peaks, mix in lemon juice and glycerine.

9. Swirl over top and sides of cake and transfer to a board. When half set, add seasonal decorations to taste. Leave 1 day before cutting.

Devil's Food Cake   Serves 8 generously (F)

American inspired, this is a dark-as-night chocolate cake with the texture of velvet and flavour of heaven. It converts easily into a party gateau, just as easily into a teatable centrepiece or, with a dusting of icing sugar, into a family-style cake which the children will adore. Best whizzed in a food processor, you can have the whole thing made and cooked in well under 30 minutes.

$3\frac{1}{2}$oz (100g) plain chocolate, at kitchen temperature

1oz (25g) cocoa powder

8oz (225g) plain flour

1 level tsp bicarbonate of soda

5oz (150g) butter, at kitchen temperature

7oz (200g) light brown soft sugar

2 Grade 2 eggs

$\frac{1}{2}$ tsp vanilla essence

$\frac{1}{4}$pt (150ml) buttermilk

3 tblsp cold milk

1. Line a 7 by $3\frac{1}{2}$ inch (17 by 9cm) soufflé-type dish with cling film, making sure it lies smoothly over base and sides.

2. Break up chocolate and put into a glass or pottery dish. Leave uncovered and melt 3 to $3\frac{1}{2}$ minutes at defrost setting. When ready, the chocolate will remain in its original shaped pieces but should be soft when touched. Remove from microwave and scrape into food processor bowl.

3. Add all remaining ingredients and blend until smooth. Stop machine, wipe down sides of bowl with spatula and continue to run machine for a further $\frac{1}{2}$ minute.

4. Transfer to prepared dish, leave uncovered and cook 8 minutes at full power, turning dish 4 times unless oven has a turntable.

5. Remove from oven. Cool to lukewarm in the dish (the cake drops to $2\frac{1}{2}$ inches or 6·25cm in depth and shrinks away from the sides but this is quite in order) then carefully lift out on to a wire cooling rack. Peel back film and leave until completely cold.

FAMILY DEVIL'S FOOD CAKE   Serves 8 generously

Cover top with a lacy doyley then dredge with icing sugar, first tipped into a fine mesh sieve. Carefully lift off doyley and the pattern will remain on top.

CHOCOLATE RUM GATEAU   Serves 8 to 10

Make cake as previously directed then cut in half horizontally and leave aside temporarily. To make Rum Butter Cream, beat 6oz (175g) softened butter until very light in texture. Gradually beat in 12oz (350g) sifted icing sugar alternately with 2oz (50g) melted plain chocolate and 1 tablespoon dark rum. When cream is fluffy in consistency, set aside one quarter then use remainder to fill cake and cover top and sides. Coat sides with finely chopped walnuts or toasted almonds and transfer to a plate. Decorate top with a piping of remaining cream then stud with walnut or toasted almond halves and halved glacé cherries coloured green. Chill lightly in the refrigerator before serving.

MOON DUST CAKE   Serves 8 (F)

Make cake as previously directed and halve horizontally. Whip $\frac{1}{4}$pt (150ml) double cream until thick then stir in 2oz (50g) grated milk chocolate, 1 level tablespoon caster sugar and 1 level teaspoon finely grated lemon peel. Sandwich cake together with cream then swirl remainder thickly over the top. Chill lightly in the refrigerator before serving.

Spirited Christmas Cake   Serves about 15 to 16 (F)

A special cake laden with fruit and alcohol, this will suit any festive occasion from Christmas to birthdays. I have to admit it is very extravagant but the mixture not only makes one family-sized cake, but also converts into 2 succulent Christmas puddings, each of which will serve at least 10 people. When cold, the cake should be wrapped in greaseproof paper, overwrapped with foil and stored in the cool until ready for coating with almond paste and, subsequently, white icing.

¾pt (425ml) sweet sherry

¼pt (150ml) brandy

2 rounded tsp mixed spice

1 tsp vanilla essence

1 rounded tblsp dark brown soft sugar

8oz (225g) sultanas

8oz (225g) seedless raisins

8oz (225g) currants

2oz (50g) chopped mixed peel

2oz (50g) glacé cherries, chopped

4oz (125g) dried apricots, well-washed then snipped with scissors into small pieces

4oz (125g) cooking dates (in a block), finely chopped

finely grated peel of 1 medium orange

4oz (125g) walnuts or toasted almonds (page 224), coarsely chopped

8oz (225g) unsalted butter, melted

12oz (350g) dark brown soft sugar

8oz (225g) self-raising flour

5 Grade 2 eggs, well-beaten (at kitchen temperature)

1. Put sherry and brandy into a *large* bowl. Cover and bring to the boil, allowing 6 to 7 minutes at full power.

2. Add spice, essence, the 1 tablespoon of sugar, sultanas, raisins, currants, mixed peel, glacé cherries, apricots, dates, orange peel and nuts. Mix in very thoroughly.

3. Cover with a plate and warm through for 15 minutes at defrost setting. Stir 4 times.

4. Remove from oven and cover. Leave to stand overnight for flavours to mature. Work in melted butter, sugar, flour and the eggs.

5. Spoon half the mixture into an 8 inch (20cm), 3pt (1·75 litre) capacity soufflé or other similar glass or pottery dish, first lined completely with cling film.

6. Leave uncovered and cook for 30 minutes at defrost setting, turning dish 2 or 3 times unless oven has a turntable. Leave to stand inside the oven for a further 10 minutes.

7. Remove from oven and cool to lukewarm. Carefully lift out of dish with the aid of the film and transfer cake to a wire cooling rack.

8. Peel away film and leave cake until completely cold before wrapping as previously directed. Allow to mature for at least 2 weeks before covering with almond paste.

Coffee Apricot Gateau   Picture p. 191   Serves 8 (F)

A showpiece for special occasions, this luscious gateau can be made in next to no time and is much less complicated to put together than it looks. To freeze, keep unwrapped and leave overnight until hard. Afterwards wrap carefully and place in a box. Unwrap before defrosting to prevent spoiling the coating.

4 digestive biscuits, finely crushed

8oz (225g) butter or block margarine, at kitchen temperature and soft

8oz (225g) dark brown soft sugar

4 Grade 3 eggs, at kitchen temperature

8oz (225g) self-raising flour

3 tblsp coffee and chicory essence

FILLING AND TOPPING

1 can (15oz or 425g) apricot halves

½pt (275ml) double cream

2 tblsp coffee and chicory essence

3oz (75g) flaked and toasted almonds

1. Have ready 2 round glass or pottery buttered dishes, each 8 to 8½ inches (20 to 21·5cm) in diameter by 1 to 1½ inches (2·5 to 3·75cm) in depth. Dust base and sides with crushed biscuits.

2. Cream butter or margarine and sugar together until light and fluffy. Beat in eggs singly, adding a tablespoon of flour with each. Fold in rest of flour alternately with coffee and chicory essence.

3. When smooth and evenly combined, divide evenly between the 2 dishes. Leave uncovered. Bake individually, allowing 5 minutes at full power and turning each 3 times unless oven has a turntable.

4. Leave in dishes until lukewarm then carefully turn out and cool on a wire rack.

5. To complete, drain apricots (keep syrup for drinks, etc.) and coarsely chop up 2 of the halves. Whip cream until thick. Fold in coffee and chicory essence.

6. Take out a quarter of the cream and gently stir in chopped apricots. Use to sandwich both layers of cake together. Transfer to a serving plate.

7. Spread rest of cream over top and sides of cake then decorate top with apricots. Press almonds against sides then refrigerate about 1 hour before serving.

Best Brownies

Makes 12 (F)

Moist and out-of-this-world are the only ways in which I can describe these American-style chocolate squares, my best yet.

3oz (75g) self-raising flour
1oz (25g) cocoa powder
4oz (125g) butter or margarine, at kitchen temperature
8oz (225g) dark brown soft sugar
1 tsp vanilla essence
2 Grade 3 eggs, at kitchen temperature
3 tblsp milk
icing sugar for the top

1. Line an oblong dish, with a base measurement of 12 by 6 inches (30 by 15cm), smoothly with cling film.

2. Sift flour and cocoa powder on to a plate. Put butter or margarine and sugar into a bowl. Add essence and beat until creamy and soft.

3. Beat in eggs individually then, with a metal spoon, stir in flour mixture alternately with milk.

4. When evenly combined, spread smoothly into the prepared dish and cover with cling film. Puncture twice with the tip of a knife.

5. Cook for 6 minutes at full power, turning dish once unless oven has a turntable. Remove from oven and remove cling film cover. Leave Brownies in the dish until lukewarm.

6. Lift out, with cling film lining, on to a wire rack. Allow to cool completely, cut into 12 squares and turn upside down. Sprinkle thickly with icing sugar before serving. Store leftovers in an airtight container.

Chocolate Crunch Cake　　　　　Serves 12

For the grand occasion, when entertaining special friends, even for Christmas, here is a sumptuous chocolate cake made from melted chocolate and butter, enriched with eggs and liqueur, and patchworked with biscuits, fruits and nuts. It cooks, literally, in the refrigerator but the microwave makes fast work of melting the necessary ingredients and, where the chocolate is concerned, prevents overheating and spoilage.

7oz (200g) plain chocolate, at kitchen temperature

8oz (225g) unsalted butter (not margarine as cake may not set), at kitchen temperature

2 Grade 2 eggs

2oz (50g) coarsely chopped nuts, either walnuts, hazels, brazils, toasted cashews or toasted almonds

3oz (75g) mixture of halved glacé cherries and pieces of crystallised pineapple or papaya

1 to 2oz (25 to 50g) crystallised ginger, coarsely chopped (optional)

1 rounded tblsp sifted icing sugar

1 tblsp fruit liqueur – apricot, cherry, banana or the new melon liqueur called Midori

8oz (225g) milk chocolate digestive biscuits, each broken into 8 pieces

1. Line an 8 by 2 inch (20 by 5cm) round or glass pottery dish with cling film.

2. Break up chocolate and put into a large bowl. Leave uncovered and melt 4 to 5 minutes at defrost setting. When ready, the chocolate will remain in its original shaped pieces but should be very soft when touched. Remove from microwave and leave on one side temporarily.

3. Cut butter into chunks and put into a dish. Leave uncovered and melt 2 to $3\frac{1}{2}$ minutes at defrost setting. Beat into the chocolate.

4. Carefully break eggs into a cup and lance the yolk of each with the tip of a knife. Leave uncovered and warm $\frac{1}{2}$ a minute at defrost setting. Beat well.

5. Stir into chocolate and butter mixture then work in nuts, glacé and crystallised fruits, ginger (if used), sugar and liqueur. Finally and gently fold in the biscuits with a large metal spoon.

6. Transfer as smoothly as possible to prepared tin or dish, cover with foil and chill overnight in the refrigerator.

7. Lift out, peel away cling film and transfer to an attractive serving plate. Cut into small wedges to serve.

TIP: Leave cake in the refrigerator in between servings as it tends to soften at room temperature.

CHOCOLATE CRUNCH RUM CAKE　　　　Serves 12
Make as previously directed but use rum instead of fruit liqueur.

CHOCOLATE CRUNCH COFFEE CAKE　　　　Serves 12
Make as previously directed but use coffee liqueur instead of fruit. Alternatively, and for a cake without alcohol, dissolve 2 rounded teaspoons instant coffee powder in hot water and use instead of liqueur.

Golden Spice Cake   Cuts into 10 pieces

A delight for all those on low animal fat diets – this cake is based on vegetable oil and has a remarkably light texture.

8oz (225g) golden syrup
$\frac{1}{4}$pt (150ml) water
3 fluid oz (75ml) salad oil (all vegetable)
2 Grade 3 eggs
2 heaped tblsp apricot jam
8oz (225g) self-raising flour
$\frac{1}{2}$ level tsp bicarbonate of soda
1 level tsp cinnamon
1 level tsp ground ginger

1. Line closely with cling film an oblong glass dish measuring 12 by 7$\frac{1}{2}$ inches (30 by 19cm) at the top, sloping to a base measurement of 10 by 6$\frac{1}{2}$ inches (25 by 16·25cm).

2. Put syrup into a bowl and melt 2 minutes, uncovered, at defrost setting. Beat in water, oil, eggs and jam.

3. Sift in dry ingredients and mix briskly together until smooth. Spread smoothly into prepared dish. Cover with cling film, then puncture twice with the tip of a knife.

4. Cook 7 minutes at full power, turning once. Remove from oven and uncover. Leave until almost cold then invert on to an oblong or oval dish or plate, dusted with icing sugar.

5. If top seems very damp and cake obviously undercooked, return to oven and continue to cook a further 2 minutes or until just dry.

6. Leave until cold and dust top with sifted icing sugar. Cut into 10 pieces. Store leftovers in an airtight container.

Toffee Triangles   Makes 8

A version of flapjack, but this time moist and succulent. Ideal for coffee mornings and informal winter parties.

4oz (125g) butter
2oz (50g) golden syrup
1oz (25g) black treacle
4oz (125g) dark brown soft sugar
8oz (225g) porridge oats

EXCELLENT

1. Well-grease an 8 inch (20cm) round glass or pottery dish of about 2 inches (5cm) in depth.

2. Put butter, syrup, treacle and sugar into a bowl. Leave uncovered and heat for 5 minutes at defrost setting. 4

3. Stir in oats then spread evenly into prepared dish. Leave uncovered and cook 4 minutes at full power.

4. Stand 3 minutes then cook a further 1 minute at full power. Leave until quite cool then cut into 8 triangles with a sharp, round-topped knife.

5. Remove from dish when cold and store in an airtight container.

MUESLI TOFFEE TRIANGLES   Makes 8

Just as delicious but made with muesli. Follow above recipe but use *unsweetened* muesli mix instead of oats.

Gingerbread

Cuts into 8 healthy pieces (F)

Come Hallowe'en and who can resist the heart-warming aroma of Gingerbread wafting from the kitchen? It's a lovely winter cake and cooks in 3 to 4 minutes in the microwave – magically quick, beautifully moist and tender, fragrantly-flavoured.

6oz (175g) plain flour
2 rounded tsp ground ginger
1 level tsp mixed spice
$\frac{1}{2}$ level tsp bicarbonate of soda
4oz (125g) golden syrup
1oz (25g) black treacle
1oz (25g) dark brown soft sugar
1$\frac{1}{2}$oz (40g) lard or white cooking fat
1 Grade 1 or 2 egg, well-beaten
4 tblsp cold milk

V. G.

1. Have ready an oblong pie dish with rim, the inside measuring about 7$\frac{1}{2}$ by 5 by 2$\frac{1}{4}$ inches (19 by 12·5 by about 6cm). Line base and sides smoothly with cling film. Alternatively, use a 6 inch (15cm) glass or pottery soufflé-type dish.

2. Sift flour, ginger, spice and bicarbonate of soda into a fairly large mixing bowl.

3. Put syrup, treacle, brown sugar and lard or cooking fat into a separate bowl. Heat 2 to 3 minutes at full power or until fat has just melted. Do not cover.

4. Remove from oven and stir well to blend. Add to dry ingredients with egg and milk.

5. Mix to a fairly soft consistency with a fork, stirring briskly without beating. Pour into dish and leave uncovered. Cook 3 to 4 minutes at full power, turning dish 4 times unless oven has a turntable. When ready, Gingerbread should be well-risen with a hint of a shine across the top.

6. Leave to stand 10 minutes inside or outside the oven, whichever is the most convenient. Lift out of dish and stand on a wire rack.

7. Peel away film from sides to allow steam to escape. Remove film from underneath when Gingerbread is cold. Store in an air-tight container, and leave 1 day before cutting.

Lemon Cheesecake   Serves 10

A party-sized cheesecake with a dairy fresh flavour and moist, creamy texture. It is best made one day and eaten the next, left in the refrigerator about 12 hours to firm up. A strawberry and raspberry version follow, the former discovered in America's deep south at Patout's restaurant in Louisiana.

BASE

3oz (75g) butter, at kitchen temperature

6oz (175g) digestive biscuits, crushed

2oz (50g) caster sugar

FILLING

2 packets (each 7oz or 200g) cream cheese or 1lb (450g) medium fat curd cheese (available from delicatessens and some supermarkets)

3oz (75g) caster sugar

2 Grade 1 or 2 eggs, at kitchen temperature

1 tsp vanilla essence

1 level tblsp cornflour

finely grated peel and juice of 1 lemon weighing 4oz (125g)

$\frac{1}{4}$pt (150ml) double cream

1 carton (15oz or 142ml) soured cream

1. Melt butter, uncovered, for 2 to $2\frac{1}{2}$ minutes at defrost setting. Stir in biscuit crumbs and sugar. Line an 8 by 2 inch (20 by 5cm) round glass or pottery dish with cling film. Cover base and sides evenly (and the evenly bit is quite important otherwise parts of the cake will be more crusty on the outside than others) with biscuit mixture, bringing it right to the top of the dish. Leave uncovered and cook $2\frac{1}{2}$ minutes at full power.

2. For filling, beat cheese until soft and light then whisk in sugar, eggs, essence, cornflour, lemon peel, lemon juice and the unwhipped cream.

3. When smooth and evenly combined, pour into crumb crust case. Cook 10 to 12 minutes at full power, turning 4 times unless oven has a turntable. The cake is ready when there is some movement to be seen in the middle and the top rises up slightly and just beings to crack.

4. Remove from oven and spread with soured cream which will set on top as the cake evens out and cools.

STRAWBERRY CHEESECAKE   Serves 10

Make exactly as Lemon Cheesecake but omit vanilla essence and the lemon. In their place, add 4oz (125g) fresh or frozen and defrosted strawberries, first puréed in a food processor or blender goblet, or rubbed through a mesh sieve.

RASPBERRY CHEESECAKE   Serves 10

Make as Strawberry Cheesecake, but use raspberry purée instead of strawberry.

Shortbread — Cuts into 12 wedges

Because Shortbread should, traditionally, remain pale after cooking, a microwave oven does it full justice and the results are excellent.

8oz (225g) butter, at kitchen temperature

4oz (125g) caster sugar

12oz (350g) plain flour, sifted

extra caster sugar

1. Grease the base and sides of an 8 by 2 inch (20 by 5cm) round glass or pottery dish with butter.

2. For Shortbread, beat butter and sugar until light and creamy. Stir in flour and spread into prepared dish. Prick all over with a fork.

3. Leave uncovered and cook 20 minutes at defrost setting, turning dish 4 times unless oven has a turntable.

4. Remove from oven and sprinkle with 2 to 3 level teaspoons extra caster sugar.

5. Cut into 12 wedges and leave in the dish until cold. Carefully lift out and store in an airtight container.

Extra Crisp Shortbread — Cuts into 12 wedges

The addition of semolina to the ingredients, and a different method of making, results in a somewhat more crisp shortbread than the one above with a slightly coarse-grained texture.

11oz (325g) plain flour

1oz (25g) semolina

8oz (225g) butter, at kitchen temperature

4oz (125g) caster sugar

extra caster sugar

1. Sift flour into a bowl then toss in semolina. Rub in butter finely. Add sugar.

2. Knead by hand to a dough and spread over a buttered round glass or pottery dish measuring 8 by 2 inches (20 by 5cm). Use fingers to ease dough over base of dish then spread evenly with a knife to make sure there are no thin patches.

3. Prick well all over with a fork. Leave uncovered and cook 20 minutes at defrost setting, turning dish 4 times.

4. Remove from oven and sprinkle with 2 to 3 level teaspoons extra caster sugar.

5. Cut into 12 wedges and leave in the dish until cold. Carefully lift out and store in an airtight container.

ORANGE OR LEMON SHORTBREAD — Cuts into 12 wedges

If making version 1, add the finely grated peel of 1 medium orange or lemon whilst beating butter and sugar.

If making version 2, add the same amount of peel at the same time as the 4oz (125g) caster sugar.

Dutch-Style Cinnamon Shortbread   Cuts into 12 wedges

Sift flour with 3 rounded teaspoons cinnamon. After spreading either version of Shortbread smoothly into dish, brush top with double cream instead of sprinkling with sugar. Leave it for a few minutes to sink in. Gently press 1oz (25g) flaked and toasted almonds (page 224) on to top of Shortbread by way of decoration. Cook, cool and store as directed.

Cake Mixes (Sandwich varieties)

Make up as directed, whisking for *half* the time recommended to prevent over-aeration and a texture full of holes. When adding the second amount of water, *include 1 extra tablespoon*. Divide mixture between 2 by 8 inch (20cm) round glass dishes lined with cling film. Cover with more film and puncture twice with tip of a knife. Cook individually, allowing $2\frac{1}{2}$ to 3 minutes each at full power. Cool about 5 minutes then uncover. Invert on to a wire cooling rack and leave until completely cold before filling as specified on the packet. Dust with icing sugar or ice as directed.

Breads, Buns and Pizzas

Yeast mixtures take well to microwave treatment, the dough rises in about half the time normally needed in a sink of hot water or airing cupboard (favourite warm places), and the resultant dough is well-textured, good-natured and easy to handle. It depends for its success on short bursts of microwave energy followed by periods of standing time. This technique warms the dough in a controlled way, the heat is evenly distributed while the dough is standing, and the process is clean and carefree. Because yeast is quickly killed by excessive heat and immediately stops acting as a raising agent, times given should be closely followed; overheating is damaging.

The risen dough may subsequently be shaped as desired and baked conventionally or, in some cases, cooked in the microwave. What *is* important to remember is that once the dough is in a tin or tins, it must be allowed to rise – or prove – the second time round in a warm place *outside* the microwave oven.

Included in this section, in addition to yeasted goods, are traditional-style soda breads, some rather super bun scones for the tea table, and an old-fashioned fruited malt loaf.

White Bread Dough
Makes 1 loaf or 16 rolls

A standard dough which can be used to good advantage in the microwave for Bap loaves and rolls.

1 level tsp caster sugar

½pt (275ml) water, with the chill off

1 level tsp dried yeast

1lb (450g) plain strong flour

1 level tsp salt or salt substitute (the latter useful for those on low sodium diets)

1oz (25g) butter or margarine

1. Put sugar into a large cup or jug and mix with 6 tablespoons of water. Warm in the microwave for 1 minute at defrost setting, leaving uncovered. Remove from oven.

2. Stir in yeast. Stand about 10 minutes when yeast brew should foam up in the cup or jug and look like a glass of beer with a head.

3. Meanwhile sift flour and salt into a bowl. Warm in the microwave, uncovered, for 1 minute at defrost setting.

4. Rub in butter or margarine finely then mix to a dough with yeast mixture and remaining water.

5. Knead thoroughly until no longer sticky and satiny-smooth, allowing about 10 minutes.

6. Place in a lightly greased or oiled large bowl then cover bowl, not dough itself, with a piece of greased or oiled cling film. Puncture twice with the tip of a knife.

7. Warm in the microwave for 1 minute at defrost setting. Rest 5 minutes. Repeat 3 or 4 times until dough has doubled in size. Re-knead briefly then use conventionally or in the recipes which follow.

BROWN BREAD DOUGH

Follow recipe for White Bread Dough, substituting brown flour or granary meal. Alternatively, use half brown flour and half white.

Bap Rolls   Makes 16 (F)

Use white or brown risen dough for these and knead lightly after the first rising. Divide into 16 equal-sized pieces and shape into flattish rounds. Arrange round the edge of 2 large greased and floured dinner plates, putting 8 rounds on to each. Cover with kitchen paper and return to the microwave. Warm 1 minute at defrost setting then rest for 4 minutes. Repeat 3 or 4 times or until Baps double in size. Sprinkle with white or brown flour and leave uncovered. Cook each plate of rolls for 3 minutes at full power, turning once unless over has a turntable. Cool Baps on a wire rack.

BAP LOAF   Makes 1 (F)

Use white or brown risen dough, knead lightly after first rising then shape into a round of about 2 inches (5cm) in height. Transfer to a greased and floured dinner plate. Cover with kitchen paper and return to microwave. Warm 1 minute at defrost setting then rest for 4 minutes. Repeat 3 or 4 times or until loaf doubles in size. Sprinkle with white or brown flour and leave uncovered. Cook 4 minutes at full power. Cool on a wire rack.

FRUIT BAPS   Rolls or loaf variation (F)

Make as above, tossing in 2oz (50g) dried fruit and 1oz (25g) caster sugar after rubbing in butter or margarine. Cook rolls an extra $\frac{1}{2}$ minute per plate and the whole loaf an extra $\frac{3}{4}$ minute.

Seed Bread   Makes 1 loaf (F)

Use white or brown risen dough, knead lightly after first rising then shape into a ball. Put into a $\frac{3}{4}$pt (375ml) straight-sided, greased round dish. Return to microwave and warm 1 minute at defrost setting then rest for 4 minutes. Repeat 2 or 3 times until dough has doubled in size. Brush with milk or beaten egg and sprinkle with poppy seeds, caraway seeds or toasted sesame seeds (page 225). Cover with kitchen paper and cook 5 minutes at full power, turning dish once unless oven has a turntable. Cook a further 2 minutes. Leave in the dish $\frac{1}{4}$ hour then carefully turn out on to a wire cooling rack.

TIP: Do not eat breads or rolls until completely cold.

TO FRESHEN CONVENTIONALLY BAKED BREAD THAT SEEMS STALE

Put into a paper bag or stand between folds of a clean tea towel. Transfer to the microwave and heat at defrost setting until bread feels slightly warm on the surface. It is now ready for eating.

Fruited Malt Loaf   Makes 2 (F)

A genuine 'golden oldie' for all those who love sticky fruit bread! It is at its best when served sliced and buttered.

1 level tsp caster sugar
$\frac{1}{4}$pt (150ml) water, with the chill off
2 level tsp dried yeast
1lb (450g) plain strong flour
$\frac{1}{2}$ level tsp salt
3oz (75g) mixture of sultanas and raisins
4 level tblsp malt
1 level tblsp black treacle
1oz (25g) butter or margarine
2 to 3 tblsp skimmed milk

1. Put sugar into a large cup or jug and mix with the water and dried yeast. Warm in the microwave for 1 minute at defrost setting, leaving uncovered. Remove from oven.

2. Leave to stand about 10 minutes when yeast brew should foam up in the cup or jug and look like a glass of beer with a head.

3. Meanwhile, sift flour and salt into a bowl then toss in the dried fruits.

4. Put malt, treacle and butter or margarine into a small basin, leave uncovered and melt 3 minutes at defrost setting.

5. Add to flour with yeast liquid and sufficient milk to make a soft dough. Knead thoroughly for 10 minutes then divide into 2 equal-sized pieces.

6. Shape to fit 2 by $1\frac{1}{2}$pt (850ml) oblong glass or pottery dishes, first well-greased. Cover dishes, not dough, with greased or oiled cling film. Puncture twice with the tip of a knife.

7. Warm in the microwave for 1 minute at defrost setting then rest 5 minutes. Repeat 3 or 4 times more or until loaves have doubled in size. Remove film.

8. Place side by side in the oven. Leave uncovered and cook 2 minutes at full power. Reverse position of dishes and cook a further 2 minutes. Repeat once more. Leave to stand 10 minutes then turn loaves out on to a wire cooling rack.

Soda Bread

Makes 4 small triangular loaves (F)

I hesitate to call this Irish Soda Bread because on my visits to Ireland – North and South – I soon discovered they use special flour to achieve a wholesome, nutty-flavoured bread with a dense texture. Mine, I believe, comes a close second and cooks to perfection in the microwave in a matter of minutes.

7 fluid oz (200ml) buttermilk
5 tblsp ordinary milk
12oz (350g) wholewheat flour
4oz (125g) plain white flour
2 level tsp soda bicarbonate
1 level tsp cream of tartar
1 level tsp salt
2oz (50g) butter, margarine or white cooking fat, at kitchen temperature

1. Well-grease a 10 inch (25cm) dinner plate. Beat buttermilk and milk well together.

2. Tip wholewheat flour into a bowl. Sift in white flour with soda bicarbonate, cream of tartar and salt. Rub in fat finely.

3. Add liquid in one go then fork-stir to a soft dough. Gather together with well-floured hands and stand on centre of plate. Shape into a 7 inch (17·5cm) round then make a deepish cross-cut on top with a knife.

4. Dust lightly with white flour and leave uncovered. Cook for 7 minutes at full power, turning plate 4 times unless oven as a turntable. Bread will rise and spread.

5. Leave to stand 10 minutes inside or outside the oven, whichever is the most convenient. When lukewarm, lift on to a cooling rack with the help of a fish slice.

6. Separate into 4 sections and cool completely before cutting. Store in a bread bin up to 2 days only as this type of bread is at its best when eaten freshly made.

SODA BRAN BREAD   Makes 4 small triangular loaves (F)

For all those who find bran helpful in the diet, this loaf should be very welcome. Make exactly as above, adding 4 level tablespoons coarse bran before mixing in liquid.

WHOLEMEAL SODA BREAD   Makes 4 small triangular loaves (F)

Make as basic Soda Bread but use all wholewheat flour and no white.

GRANARY SODA BREAD Makes 4 small triangular loaves (F)

Make as basic Soda Bread but use all granary meal (flour) and no white. Increase milk by 1 tablespoon.

Pizzas Neapolitan   Makes 4

Child's play – almost – in the microwave, these are vibrant and vivacious Pizzas, reminiscent of the people of Naples and its off-shore islands.

2 tblsp salad or olive oil
4oz (125g) onions, peeled and chopped
1 garlic clove, peeled and crushed
5oz (150g) tomato purée
white or brown risen dough
12oz (350g) Mozzarella cheese, grated
2oz (50g) anchovies in oil, drained and separated
4oz (125g) small black olives

1. Put oil, onions and garlic into a 1pt (575ml) dish, leave uncovered and cook 5 minutes at full power, stirring once.

2. Mix in tomato purée and leave on one side temporarily.

3. Knead dough lightly and divide into 4 equal pieces. Roll out into rounds, large enough to cover 4 greased and floured 8 inch (20cm) dinner plates.

4. Ease dough out towards the edges then warm, one plate at a time, for $\frac{1}{2}$ minute at defrost setting. Rest 4 minutes. Repeat 3 or 4 times or until dough doubles in size. Leave uncovered throughout.

5. Spread each with tomato mixture then top with grated cheese. Garnish attractively with anchovies and olives then cook individually, allowing 5 minutes at full power and turning plate twice unless oven has a turntable. Serve piping hot.

Teatime Bun Scones   Makes 8 (F)

On a nippy winter's day, what could be more cheering than a pot of freshly brewed tea and these indulgent Bun Scones, eaten while still warm, drenched in butter and topped with summer strawberry jam or some exotic honey?

8oz (225g) wholemeal flour
1 level tsp cream of tartar
1 level tsp bicarbonate of soda
$\frac{1}{4}$ level tsp salt
1 rounded tblsp caster sugar
1oz (25g) butter or margarine, at kitchen temperature
$\frac{1}{4}$pt (150ml) buttermilk
fresh milk or beaten egg for brushing
extra caster sugar mixed with cinnamon for sprinkling

1. Tip flour into a bowl then sift in cream of tartar, bicarbonate of soda and salt. Toss in sugar then rub in butter or margarine finely.

2. Using a fork, mix to a soft dough with buttermilk. Turn out on to a floured surface and knead quickly and lightly until smooth.

3. Pat or roll out to $\frac{1}{2}$ inch (1·25cm) in thickness then cut into 8 rounds with a $2\frac{1}{4}$ inch (about 4cm) fluted biscuit cutter. Use re-rolled trimmings to make the required number.

4. Place round the edge of a greased 10 inch (25cm) dinner plate. Brush with milk or beaten egg then sprinkle with sugar and cinnamon. Leave uncovered.

5. Cook for 4 minutes at full power, turning plate 4 times unless oven has a turntable. Leave to stand 3 or 4 minutes then transfer to a wire cooling rack. Eat while still warm as suggested above.

Confectionery

Microwave ovens weave their own especial magic where sweet making is concerned and I am constantly surprised at how quick and fuss-free it is to produce the sort of confectionery one can pack up and give as gifts, offer round at home or sell at stalls gracing garden fêtes, school open days and fund-raising events for charity. A short selection follows with these major advantages:

1. They can be made in dishes instead of pans so there is less messy washing up.

2. The mixtures do not boil over.

3. The danger of burning oneself is reduced.

4. The mixtures need not be stirred all the time as when cooked conventionally – just occasionally.

Walnut Candy   Makes 1 lb or 450g

A cross between toffee and fudge, this is a super confection with a lovely, old-fashioned flavour and crumbly texture.

12oz (350g) light brown soft sugar
¼pt (150ml) milk
2oz (50g) golden syrup
1oz (25g) butter
1 tsp vanilla essence
2oz (50g) walnuts, coarsely chopped

1. Well-butter a shallow dish of 1¾pt (1 litre) capacity. It makes no difference whether it is square or round.

2. Put all ingredients, except nuts, into a 3pt (1·75 litre) dish. Leave uncovered and cook 14 minutes at full power, stirring 4 or 5 times.

3. Remove from oven, cool 5 minutes, then stand in the sink. Add cold water to come half way up sides of dish.

4. Leave for a further 8 minutes then lift out and wipe base and sides dry.

5. Add walnuts and beat candy (hard work!) for a few minutes until it starts to lighten.

6. Spread into prepared dish and allow to set. Remove from dish by lifting up with a knife then break candy into pieces.

7. Store in a polythene bag or tin.

BRAZIL NUT CANDY   Makes 1 lb or 450g

Use coarsely chopped brazils instead of walnuts.

Coffee Truffles   Picture p. 192   Makes 15

Classy affairs, with their roots deep set in France! They are decidedly on the rich side and, as can be seen from the photograph, look elegant and presentable in paper sweet cases. The best Truffles I know!

1 bar (3½oz or 100g) plain chocolate
2oz (50g) butter
2 rounded tsp instant coffee powder
4oz (125g) icing sugar, sifted
cocoa powder sifted on to a piece of paper

1. Break up chocolate and put into a bowl with butter. Stir in coffee powder.

2. Leave uncovered and melt 4 minutes at defrost setting. Stir until ingredients are well mixed, making sure the coffee has dissolved.

3. Mix in icing sugar thoroughly. Leave about 5 minutes then roll into 15 balls.

4. Toss in cocoa powder and transfer to paper sweet cases. Store in the cool but not in a refrigerator as the Truffles will become too hard.

PLAIN TRUFFLES   Makes 15
Make as above but omit coffee.

RUM OR SHERRY TRUFFLES   Makes 15
Make as Coffee Truffles but omit coffee and add 1 teaspoon rum or sherry essence instead.

VANILLA TRUFFLES   Makes 15
Make as Coffee Truffles but omit coffee and add 1 teaspoon vanilla essence instead.

Rose or Pistachio Fondants   Makes about 1¼lb or 575g

A touch of gracious living and nostalgia with these delicately-flavoured and pastel-tinted fondants.

2oz (50g) butter

2 tblsp milk

1 tsp rose or pistachio essence

1lb (450g) icing sugar, sifted

red or green food colouring

1. Put butter, milk and essence into a 3pt (1·75 litre) dish and heat 3 minutes at defrost setting.

2. Work in icing sugar then add a few drops of red or green colouring, mixing until evenly tinted.

3. Knead until smooth then roll out to ½ inch (1·25cm) in thickness on a surface dusted with sifted icing sugar.

4. Cut into about 30 rounds with a 1 inch (2·5cm) fluted cutter or 70 rounds with a ½ inch (1·25cm) cutter. Leave 2 or 3 hours to dry out then drop into paper sweet cases.

DINNER PARTY MINTS   Makes about 1¼lb or 575g

Follow recipe for Rose or Pistachio Fondants, but use peppermint essence. Tint pale green. If liked, brush one side of each with melted chocolate.

FRUIT CREAMS   Makes about 1¼lb or 575g

Follow recipe for Rose or Pistachio Fondants, but use orange, lemon, strawberry, raspberry or pineapple essence. Tint with matching colours.

TIP: In order to make the full number of sweets, either 30 or 70, knead trimmings together then re-roll and re-cut.

Marshmallow Raisin Fudge   Makes 12oz or 350g

Almost fool-proof, this is my favourite recipe for a speedy fudge.

2oz (50g) butter

2oz (50g) light brown soft sugar

2 tblsp milk

4oz (125g) marshmallows (pink or white)

4oz (125g) icing sugar, sifted

2oz (50g) raisins

1. Put butter into a 3pt (1·75 litre) dish with sugar and milk. Heat 4 minutes at defrost setting, stirring twice.

2. Continue to cook a further 4 minutes at full power, stirring twice.

3. Mix in marshmallows. Cook $\frac{1}{2}$ minute at full power. Stir and continue to cook for a further $\frac{1}{2}$ minute.

4. Stir briskly a few times, add raisins then spread into a $1\frac{3}{4}$ pt (1 litre) buttered dish, shallow for preference. Leave about 2 hours in the cool or until Fudge is set.

5. Cut-up and store in an airtight tin or polythene bag.

Marshmallow Nut Fudge   Makes 12oz or 350g

Add 2oz (50g) chopped walnuts or toasted almonds instead of raisins.

Cherry Petit Fours   Makes about 12

Ideal for serving with after-dinner coffee, these are fanciful little mouthfuls designed for entertaining.

1 bar)3$\frac{1}{2}$oz or 100g) plain chocolate

2oz (50g) digestive biscuits, finely crushed

6 glacé cherries, halved

1. Break up chocolate, put into a bowl and melt 3 to 3$\frac{1}{2}$ minutes at defrost setting. Leave uncovered.

2. Stir in biscuits then transfer equal amounts to 12 paper sweet cases.

3. Top with halved cherries and leave in the cool until quite firm before serving.

Preserves

Making preserves in a microwave is quick, clean and safe. There are no pans of very hot jam or marmalade to contend with, no boiling over and no hassle. The technique is reliable, the preserve a bright colour and the taste is impeccable.

The same maxims apply to preserves made in the microwave as those cooked conventionally on the hob:

1. Choose sound fruit; not over-ripe.

2. Wash well.

3. Stone where possible before cooking.

4. To test for setting, use a sugar thermometer which should register 220°F (110°C). Alternatively, pour a little preserve on a cold sau-cer. Leave 2 minutes. If a skin forms on top which wrinkles when touched, preserve is ready. If not, cook a little longer, checking at the end of every minute.

5. Skim.

6. Spoon into clean and dry jars. Top with waxed discs. Cover and label when cold.

7. To sterilise and warm empty glass or pottery jars, pour about 3 tablespoons water into each. Heat $1\frac{1}{2}$ to 2 minutes at full power. Pour out water. Turn jars upside down to drain on a clean tea towel. If traces of water remain inside, wipe dry with kitchen paper.

8. Store in a cool, dark and dry place.

Jam
Yield about $1\frac{1}{2}$lb (675g)

To make jam in the microwave, keep to smallish quantities of fruit (1lb or 450g). Put the fruit in a 4pt (2·25litre) dish and cook to the pulpy stage with water, *but no sugar*, as given in the chart Cooking Fresh Fruit on page 162. Afterwards add the amount of boiling water and granulated or preserving sugar etc., given below. Stir well, return to microwave and leave uncovered. Cook 5 to 7 minutes at full power until sugar has completely dissolved, stirring twice. Continue to cook, uncovered, for 20 to 40 minutes at full power (time will depend on fruit) or until jam sets. To test, pour a small quantity of to a cold saucer and leave to stand for 2 minutes. If a skin forms on top which wrinkles when touched, the jam is ready. If not, continue to cook until setting point is reached. Stir frequently throughout cooking. Skim at the end. Pot, cover and label.

APPLE AND BLACKBERRY
Add 1 tablespoon water and 1lb (450g) sugar.

APRICOT
Add 1 tablespoon water, 1lb (450g) sugar and juice of $\frac{1}{2}$ medium lemon.

BLACKBERRY

Add 1lb (450g) sugar and 1 tablespoon lemon juice but *no* additional water.

RASPBERRY

Cook to pulp as given in chart under Apples, allowing 4 to 6 minutes but with *no* water. Add 1lb (450g) sugar.

STRAWBERRY

Cook to pulp as given in chart under Apples, allowing 4 to 6 minutes but with *no* water. Add 13½oz (390g) sugar and juice of half a small lemon.

BLACKCURRANT

Add ½pt (275ml) water and 1lb 3oz (525g) sugar.

GOOSEBERRY

Add ¼pt (150ml) less 1 tablespoon water and 1lb (450g) sugar.

PEACH

Add 3 tablespoons water, 13½oz (390g) sugar and juice of 1 small lemon.

PLUMS AND GREENGAGES

Add 1 tablespoon water and 1lb (450g) sugar. Preferably remove stones before cooking.

Dried Apricot Jam   Makes 2lb or 900g

A handsomely-flavoured jam with a thousand and one uses.

8oz (225g) dried apricots, well-washed and soaked overnight in 1pt (575ml) water

2lb (900g) granulated or preserving sugar

strained juice of 1 large lemon

1. Put apricots and water into a large bowl. Cook, uncovered, for 15 to 20 minutes at full power or until fruit is soft and tender.

2. Add sugar and lemon juice. Return to microwave. Leave uncovered and cook about 5 minutes when sugar should be dissolved. Stir twice.

3. Continue to cook, uncovered, a further 20 to 25 minutes at full power or until setting point is reached. (See introduction.)

4. Leave until lukewarm then pot and cover.

Mixed Fruit Marmalade
Makes about 5 to 6lb or 2·5 to 2·75kg

A full flavoured marmalade which does credit to the microwave. Use plump and juicy fruits and make sure they are well-washed and dried before using.

2 medium grapefruit

2 medium oranges

2 medium lemons

1½pt (850ml) boiling water

4lb (1·8kg) granulated or preserving sugar

1. Peel fruit thinly and cut skin into fine, medium or thick strips, depending on personal taste.

2. Halve each piece of fruit and squeeze out the juice. Pour into a *large* bowl. Save all the pips and tie in a clean cloth with cut-up white pith. Add to bowl.

3. Add ½pt (275ml) boiling water and leave to stand 1 hour. Pour in remaining water then cover bowl with cling film. Puncture twice with the tip of a knife.

4. Cook 20 to 30 minutes at full power, time depending on the thickness of the skin. Turn bowl 3 times unless oven has a turntable.

5. Uncover. Stir in sugar and return to microwave. Leave uncovered and cook about 8 minutes or until sugar dissolves, stirring 4 times.

6. Continue to cook, uncovered, for another 30 to 35 minutes or until setting point is reached. (For testing, see Jam.) Stir every 7 to 10 minutes.

7. Leave until lukewarm, remove and discard tied-up pips and pith then transfer marmalade to clean, dry jars. Cover and label when cold.

TIP: It is important to leave marmalade until lukewarm before potting to prevent the peel from rising up in the jars on cooling.

Lemon Curd

Makes about 1lb or 450g

Very fresh, very lemony and quite delicious! Make in small quantities and store in the refrigerator to prevent spoilage. Based on eggs and butter, the curd quickly deteriorates if left out and about.

4oz (125g) butter
3 Grade 3 eggs *plus* 1 extra yolk
8oz (225g) caster sugar
finely grated peel and juice of 3 medium lemons, first washed and dried

1. Put butter into a 2pt (1·25 litre) basin and heat 4 minutes at defrost setting.

2. Add rest of ingredients, first beaten well together.

3. Leave uncovered and cook 5 minutes at full power, beating at the end of every minute with a wooden spoon.

4. When curd is thick and coats the back of a spoon in an even layer, remove from oven and spoon into 1 or 2 small jars or pots. Cover as for Jam (page 218).

TIP: If curd looks a little too thin, cook for a further $\frac{1}{2}$ to 1 minute.

Apple Chutney

Makes about 2lb (900g)

Made from garden windfalls – or even your best crop – and with the full taste of autumn behind it, chutney fares well in a microwave as you will find out when you try the recipe. A few variations follow.

1lb (450g) cooking apples, peeled and chopped
4oz (125g) onions, peeled and chopped
3 level tsp salt
4 tblsp water
12 fluid oz (350ml) malt vinegar
8oz (225g) dark brown soft sugar
1 garlic clove, peeled and crushed
4oz (125o) chopped dates
4oz (125g) raisins
3 level tsp ginger
1 level tsp cinnamon
1 level tsp mixed spice
$\frac{1}{4}$ to $\frac{1}{2}$ level tsp cayenne pepper (fiery!)
1 bouquet garni bag

1. Put apples and onions into large bowl. Mix in salt and water. Cover with a plate and cook 5 minutes at full power.

2. Mix in all remaining ingredients. Leave uncovered and cook 30 to 40 minutes at full power until chutney has thickened to a jam-like consistency.

3. Stir often and cook an extra 5 to 10 minutes if necessary. Remove and discard bouquet garni bag. Leave chutney, covered with a lid, overnight for flavours to blend and mature.

4. The next day pot and cover as for Jam (page 218).

APPLE AND PEAR
Follow basic recipe but use half apples and half pears.

APPLE AND GOOSEBERRY
Use half apples and half topped and tailed gooseberries.

APPLE AND GREEN TOMATO
Use half apples and half chopped-up green tomatoes.

APPLE AND APRICOT
Use all apples but substitute scissor-snipped washed dried apricots for dates.

Drinks

Milk

Milk is easily heated up in the microwave and runs less risk of boiling over than if warmed conventionally in a saucepan on the hob.

To heat until hot, pour ½ pint (275ml) milk into a glass or pottery jug. Leave uncovered and heat 1½ to 2 minutes at full power.

To bring milk just up to the boil, follow directions above and heat 2½ to 3 minutes at full power.

Cocoa   1 cup

Put 3 to 4 level teaspoons cocoa powder into a large cup or mug (not teacup size as it is a bit too small). Mix smoothly with 1 or 2 tablespoons cold milk. Add a further ¼ pint (150ml) cold milk and whisk gently to ensure even mixing. Leave uncovered and heat 1¾ to 2 minutes at full power or until cocoa just comes up to the boil. Add sugar to taste (or not), stir round and drink.

HOT CHOCOLATE   1 cup

Make as above, using drinking chocolate powder instead of cocoa. Leave uncovered and heat 1¾ to 2 minutes or until very hot. Stir round, sweeten to taste if necessary and drink.

Coffee with Milk   1 cup

Make as cocoa, using 1 to 2 teaspoons instant coffee powder instead of cocoa.

FOAMY COFFEE

Fill a fairly large cup with cold, leftover coffee. Add 2 or 3 rounded teaspoons low fat milk powder mixed smoothly with 2 teaspoons cold water. Heat about 1½ minutes at full power or until very hot and foamy. Sweeten as desired, stir round and drink.

REHEATING LEFTOVER COFFEE

Because of speed, there is no stale flavour when remains of a pot of coffee are reheated. Pour into cups and reheat, individually, for about 1 minute at full power. Add milk or cream and sugar to taste.

Jaffa Wine Mull   Serves 5 to 6

Tangy, zesty and spicy – all the ingredients needed for a microwaved mulled wine which 'cooks' in 6 to 8 minutes.

2 large grapefruit
1pt (575ml) medium dry red wine
2 inch (5cm) piece of cinnamon stick
3 cloves
4oz (125g) granulated sugar
2 tblsp whisky or brandy

1. Halve grapefruit and squeeze out juice. Strain into a large bowl then add wine, cinnamon stick, cloves and sugar.

2. Cover with a plate and heat 6 to 8 minutes at full power, stirring at least twice. Remove from oven and leave to stand 5 minutes.

3. Stir round again and add whisky or brandy. Ladle into handled cups or glasses and serve.

Winter Punch   Serves about 6

A Punch to thaw you out in a very civilised way!

¾pt (425ml) apple juice
¼pt (150ml) ruby port
½pt (275ml) orange juice
½ level tsp cinnamon

1. Put all ingredients into a large bowl and cover with a plate.

2. Heat at full power for about 5 to 8 minutes when Punch should be hot but not boiling.

3. Leave to stand 5 minutes, then stir round.

4. Ladle into handled cups or glasses and serve.

Odds and Ends

Toasting Nuts, Other Cereals and Seeds

Although microwave ovens are reputed not to brown – and for many dishes this holds perfectly true – they nevertheless have a marvellous effect on nuts, as demonstrated by the short selection of ideas below. Even if the toasting process is no swifter than it would be in a conventional oven or under the grill, the saving in fuel is appreciable, the whole operation is clean and tidy, and the browning is evenly distributed with minimal effort.

The type of dish or plate used will affect the cooking time to some extent, and nuts on a pottery plate will take marginally longer – about $\frac{1}{2}$ to 1 minute – than those in a glass dish such as Pyrex.

Toasted Flaked Almonds

Spread 4oz (125g) flaked almonds on to a 10 inch (25cm) pottery plate or put into a 7 inch (17·5cm) round glass dish. Leave uncovered. Toast in the microwave for 6 to 7 minutes at full power or until nuts become light golden brown. Move about with a wooden spoon or fork at the end of every minute. Remove from oven but leave on the plate or in the dish so that they go on gently cooking and crispening. When cold, store in an airtight jar or tin.

Buttered Flaked Almonds

Superb sprinkled over cooked vegetables such as cauliflower or broccoli, buttered almonds take a few minutes to prepare in the microwave and work well every time.

Put $\frac{1}{2}$oz (15g) butter into an 8 inch (20cm) round and fairly shallow dish. Melt, uncovered, $\frac{3}{4}$ to 1 minute at full power. Add 2oz (50g) flaked almonds. Cook, uncovered, for 6 minutes at full power or until golden brown, turning every 2 minutes unless oven has a turntable. Use straight away, otherwise the butter congeals.

TOASTED WHOLE ALMONDS

Blanch and dry. Make as Toasted Flaked Almonds but use 4oz (125g) blanched almonds instead. After blanching, wipe dry in a tea towel.

TOASTED CASHEWS

Make as Toasted Flaked Almonds but use 4oz (125g) cashews instead.

TOASTED HAZELNUTS

This technique will give you toasted nuts with skins which are easy to rub off.

Make as Toasted Flaked Almonds but use 4oz (125g) hazelnuts instead. Cook for 10 minutes at full power, moving nuts with a wooden spoon or fork at the end of every $1\frac{1}{2}$ minutes.

TOASTED PINE NUTS

Make as Toasted Flaked Almonds but use 4oz (125g) pine nuts instead.

TOASTED DESICCATED COCONUT

Make as Toasted Flaked Almonds but use 4oz (125g) desiccated coconut instead and cook 5 minutes at full power.

TOASTED SHREDDED COCONUT

These are curling coconut strips which look a bit like narrow noodles. To brown, make as Toasted Flaked Almonds but use 4oz (125g) shredded coconut instead and cook $5\frac{1}{2}$ to 6 minutes at full power.

TOASTED PORRIDGE OATS

Make as Toasted Flaked Almonds but use 4oz (125g) porridge oats instead and cook $6\frac{1}{2}$ to 7 minutes at full power.

TOASTED SESAME SEEDS

As these can brown suddenly and burn, a pottery plate slows down the cooking process which, in this instance, is more beneficial than glass. Make as Toasted Flaked Almonds but use 4oz (125g) sesame seeds instead and cook 12 minutes at full power, moving seeds with a wooden spoon or fork at the end of every 2 minutes.

226

Toasted Peanuts

No speedier in a microwave than a conventional oven or under the grill, the main advantage here is a great saving in fuel and first-class results.

Spread 1lb (450g) shelled peanuts over the base of glass tray in oven or put into a large round or square dish. Cook, uncovered, for 15 to 17 minutes at full power. Carefully turn nuts over with a spatula every 5 minutes to ensure even browning. Remove when cool to the touch. If nuts have brown skins, rub off between palms of hands. Store in an airtight tin when cold. Peanuts have a natural sodium (salt) content and, when treated this way, you will find they taste as though they are very slightly salted.

Crème Frâiche   Makes $\frac{1}{2}$pt or 275ml

From France, with flair and that famous style, comes a wonderful thick cream which adapts happily to sweet and savoury uses. It has a slightly tart taste but is still mild enough to be used as a gloriously rich filling and icing for fancy gateaux, as a topping for soft summer fruits, in a savoury dip – with personally chosen embellishments – for crudités, in all manner of sauces to give them added panache, over freshly cooked vegetables in place of butter and, of course, in paprika and goulash dishes, in stews and braises, in broths and soups, in ice creams and pancakes.

Not available, as yet, in shops over here, you can make your own simply enough in the microwave and, provided it's kept covered in the refrigerator, use it for up to 2 weeks – it has good staying powers.

$\frac{1}{4}$pt (150ml) double cream
1 carton (5oz or 142ml) soured cream
both taken from refrigerator

1. Tip both creams into a bowl and whisk gently together until smooth.

2. Cover with an inverted plate and warm 3 minutes at defrost setting.

3. Stir round, cover securely with cling film and refrigerate. Leave overnight before using.

TIP: As Crème Frâiche does not curdle, it can quite safely be brought to the boil in cooking.

Drying Herbs

If you grow your own herbs, you will know the tedium of trying to dry them successfully for winter use, especially if you are dependent on hot sun in our unpredictable climate. This is where a microwave reduces the hassle to nil and carries out the process quickly and efficiently, ensuring that your annual crop can be dealt with in minutes. Each variety of herb should be dried separately and stored in airtight jars.

Cut herbs off shrubs, remove leaves from stalks (needles in the case of rosemary) and loosely pack into a ½pt (275ml) measuring jug, filling it almost to overflowing. Tip into a colander and rinse quickly and gently. Leave to drain then dry thoroughly between a clean, folded tea towel. Transfer to 2 sheets (one on top of the other) of kitchen paper, placed on floor of oven. Spread out to form an even layer. Heat for 5 to 6 minutes at full power, carefully moving herbs about on the paper 2 or 3 times. As soon as they sound like the rustle of autumnal leaves and lose their bright green colour, you can take it the herbs are dried through. If not, given them a further 1 to 1½ minutes. Remove from oven and crush by rubbing between hands. Tip into jars with airtight stoppers, label, and store away from bright light.

Dried Chestnuts

Easier, I believe, to cope with than jacketed ones, the microwave renders dried chestnuts cooked and usable in about 1¾ hours, without either soaking overnight or prolonged cooking.

Wash 9oz (250g) packet of dried chestnuts thoroughly. Put into a 3pt (1·75 litre) dish and mix in 1 pint (575ml) boiling water. Cover with a plate and cook 15 minutes at full power. Leave to stand 15 minutes inside or outside the oven, whichever is the most convenient. Cook a further 15 minutes at full power then stand for another 15 minutes. Add an extra ¼ pint (150ml) boiling water and cook a further 10 minutes at full power. Remove from oven and stir round. Cover again with a plate and leave to stand for a final ¼ hour.

TIP: To ensure even distribution of heat, stir chestnuts twice every time they are cooking.

Couscous   Serves 4 to 6 (F)

Typically North African, Couscous is a traditional accompaniment to hearty meat stews laced with every vegetable under the hot desert sun. Now that packeted Couscous is readily available, it can be cooked separately in the microwave and takes little more than 3 to 4 minutes.

8oz (225g) couscous
1pt (575ml) boiling water
½ level tsp salt
½oz (15g) butter or margarine

1. Put all ingredients into a 3pt (1·75 litre) glass or pottery dish.

2. Cover with a plate and cook 4 minutes at full power, turning dish twice unless oven has a turntable.

3. Uncover and fluff up with a fork. Serve very hot with stews of chicken, beef or lamb.

Crisp Breadcrumbs

There is no better place than a microwave oven for making fine white or brown breadcrumbs, the kind top haute cuisiners always recommend for coating foods such as turkey escalopes or fish fillets, destined to be fried conventionally in deep fat or oil. Not only is crumbing in the microwave a marvellous way of using up stale bread and end crusts of loaves, but the resultant crumbs become dry and crisp without deepening in colour to the goldfish yellow often found in packeted varieties. Once cold and popped into an airtight cannister, the crumbs will keep almost indefinitely in the cool.

Turn 4oz (125g) bread (white, brown or a mixture) into crumbs, the finer the better. Tip into a 10 inch (25cm) round dish which is not too deep – about 2 inches (5cm) only. Cook, uncovered, at full power for 5 to 6 minutes, stirring 4 times. Remove from oven and leave until the crumbs crispen and cool, stirring occasionally. Store as recommended above.

TIP: If bread is very fresh and there is more moisture to be driven off, cook for a further 1 to 1½ minutes.

Fondue   Serves 6

The après-ski favourite of European Alpine resorts, Fondue is a hearty, sustaining meal and well-suited to blustery days and nights. It's a hospitable dish too, in that everyone circles round it and literally dips in, formality going to the winds. Fondue is quick and simple to make in the microwave.

1 garlic clove, peeled
6oz (175g) Emmental cheese, grated
1lb (450g) Gruyère cheese, grated
1 level tblsp cornflour
½pt (275g) dry white wine
1 tsp lemon juice
2 tblsp Kirsch
salt and pepper to taste
French bread cut into cubes for serving

1. Crush garlic into a 4pt (2·25 litre) glass or pottery dish. Add both cheeses, cornflour, wine and lemon juice.

2. Leave uncovered and cook until Fondue bubbles gently; about 7 to 8 minutes at full power. Stir at least 3 times.

3. Remove from oven then stir in Kirsch. Season to taste and eat by spearing a cube of bread on to a fork and swirling it round in the cheese mixture. Accompany with tots of Kirsch and hot tea – no cold drinks whatever.

TIP: If a man drops his cube of bread into the cheese mixture, his forfeit is to kiss one of the ladies. Twice, and he has to organise the next Fondue party.

FONDUE BRITISH-STYLE   Serves 6

Make as previous recipe but use Cheddar cheese and cider instead of wine. Whisky may replace Kirsch but no strong spirit is actually necessary.

Hints and Tips

1. To have plate meals ready on tap, arrange cooked foods (such as meat and two or more vegetables) on individual dinner plates. Place the meat, poultry, bacon, sausages, hamburgers or fried fish in the centre *without piling up*, coat with gravy or sauce then surround with a ring of assorted vegetables, pasta or rice. Cover with cling film. To serve, puncture film twice with the tip of a knife then reheat each plate individually from frozen. Allow 6 to 7 minutes at full power, depending on the dish. Turn plate 4 times unless oven has a turntable. Food is ready when gravy or sauce begins to bubble in the centre. Leave to stand 3 to 5 minutes before serving.

2. To soften ice cream and loosen jellies (provided they are not in metal tins or moulds), heat 45 seconds at defrost setting. Stand 2 to 3 minutes.

3. To melt golden or other syrups and honey which have become grainy (crystallised), take metal caps off jars and warm, individually, for about 3 minutes at defrost setting.

4. Sometimes dishes become too hot to handle as they absorb heat from the cooked food. For comfort, therefore, remove from oven with gloves.

5. To soften 8oz (225g) brown sugar that has become lumpy, put into a dish with half a slice of very fresh bread. Cover and warm $1\frac{1}{2}$ minutes at defrost setting. Alternatively, heat sugar with a wedge of cut fruit (pear or apple) instead of bread. Another method is to cover sugar with a piece of wet kitchen paper and use neither bread nor fruit.

6. To clean the interior of the microwave easily, dampen a dish cloth and heat for 30 to 45 seconds at defrost setting. Wipe over top, base and sides of oven then dry with a clean tea towel. Do this frequently to prevent food spills from sticking to the inside. Alternatively, and to freshen the oven at the same time, put about $\frac{1}{2}$ pint (275ml) bowl of cold water inside the oven. Add a slice or two of fresh lemon or lime. Heat at full power for 3 minutes or until boiling fast and oven steams up. Wipe interior clean with a dish cloth then dry with a tea towel.

7. To avoid dishes which overheat and therefore detract from the efficiency of the cooking programme (the food will take longer), test by pouring $\frac{1}{2}$ pint (275ml) water into the dish to be used. Heat for 1 minute at full power. If it becomes hot, it is unsuitable and another dish should be chosen.

8. To soften 14oz (397g) of frozen pastry, warm for 2 minutes at defrost setting. Stand 5 to 10 minutes or until pastry is soft enough to roll out.

9. To achieve best results when reheating soups, do so on full power for clear soups and at defrost setting for thick or creamy soups.

10. To rehydrate dried fruits, such as apple rings or prunes, without soaking overnight, put about 8oz (225g) into a glass bowl. Cover with water (only just) and bring up to the boil; $5\frac{1}{2}$ to 8 minutes at full power. Leave to stand 10 minutes, covered, then drain and use as desired.

11. To plump up raisins, currants or sultanas, treat as dried fruits above but reduce cooking time to about 4 to 6 minutes at full power. Stand 5 minutes. Drain and dry.

12. To release and extract more juice from citrus fruits and pomegranates, warm for 15 to 30 seconds (depending on size) at full power. Stand 5 minutes.

13. To bring refrigerated cheeses to room temperature quickly, warm about 4 to 6oz

(125 to 175g) for 15 to 30 seconds at defrost setting. If it still feels cold and hard (Brie for example) allow an extra few seconds *but watch carefully* to see that cheese does not begin to melt.

14. To prevent chicken livers from popping, pierce each piece with the tip of a knife.

15. To refresh dinner rolls, place in a serviette-lined basket and warm through until the surfaces feel very slightly warm; about 1 to 3 minutes (depending on quantity) at defrost setting.

16. To warm jars of baby foods, remove metal lids. Heat individually, allowing about $1\frac{1}{2}$ minutes at defrost setting.

17. To warm baby lotions, beauty lotions, shampoos and hair conditioners in the winter, remove caps and heat each for about 40 to 50 seconds at defrost setting.

18. To prevent a face full of steam, tilt the dish or bowl *away* from yourself when uncovering and removing either the lid, plate or cling film.

19. To improvise on a ring mould, cover the outside of a tumbler (straight-sided and smooth) with cling film. Stand in the middle of a round, soufflé-type dish with open end of tumbler facing.

20. To remove plastic wrap easily from foods, warm for a few seconds at defrost setting, or until the plastic looks moist.

21. To soften legumes (dried peas and beans etc.) and eliminate soaking overnight, wash 8oz (225g) of the dried vegetables under cold, running water. Put into dish and add 2 pints (1·25 litres) boiling water. Cover dish with cling film, then puncture twice with the tip of a knife. Cook 4 minutes at full power. Leave to stand 2 hours. Drain and use as required.

Acknowledgements and thanks to :

Anchor Dairy Products
Bejam frozen foods
Butterball Turkey Products
Button Geese
Buxted Chicken Products
Brittany Artichokes
Cadbury-Schweppes
Campbell's Soups
Colman's Products
Cherry Valley Duckling
Corningware/Pyrex
Dairy Crest Products
Davis Gelatine
Central Bureau of Fruit & Vegetable Auctions in Holland
Kraft Foods
Lakeland Plastics
McCormick Herbs & Spices
Bernard Matthews Turkey Products
Scottish Salmon Information Service
Suchard Chocolate
Schwarz Herbs & Spices

Photographic acknowledgements

American Rice Council (pages 51, 55, 56, 96, 145, 149 and 150)
Heinz (page 49)
John West (page 50)
Central Bureau of Fruit and Vegetable Auctions in Holland (pages 52 and 148)
Farmhouse English Cheeses (page 53)
Campbell's Soups (pages 54 and 151)
New Zealand Lamb (page 89)
Mushroom Growers' Association (page 90)
Gale's Honey (page 91)
Bovril (page 92)
British Chicken (page 93)
Pyrex Clear Bake-Ware (page 94)
Knoor Bread Sauce Mix (page 95)
Vanden Bergh's Margarine (page 146)
Dutch Dairy Bureau (page 147)
McCormick's Herbs and Spices (pages 152 and 187)
Ambrosia Custard (page 185)
Stork Margarine (page 186)
Bacofoil Roastabags (page 188)
Brown & Polson Blancmange (page 189)
Flour Advisory Bureau (pages 190 and 191)

Line drawings by John Grimwade

Index

C

236